A Revisionary History
of Portuguese Literature

HISPANIC ISSUES
VOLUME 18
GARLAND REFERENCE LIBRARY OF THE HUMANITIES
VOLUME 2122

Hispanic Issues

Nicholas Spadaccini, *Series Editor*

A Revisionary History
of Portuguese Literature

Edited by
Miguel Tamen and Helena C. Buescu

Garland Publishing, Inc.
a member of the Taylor & Francis Group
New York and London
1999

Library of Congress Cataloging-in-Publication Data

A revisionary history of Portuguese literature / Miguel Tamen & Helena
    C. Buescu, editors.
            p.   cm. — (Garland reference library of the humanities ; 2122.
    Hispanic issues ; v. 18)
        Includes bibliographical references and index.
        ISBN 0-8153-3248-3 (hc : alk. paper)
        1. Portuguese literature—History and criticism.   I. Tamen, Miguel.
    II. Buescu, Helena Carvalhão.   III. Series: Garland reference library of
    the humanities ; vol. 2122.   IV. Series: Garland reference library of the
    humanities. Hispanic issues ; v. 18.
    PQ9016.R48   1999
    869.09—dc21   98–41980
                                                                            CIP

The editors gratefully acknowledge assistance from Indiana University and the
    Department of Spanish and Portuguese at the University of Minnesota.

Printed on acid-free, 250-year-life paper
Manufactured in the United States of America

Hispanic Issues

Contents

◆ Preface

Miguel Tamen and Helena C. Buescu

This project arose out of the Editors' belief that, in the English-speaking academic communities, no updated historical overview of Portuguese literature nor any updated review of the state of current discussions within the field of Portuguese literature had been produced for many years. Our volume tries to address these two issues. The twelve essays included herein are presented in a chronological order, so that the possibility of a diachronic perspective on Portuguese literature is preserved, without for that matter sacrificing the putative strength of the individual contributions.

As it stands, the volume can provide beginning students of Portuguese literature with a series of assessments, in a chronological order, that, when taken together, constitute some sort of updated version of the state of Portuguese Literature Studies as well as a version of the development of Portuguese literature. Advanced students and scholars, meanwhile, will not fail to establish a connection between the individual pieces and some of the best known, ongoing or endemic, controversies in the domain of Portuguese literature. The adjective "revisionary" in our title is therefore doubly justified: to beginning students, it warns them that, rather than "the facts" about Portuguese literature, this issue presents chronological interpretations; to more specialized audiences, it signals the lack of satisfaction most of the scholars represented here feel vis-à-vis some of the accepted truths in the field of Portuguese literature. As the editors believe that the problem of the relationship between literary history and revisionism can be of some interest, each of them has decided to write a short essay on the topic.

All essays except M. S. Lourenço's, A. M. Feijó's, and M. Tamen's were translated by Richard Zenith. The translation was made possible by a generous grant from the Fundação Luso-Americana para o Desenvolvimento, later complemented by another grant from the Calouste Gulbenkian Foundation. The editors are also very grateful to Professors Edward Friedman and Nicholas Spadaccini, who were responsible for the proposals that gave birth to this volume (though certainly not for its shortcomings), and enthusiastic supporters of the whole project.

As overviews and reviews are precarious products, with stringent expiration dates attached to them, it is also our belief that this book will in its turn be reviewed and superseded. If so, its ultimate demise would certainly be a good omen for the advancement of Portuguese studies in America.

When this volume was already in production, the editors were surprised by the untimely death of one of its contributors, Margarida Vieira Mendes. They would like to dedicate it to her memory and to the memory of the superb teacher and scholar she was.

Stanford and Lisbon, July 1997

Ghosts Revised: An Essay on Literary History

Miguel Tamen

Professor Parkins, the protagonist of an all but forgotten ghost story by an all but forgotten ghost story writer (M. R. James), unsurprisingly enough, sees a ghost. The narrator judiciously concludes:

> . . . I gathered that what he chiefly remembers about it is a horrible, an intensely horrible, face *of crumpled linen.* What expression he read upon it he could not or would not tell, but that the fear of it went nigh to maddening him is certain. (148)

A curious thing about the narrator's stance in the passage above is that he is only certain about the *effect* of a certain face. What Professor Parkins actually *read* in that face, the narrator says, is not even a matter of conjecture for him. What Parkins "chiefly remembers" about the ghost is only the event of having seen it ("the fear of it"). From the point of view of Parkins's own remembrance, he can only testify to an appearance, not to the meaning of what has appeared. In all rigour, in the eye of the terrified beholder, a ghost is even less than an appearance, as appearances are bound to become food for what Kant (a notorious denouncer of ghost-seers as well as a contemporary of the rise of the gothic novel) called one's Understanding; a ghost is an *apparition*, a force from the past, from which nothing but its incalculable, if invariably unpleasant, effect may follow. Such is, among many others, the version of another early twentieth-century writer, Raúl Brandão, who, at the outset of his memoirs, grimly declares that we are simply the prey for images of the dead. Although we "picture ourselves as people who build things, and impose ourselves on things, . . . we only obey to the incessant impulse of the dead" (Brandão 1: 18). My contention in much of what follows will be that history and history-writing are versions of an aspect of this basic predicament which, apart from the late Freud of *Beyond the Pleasure Principle*, and from the late Marcel of *La Fugitive*,[1] has mainly survived in ghost stories, namely, that of the dissociation between meaning and event, between identifiable faces and unreadable effects. The meager implication of my concerns is that there are some puzzles that affect the notion of history-writing which can help us understand why the most substantial part of the articles that follow my own essay present themselves as *revisions*, rather than as definitive visions about well-established topics. As the reader might have guessed by now, I will be proposing yet another revision of the notion of "revision." The only purpose this essay can claim to have, therefore, is that of a momentary dilution of some of the more exuberant hopes for something like a positive literary and historical knowledge.

What Is a Ghost?

Among the many available classical words for witnessing through contemplation, there are two particularly well known and much glossed over: *theoria* and *revisio*, which of course gave "theory" and "revision." Commenting on the use of the first term by John Ruskin in his *Modern Painters* ("the exulting, reverent, and grateful perception [of pleasantness]"), while acknowledging that there is indeed a link between theory and jubilation, Wlad Godzich emphasizes both the public aspect of theoretical verification, and its relationship with death. "We may recall here," he writes, "the role of witnesses to the execution of death sentences in the American judicial system" (165). A *theoria*, a set of professional witnesses, performs in this case the function of certifying that a certain event has taken place (incidentally without making, or making public, any enquiries as to its meaning). The theoretical point of view is therefore what constitutes certain facts. A person is not legally dead until *pronounced* dead and such is a *theoretical* pronouncement proper.

As to the second term, *revisio*, it derives from *visio*, usually translated as "vision." Ernout and Meillet, in their indispensable *Dictionnaire etymologique de la langue latine* (s.v. *uideo*), remark that the term ("a rare and technical term"), among other things, translates the Greek *theoria*. "It belongs," they add, "to the philosophical language which has undoubtedly created it to translate *phantasia* and *phantasma*." And so we are back to ghost-language or, rather, the ghost of ghost-language has reappeared in our argument.

We are quite familiar by now with the notion that theories put forward helpful visions, visions which help us to do things we would not be able to do otherwise, such as flying rockets and treating retroviral diseases: less so with the notion that such visions are, etymologically at least, ghosts, and therefore that the creation of a public degree of evidence for certain visions involves the delicate task of controlling ghosts. It seems that the control of a vision implies the notion that in a certain sense we already possess, at least potentially, its ultimate meaning, a foreknowledge of its ultimate consequences. *Useful* ghosts, one could say, are perhaps ghosts about which the dissociation between meaning and event is not a problem. Needless to say, in the land of Pragmatism only useful ghosts are allowed in the city—*in theory*, at least, for all visions are open to very real possibilities of misunderstanding and so the law and order in the republic of theory proves to be yet another vision.

Of course, in a trivial sense *anything* can be misunderstood as, say, the structure and the shape of a hammer do not preclude that I might want to brush my teeth with it. Theories, however, are liable to misunderstanding in another sense: the sense in which they have nothing which is granted the kind of resilience comparable to that of the shape of a hammer. Matter, so to speak, does not provide theories with any instruction manual: visions, whether theories or ghosts, come up with no meaning whatever. That theories can be misunderstood is probably coextensive with the fact that theories can be used.

All this (allegedly oversimplified) situation allows me into the main purpose of this section, namely, a serious discussion of the question "What is a ghost?" I shall reserve for the next section the even more serious matter of history. On the former matter (the definition of "ghost") there are again many available terms. The French term *revenant* (someone who *revient*, who comes *back*) has for me the advantage of suggesting that a phantasm, a vision, is indeed a *re*vision. As Plato knew well, what appears is at best the first copy (and at worst the last copy) of something else. The Latin rendering of *phantasma* by the word "visio" effaces the only substantial fact there is about ghosts, namely, that ghosts are always second to something. The appearance of an Idea, as Plato also saw, would be far from triumphant, as it would not be recognizable as such. Ideas survive in M. R. Jamesian "crumpled" (and often frightening) versions of their former selves. The consequence of this point for my incipient phenomenology of the ghost is simply that, in Scottish castles and at M.I.T. alike, the only possible form of contemplation is revision.

Words such as "revision" and "revisionism" have a bad name, at least for Europeans. Perhaps there is something akin to a "metaphysics of the first time" at work there, for which no repetition, let alone the kind of repetition with a twist that appears to be truly revisionist, can bring good news. The word "revisionist" has mostly been used as a slur, directed, for good and bad reasons alike, against all sorts of putative weakeners of a truth that, instead of straightforwardly denying that very truth, often rewrite that truth in a weakened, ghastly and therefore ghostly way. The word belongs thus to a tradition of exorcism of undesired repetitions and its specific use betrays a nostalgia of pure beginnings, of a world in which affirmation and denial are the only possible modes of argument.

The term "revisionist" has of course been made famous in literary criticism by Harold Bloom, whose often revised descriptions of "revisionary ratios" are first and foremost descriptions of oblique ways of both affirmation and denial through which what he calls strong poets create room for their poetry. "The revisionist," writes Bloom, "strives to *see* again, so as to *esteem* and *estimate* differently, so as then to *aim* 'correctively'" (Bloom, *Map* 4). For Bloom, "we read to usurp, just as the poet writes to usurp . . . [a] place, a stance, a fullness, an illusion of identification or possession" (Bloom, *Agon* 17). Minus the pathos, altogether different, the emphasis on the notion of "mistake" as well as on the transcendental role of mistakes is what brings Karl Popper's philosophy of science close to Bloom's criticism, and apart from other available contemporary philosophies of science, namely, from those that claim to have superseded his own.[2] In their own very different ways,[3] both Bloom and Popper have denounced as an illusion the idea that poetry and knowledge, even meaning, are logically independent from previous mistakes, purified, as it were, from their own past by some miraculous linguistic or epistemological break, in short, *incommensurable* vis-à-vis their own past. Nor for that matter do they endorse the neoclassic alternative of a timeless tradition where continuity is achieved at the price of indifference, that is, where Dante and Yeats, Plato and Heisenberg, belong to one happy family, each contributing, in his own way, to a common pursuit. Seen in this light, well-known metaphors such as that of the poet as the creator of a pristine world (not to mention the metaphor of the poet as the organic part of a larger tradition), or that of the scientist as the inhabitant of an ultimately self-enclosed monadic paradigm (not to mention that of the scientist as the aquiescent member of a timeless brotherhood of knowledge) appear to be protections against the possibility of repetition or, better even, against contamination by revision, against an undesired proximity between error and truth, as if truth were attainable without debt, either through illumination or through membership of the oldest club in town.

There is perhaps a method to revisionism, albeit a minimal one. In every revision, the past gets apprehended through visions. Deceptively varied as the latter might be, however, each and every vision consists primarily in the ascribing of mistakes to previous visions, in what Bloom calls acts of limitation, substitution, and representation. Such acts, of course, open up the disturbing possibility of no revision's being able to claim any form of exemption for its own status: all revisions get revised, as my own dear and *truly* true ghost-descriptions will inevitably become someone else's ghost. That, as Oscar Wilde once remarked, truth is never pure means that, contrary to what Wilde believed, and to revise a quote from W. V. Quine, a curious thing about it is its simplicity.

Historical Truth

All these caveats should not have to appear in a discussion of the simplest variety of simple truth, namely, historical truth. However, surprising as it may seem, thinking about history has often depended on the assumption that history as a whole is given in its entirety at some early point in time and hence that both our visions of it and the so-called historical events are merely the illustration of some previously written laws. Such an assumption lies at the core of historical prediction, as no predictions of historical events would be possible without assuming some sort of causality in history, whose principles would then be inevitably reproduced in our visions of it.

Any attempt to think history-writing as revision is therefore incompatible with the very notion of historical laws and so of historical prediction. The notion, which Nietzsche helped to make known, but not popular, in his second *Untimely Meditation* ("On the Uses and Disadvantages of History for Life"), that history is "an attempt to give oneself, as it were *a posteriori*, a past in which one would like to originate" (Nietzsche 77) is, on the other hand, quite close to the sense of pragmatic usurpation that we saw at work in Bloom's theory of revisionism. In this Nietzschean sense, the unity of history is not external to history-writing, just as the virtues of history-writing are not measured against some set of external laws. Rather, what we call the unity of history is in itself part of the strategy, and indeed of the very possibility, of history-writing, that is, is the product of specific revisionary ratios. A *theory* about history is in this sense a revision, haunted and made possible by the ghosts of what it purports to revise.

The ways of revision, as applied to history-writing, are numerous, and need not be discussed at this point. Perhaps they should be discussed one day according to the resistances they raise, from the inconspicuous to the outrageous, from consensual unobtrusive ghosts, to frightening specters. It appears, for instance, that most people are now prepared to grant that what is called history-writing always contains some measure of an indictment directed at other versions of it, directed at other people's mistakes. Literary history is particularly sensitive to this mode, perhaps because the notions of "literary events" and of "historico-literary causality" have typically been perceived as requiring a great deal more of argument than the notion of, say, "political event." What

Friedrich Schlegel once called the "polemical" element in criticism denotes not only the perception of art criticism as a series of endless discussions, as the little credit that notions such as "event," "law," and "causality" have always been granted by critics and even by literary historians. On the other hand, fewer people are prepared to acknowledge that, as the status of proof in historical discussions does not require and indeed cannot produce any sense of a correspondence between external events and history-writing, every indictment is always essentially mistaken. I do not mean this in any trivially sceptical sense. Rather, mistakes in history-writing are both the necessary correlates of revisions and the measure of their very adequacy. Some revisions will acquire the founding status of mistakes against which some subsequent revisions will be measured up. The so-called progress in history-writing does not correspond therefore to the superseding of previous versions, if by that one understands an *itinerarium ad veritatem*. Quite the contrary, it is simply something you call, when in a beautifying mood, to the *use* of history for life. That the notion of "use" requires the notion of "revision" and hence the notion of "mistake" should make us wary of any hasty identifications between "usefulness" and "goodness," or "usefulness" and "morality."

Literary History

Contrary to art history, literary history has always been primarily connected to the idea of *national* objects, in this case, national literatures. The contrast is apparent in the ease with which general books on art history keep being produced (even by firm believers in the contingency of history), as opposed to the relatively few, and typically flawed, attempts at a comprehensive, multinational, literary history, which in some quarters is still known as comparative literature. The typical procedure of both art history and multinational literary history is rather the procedure of geographical incarnation, which ultimately was devised by Hegel: a set of features, such as stylistic traits, simultaneously incarnates for some mysterious reason in one or, at the most, in *three*, geographical regions. Art history writing is therefore akin to a geographical parade. On matters of national literary history things are quite different, as what is paraded against a constant, idealized, geographical background instead is usually a set of terms used for historical classification (e.g., "Romanticism," "Baroque," "Middle-Ages"), which, if not incarnate everywhere, can in principle incarnate anywhere. The fact that most recent histories of Sudanese literature do not recoil from discussing Mannerism in Sudan—which, incidentally, should not make us forget that this latter phrase is just like "romanticism in Germany," that is, that both phrases share the assumption that the history of a nation partakes from transnational artistic categories—points to the special position of the concept of "nation" in literary history.

As is well known, literary history was one of the main instruments through which the very idea of a nation as a community started to be produced in nineteenth-century Europe. Should you forgive me a passing positivistic mood, I would venture to speculate that there could have been a reason for that, albeit perhaps a negative one. Indeed, history *tout court* seemed not to be enough, as, since this was a wholly European affair, very few existing nations could present unidealized explanations of their own identity which would satisfy criteria held to be verifiable such as geographic and political stability, or linguistic consistency. The deplorable result of those criteria when applied to inquiries on the identification and origin of a nation is invariably that the nation under scrutiny is neither identifiable nor the oldest European nation (always a coveted honorific prize in the contest for best-established national identity). You could still argue, as many did, that the essential qualities of France were already at work in the person of King Clovis, who was conveniently born slightly before the apocalyptic event that marked the beginning of European history, that is, the fall of the Roman Empire. That, however, would be at odds with unfortunate facts such as the large Duchy of Burgundy's becoming part of what we now call France only after 1477, not to mention the town of Calais, which was English up to 1558, and the historical fluctuations of Alsace-Lorraine, brought, who knows if only provisionally, to a halt as recently as 1945. In short, it would take a special kind of dealing with the past to produce satisfying identifications and genealogies, a dealing powerful enough to make identity work.

Unlike art history, and even historical linguistics, literary history has always been an instance of such a satisfying dealing, and for several reasons. First, there was a perfect *ersatz* for the fall of the Roman Empire in the progressive disappearance of Latin, which, when seen at a close distance, was as little apocalyptic and sudden as the fall of the Roman Empire itself, but which nevertheless explains why most works of literary history also start with the Middle Ages. Indeed, and for literary history, the Middle Ages have become not only the dominant metaphor of the origin as the very emblem of the linguistic proliferation (and of the proliferation of written languages) which became in its turn the model for the constitution of several post-Latin national identities. Secondly, there were available techniques and tricks (namely, what became, around the late eighteenth century secular interpretation) for establishing evidences of an unproblematic transition between linguistic forms and structures, and intentions and values. I believe that the idea that, say, the romance version of the *Serments de Strasbourg* is already part of the "French" heritage (up to the prose of Georges Perec) is typically concocted through notions such as those of intention and of value-attribution that have to do with a secular notion of interpretation (as the solutions to the problems of either the intention or the values of sacred texts are a priori guaranteed by the special origin of those texts). In short, given that little consistency can be expected from the applying of political, linguistic and geographic criteria to literary events, those are replaced, in literary history (as in several contemporary inventions such as the soft "-logy"-ending sciences) by consistency-making concepts such as the famed notion of "culture." Whereas the converse is not necessarily true, the sense of *national* community cannot help being cultural, this latter term being an excuse as well as a specific *use* of the past: an *identifying* use.

It can therefore be said that literary history, from its inception, and by definition, has been *national*, *communitarian* and *cultural*, as its main result was the formation of a specific, teachable knowledge of national cultural communities. The definition for "nation" that is invariably produced by literary historians is therefore neither a linguistic one, nor a political or geographic one. In fact, "culture" is the concept through which the past is made present in an unchanged form, for the simple reason that the present cannot help but being the perfect illustration of predicates already contained in the definition of a given national identity. In this sense, when literary historians get ideas about a given literary history, those are invariably ideas of *pure* entities, of pure nations, from which all hint of political, geographic and linguistic dirt has been removed. In this, and a typical nineteenth century activity, literary history is yet another form of disbelief in ghosts.

An important consolation for ghost-seers remains, nevertheless, in that notions such as that of an identifiable cultural community are produced within the revisionary framework sketched above. There appears to be therefore a ghostly substance to the idea of "nation," and certainly to the idea of "literary nation," no matter how much those ideas are reiterated, and precisely because of their very reiteration. Purity itself, so to speak, is impure, as nations resemble not so much entelechies, as the embarrassing result of the continuous work, together with all its remains, of the production of an entelechy (and I need no reminding that a produced entelechy is a contradiction in terms). This is perhaps why ostensibly accurate historical reconstructions keep making us smile, as if we all knew too well that no past could have been like *that*. This is certainly why, when it comes to the knowledge of the past, despite all our craving for meaning, we have to settle for ghosts.

I have been deviously suggesting that there are always two inextricably tied sides to literary history: the vision-proposing side, and the revisonary side. Analogously, it could perhaps be suggested that there are typically two sides to the notion of cultural community as produced by literary history: the nation-building side is always the indirect confession that a given nation had to be built through efforts, no matter how mistaken, which are just like ours. In some of these versions, nations aspire to become part of nature. Yet the naturalization of the nation, which is the final outcome of literary history, would involve a specific debt, the debt of all nations, there where the efforts, the mistakes, the accidents and the successes, and, in any case, the energy of nation building can be read. Perhaps it is only fitting that the best metaphor I can think of for it is again a literary one, namely, that of the Flaubertian yearning for "an impersonal style." The naturalness of such a style was the product of successive efforts and revisions, and Flaubert, in a perfect allegoretic mood, died with yet another final revision in his hands. What one calls the *oeuvre* of a writer such as Flaubert is indeed a heap of dirt, a heap of perfect solutions for literary problems which in the end proved to be inadequate. If I were to dream of Portugal, and if my dreams were another perfect unified explanation for things past and future, I would be dreaming that what we call Portuguese literary history is really some sub-Flaubertian plot, no more than the history of the debt of "Portugal." No strike of narration, no miracle of style or language can produce a nation. Nations, history and literature alike appear, like ghosts, literally *by mistake*, that is, through revision.

Notes

1. In *La Fugitive*, the penultimate book of Proust's *À la recherche du temps perdu,* the protagonist Marcel, in Venice after the death of Albertine (and after having received already two posthumous letters from her), receives a telegram that reads: "My friend, you must think I am dead [*vous me croyez morte*], forgive me, I am quite alive, I would like to see you, talk marriage with you, when are you coming back? Tenderly. Albertine." (Proust 3: 641, my translation.)
2. See for instance Popper.
3. Which get perhaps closer in Popper's choice of mottos for his *Conjectures and Refutations*: Oscar Wilde's "Experience is the name every one gives to their mistakes," and John Archibald Wheeler's "Our whole problem is to make mistakes as fast as possible" (Quoted in *Conjectures* vi.)

Works Cited

Bloom, Harold. *Agon. Towards a Theory of Revisionism*. New York: Oxford UP, 1982.
_____. *A Map of Misreading*. New York: Oxford UP, 1975.
Brandão, R. *Memórias. 6ª edição*. Lisboa: Aillaud & Bertrand, 1925.
Ernout, R., and A. Meillet. *Dictionnaire etymologique de la langue latine. Histoire des mots. Troisième édition revue, corrigée et augmentée d'un index*. Paris: Klincksieck, 1951.
Godzich, W. "The Tiger on the Paper Mat." *The Culture of Literacy*. Cambridge: Harvard UP, 1994.
James, M. R. "'Oh, Whistle, and I'll Come To You, My Lad.'" *Collected Ghost Stories*. Ware: Wordsworth, 1993.
Nietzsche, Friedrich (1874). "Vom Nutzen und Nachteil der Historie für das Leben." Trans. R. J. Hollingdale. "On the Uses and Disadvantages of History for Life." *Untimely Meditations*. Cambridge: Cambridge UP, 1987.
Popper, Karl. *Conjectures and Refutations: The Growth of Scientific Knowledge*. New York: Harper, 1968.
Proust, Marcel. *À la recherche du temps perdu*. Paris: Gallimard, 1956.

Chapter 1

Infractions of the Name-Hiding Rule in Galician-Portuguese Troubadour Poetry

João Dionísio

A fundamental rule for the *langue d'oc* troubadour was to keep his love a secret, not revealing the identity of his beloved lady. The rule obliged him, above all, to *celar* "hide" her name. The significance of direct allusions to the lady, in the cases when this rule was broken, is a matter that deserves careful analysis. In the working hypothesis proposed by Monson, the lady celebrated by the troubadour may actually exist—either as a woman he is courting or as a benefactress to whom he dedicates a poem in hope of some material compensation—or she may be a strictly literary figure serving a precise function within the composition (257).

In spite of its schematic character, this hypothesis suggests that Monson regards the traditional sociological view of troubadour practice to be a reductive scenario. The view generally invoked when these issues are addressed is a kind of fusion of the two situations considered in the first part of the hypothesis: the lady is married to a nobleman and has an extramarital liaison with the troubadour which, if it became public knowledge, would cause her to fall into disgrace and cause him to lose the material benefits that the relationship had thus far afforded him. Regardless of whether Monson's analysis or the traditional synthesis better describes what really took place, in either view, whatever the designation *dompna* or *midons* refers to, the troubadour is obliged not to reveal the identity of the lady he exalts in song.

Some of the *vidas* of the Provençal troubadours show that at times what was at stake, when this silence was broken, was not only a greater or lesser ensemble of material benefits but one's very own life. The *vida* of Guillem de Cabestanh, for example, tells of his sorry lot after Raimon de Castel-Roussillon discovered that his wife, Saurimonde, was loved by the troubadour and had requited his affections:

> E qan venc un dia, Raimons de Castel Rossillon trobet passan Guillem de Cabestanh ses gran compaignia et aucis lo; et fetz li traire lo cor del cors e fetz li taillar la testa; e.l cor fetz portar a son alberc e la testa atressi; e fetz lo cor raustir e far a pebrada, e fetz lo dar a manjar a la moiller. (Boutière and Schutz 532)

> [And there came a day when Raimon de Castel-Roussillon found Guillem de Cabestanh passing alone in the country and killed him, and removed his heart from his body and had his head cut off. And he had the heart brought to his home as well as the head; and he roasted the heart with pepper, and gave it to his wife to eat.]

This account, whose veracity at this point is irrelevant, is an extreme illustration of the threat that hung over the troubadour and which gave rise to an obvious technical problem: how to let a woman know that a certain composition is directed to her, that she and not some other lady is being eulogized, if her name cannot appear in the verses? The troubadour had to maintain a delicate balance between the use of words and silence (Köhler 112). In the Provençal *canso,* this difficulty was overcome by referring to the woman with a pseudonym [*senhal*] in the poem's final section [*tornada*], which was shorter than the stanzas. This achieved, in Jacques Roubaud's well-stated formula, the differentiation between the generic *I* of the troubadour and the *I* who composes the *canso*, as well as between the universal woman who receives the composition and the specific woman to whom the song is addressed (270).

In Galician-Portuguese troubadour poetry the convention of *celar* appears, not surprisingly, in the *cantigas de amor*, the genre closest to the Provençal *canso*. But the contours of the problem differ from those observed in *langue d'oc* poetry, for the *cantigas* are considerably more abstract than the *cansos*. This abstraction is especially noticeable in the qualities that the troubadour attributes to the *senhor*, the equivalent of the Provençal *dompna*, for in no *cantiga* can we find a *descriptio dominae* with the realistic traits that do appear in the *canso*. Various reasons have been posited to explain this difference. Tavani, who contends that the Galician-Portuguese composition is not directed to a real woman but to an abstract or highly idealized figure, cites sociocultural reasons, namely the concentration of Galician-Portuguese troubadour activity in a single royal court (*A poesia lírica galego-portuguesa*, 109-110). Luciana Stegagno-Picchio, while acknowledging the social causes for this phenomenon, emphasizes the different conception of sin shown by Provençal and Galician-Portuguese poets to account for the greater abstraction found in the latter (69-70). There are also those who point to a more tautological cause, apparently intrinsic to Galician-Portuguese poetry. Segismundo Spina, for instance, attributes the hazy portrayal of the beloved lady to the bashful modesty of Peninsular troubadours (426), an explanation that finds an echo in Maria da Conceição Vilhena's contention that "more than their Provençal counterparts, the Galician-Portuguese troubadours succeeded in strictly adhering to the principle of discretion" (218).

Whether for reasons more extrinsic or intrinsic to the actual texts of the Galician-Portuguese poetic corpus, one fact seems indisputable: the convention of *celar* in Peninsular poetry extends to other characteristics of the inspiring lady besides her name.

The general consensus among authors is that the Galician-Portuguese *cantigas de amor*, while deriving largely from Provençal models, did not adopt the device of the *senhal* commonly employed in the *cansos* (cf. Spina 427, for example), but no exhaustive study has been carried out to support this view. In fact some *cantigas* do have words that function in the same or a similar way to the *senhal* as it was used north of the Pyrenees. As an example we may cite the anonymous "A mais fremosa de quantas vejo" (Michaëlis I, 549), with its obscure references in the refrain:

A mais fremosa de quantas vejo
en Santaren, e que mais desejo,
e en que sempre cuidando sejo,
non ch'a direi, mais direi-ch', amigo:
 ay Sentirigo! ay Sentirigo!
 al é Alfanx' e al Seserigo!

[The fairest lady of all I've seen
in Santarém, whom I most desire
and who is always on my mind—
I won't say who, friend, and yet I'll say:
 Ah Sentirigo! Ah Sentirigo!
 Alfanx is other, and Seserigo, other!]

Taken literally, the refrain merely consists of allusions to small localities in the vicinity of Santarém (Michaëlis II, 447). The beginning of the *cantiga* and the final strophic verse, however, strongly suggest that the place names of the refrain serve to identify the lady from Santarém, for the troubadour announces that he will not publish the identity of his beloved but will do something else instead. The *senhal* consists precisely in replacing the lady's real name by another, a substitution giving rise to difficulties of comprehension foreseen by the *cantiga*: "e non sei ome tan entendudo / que m' og' entenda o por que digo" [and I don't know a man who grasps enough / to grasp why now I say] (vv. 15-16). The author, therefore, is conscious that his use of what seems to be a *senhal* creates serious interpretive problems, quite understandable in an ambit much less prone than the Provençal poets to employ this device. This consciousness is even more pronounced in the next *cantiga* recorded in the *Cancioneiro da Ajuda*, "Pero eu vejo aqui trobadores" (Michaëlis I, 550-51), which, given its textual proximity and the motifs it shares with the previous *cantiga*, is doubtlessly by the same author. The interpretive challenge is still present, though now the author is relying on an audience more skilled in exegetical difficulties, namely, the troubadours, as indicated already in the incipit. But not even this public is able to solve the riddle:

Pero eu vejo aqui trobadores,
senhor e lume d'estes olhos meus,

que troban d'amor por sas senhores
non vej' eu aqui trobador, par Deus,
   que m' og' entenda o por que digo:
al é Alfanx' e al Seserigo!

[Though here I see troubadours,
O lady and light of my eyes,
who sing of love for their ladies,
I see no troubadour here, by God,
   who understands why I say:
   other is Alfanx, and Seserigo, other!]

The author almost seems to delight in the fact that not even those most familiar with the techniques for camouflaging amorous sentiments, the poets "que troban d'amor por sas senhores," are able to grasp the refrain's meaning. And so the lady could remain grateful to her troubadour for keeping their love a secret: so secret, in fact, that not only her identity but also that of the troubadour are a complete mystery to us today.

Another possible *senhal* is discernible in the Pero Garcia Burgalês *cantiga* that begins "Ay Deus! que grave coita de soffrer" (Michaëlis I, 806), in which the troubadour laments the departure of his lady, tersely related by the monostich refrain: "Porque se foi a Rainha Franca." Carolina Michaëlis, it should be noted, admitted that the final words could be read as "a Rainh' a França," which would make the hypothesis of this being a *senhal* less likely, but she decided in favor of the first reading, a transcription also adopted by the monographic editor of the Burgalês corpus (Blasco 217).

Although the existence of a Galician-Portuguese species of *senhal* can be detected in still other *cantigas*, the number of them resorting to this device is minuscule in comparison to Provençal poetry. Apart from this limited number of texts, the concealment of the beloved lady's identity in Peninsular lyric poetry depends primarily on a *descriptio* that is vague and unspecific, almost invariably the case in the *cantigas de amor*. Thus the apparent or actual revelation of the name of the lady to whom the troubadour addresses his songs stands out far more in Galician-Portuguese than in Provençal poetry.

Keeping in mind the rare nature of such an infraction, I will attempt to show how the Galician-Portuguese troubadours break the rule of *celar*, why they might be prompted to do so, and what effects they hope to achieve. I will look especially at the *cantiga de amor* and the *cantiga de amigo*, limiting the scope of my study to those situations in which the name of the beloved lady is revealed directly. I will make only a few brief observations with respect to the satiric *cantigas* and the Marian songs and will exclude minor genres such as the Galician-Portuguese lay [*lai*] and lament [*pranto*] as well as all those texts in which the woman is identified through a periphrastic reference (e.g., "filha de don Paay / Moniz" [daughter of Don Paay / Moniz], vv. 11-12 of the famous *cantiga* "No mundo nom me sei parelha," Michaëlis I, 82).

One of the most common situations leading to the revelation of the beloved lady's name is the troubadour's feeling that his love is not requited, coupled with his languishing hope that such may yet occur one day. And so, in order to punish the woman, or simply to confirm that there is no love, the troubadour breaks the *celar*.

In the first stanza of "Pois non ei de dona 'Ivira," a *cantiga* attributed to Martim Soares, the troubadour leaves the land where the lady resides, revealing her name because he has received nothing from her except wrath (Michaëlis I, 131; Lapa 432). Pero Velho de Taveirós's *cantiga* "Par Deus, dona Maria, mia senhor ben-talhada" (Michaëlis I, 773) is likewise dominated by the discourse of one who complains of having been badly compensated for the good he offered his lady. The text of Roi Queimado that begins "Preguntou Johan Garcia" (Michaëlis I, 286) presents the curious case of the narrator's not only divulging the name of the woman for whom he dies but also, in the incipit, the identity of the one who asked him about his dying. It being a rule of courtesy not to inquire about a love that is meant to be kept secret, the troubadour reveals both the name of the beloved over whom he despaired and the name of the man who had so discourteously questioned him. In this *cantiga* as well as in the one that follows it (Michaëlis I, 287), by the same author, it is interesting to note that the lady's name is conveyed in direct discourse. In the first case it is what the troubadour himself said in the past that is quoted; in the second, what Guiomar Afonso will say once the troubadour has died. In this respect the *cantiga* of Joam Soares Somesso beginning "Ogan' en Müimenta" (Michaëlis I, 738-39; Lapa 243) has affinities with Roi Queimado's texts, being unusual insofar as only the first two verses of each stanza are ascribed to the troubadour, with all the rest consisting of direct discourse attributed to Martim Gil. Realizing he is about to lose his beloved, Urraca Abril, since her father means to marry her off, Martim Gil divulges her name and that of her possible future husband, who will indeed eventually contract marriage with Urraca (Mattoso 310, 424). Through the use of citation, the gravity of breaking the *celar* rule is attenuated in these *cantigas*. We can also speak of attenuation in the case of "Par Deus ay dona Leonor," by Roi Paes de Ribela (Michaëlis I, 383-84), if we accept as valid the interpretation of v. 9, "e Deus que vus en poder ten" [and God who has you in his power], as an allusion to Leonor's being a nun.

We may note, parenthetically, that all of these *cantigas* are transmitted by the *Cancioneiro de Ajuda*, very possibly a partial copy—containing only *cantigas de amor*—of a larger compilation in which the three main genres were represented. Be that as it may, some of these texts still raise doubts about the genre in which they are best classified, as demonstrated by Rodrigues Lapa's edition of the satiric *cantigas*, in which the aforementioned compositions of Martim Soares and Joam Soares Somesso were included.

In other texts the revelation of the lady's name is motivated by the insanity that has supposedly beset the troubadour. This situation is well illustrated by the group of *cantigas* in which Pero Garcia Burgalês makes allusions to Joana, Sancha and Maria. His "Que alongad' eu ando d' u iria" (Michaëlis I, 189-90) contains themes typically found in the *cantiga de amor*, such as the bashfulness of the lover who doesn't dare declare his love, the death he claims would be preferable to love's suffering, and also the insanity that leads him to indicate the name of his beloved lady: "Direi-a ja . . . ca ja ensandeci . . . / Joana est . . . ou Sancha . . . ou Maria" [Now I'll say who . . . for I've gone mad . . . / it's Joana . . . or Sancha . . . or Maria] (vv. 26-27). Making probable reference to this *cantiga* in another of his compositions, "Joana, dix' eu, Sancha e Maria" (Michaëlis I, 215-16), Pero Garcia pretends to have regained his senses in order to answer evident protests that one of his songs had identified his beloved lady. He points out that "non dixe por qual morria / de todas tres" [I didn't say which of the three ladies / I was dying for] (vv. 3-4). And interpreting his declaration as the fruit of insanity, he decides that his reason for indicating the three names was not after all so crazy: "Tant' ouve medo que lhe pesaria / que non dixe qual era mia senhor / de todas tres" [So afraid was I that it would weigh on her / that I didn't say who was my lady / from among the three] (vv. 8-10). In a third *cantiga* of the series (Michaëlis I, 217-18), Pero Garcia relates that a woman with one of the three names learned of the *cantiga* in which she was mentioned and realized that the troubadour loved her, for which cause she began to mistreat him. Thus the lady seems to have thwarted Pero Garcia's strategy of onomastic multiplication. The final *cantiga* of the series, "Que muitos que mi andan preguntando" (Michaëlis I, 219-220), deals with the barrage of questions demanding to know from the troubadour which of the three names in fact identifies his lady ("Se é Joana? se Sancha? se quen? / se Maria? . . . ," vv. 3-4).

There are other situations in which the beloved's name is revealed without the justification of insanity or unrequited love. Vasco Rodrigues de Calvelo reveals the name of his lady in the very first line of "Se eu ousass' a Mayor Gil dizer" (Michaëlis I, 601-02), a *cantiga* founded on the troubadour's fear to tell the good he receives from his beloved, since he would then be obliged to speak of the evil that comes along with that good. Fernam Pais de Tamalancos, on the other hand, reproaches the king for removing him far from his lady in "Gran mal me faz agora 'l rei" (Michaëlis I, 712), a seeming transposition of the *cantiga de amigo* in which the young female narrator complains that the king has retained her beloved in military operations. Worth more attention is Pero Viviaes's "A Lobatom quero eu ir" (Nunes, *Cantigas d'Amor*, 43-45), in which the troubadour falls in love with a certain Dona Joana based on what he has heard about her, without ever having met her, a scenario reminiscent of Jauffré Rudel's *amor de lonh* "distant love." The narrator directs his song to God (vv. 1-2: "A Lobatom quero eu ir, ay Deus, e tu me guya" [I want to go to Lobatom with you, God, as my guide]), which in a certain way justifies the mention of the lady's name, since the text pretends to represent intimate communication with the divinity, whose omniscience makes secrecy impossible. This justification is undermined, however, by the reference to God in the third person at the end of the stanza, when the troubadour names his beloved: "a que parece melhor / de quantas Nostro Senhor / Deus fez é dona Johanna" [the fairest looking / of all the women Our Lord / God made is Dona Johanna] (vv. 5-7). The difficulty of understanding the status of the interlocutor is compounded by the difficulty of establishing the text. According to Nunes's edition, another lady is suddenly alluded to at the end of the refrain: ". . . poys y / ffor, verrey ssair Maria." Nunes makes the following observation with respect to this passage: "I cannot make out what the troubadour means by these words: *verrey sair Maria*; if they have not been altered, do they mean that, while waiting for his beloved lady, another suddenly appeared?" (Nunes, *Cantigas de Amor*, 44, note). Instead of "sair Maria," authors such as José Pedro Machado and Elza Paxeco Machado have proposed "sa irmana," while Beltrami reads "sair mana" (cf. Beltrami 51-52, where the various possibilities are discussed). The interpretation of this text's onomastic occurrences depends, of course, on how this problem of textual criticism is resolved.

In the other genres of Galician-Portuguese poetry, the motive for breaking love's secrecy is presented in inverse fashion to what we find in the *cantigas de amor*. The inversion, however, takes different forms. In the *cantiga de amigo* there is a direct inversion of roles, with the female narrator now being expected to keep the name of her beloved a secret. Since this name corresponds to that of the troubadour himself, we are dealing in effect with a situation of *autonominatio*. As with the *cantigas de amor*, the majority of the *cantigas de amigo* in which the name of the narrator's beloved is mentioned concern situations in which there is no active love relationship—in the former genre, because no such relationship ever began; in the latter, because it has ended. But the corpus of *cantigas de amigo* in which the troubadour names himself—virtually monopolized by seven texts of Joam Garcia de Guilhade—presents various scenarios. If in "Treides todas, ai amigas, comigo" (Nunes, *Cantigas de Amigo*, 159) the *amigo* is named in connection with a panegyric for his qualities as a loyal lover, a motif that no doubt has some relation to the Provençals' typical boastfulness, in other *cantigas de amigo*—such as "Sanhud' and[ad]es, amigo" and "Vistes, mias donas, quando noutro dia" (Nunes, *Cantigas de Amigo*, 162-64), the explicit mention of the troubadour's name responds to his overly bold advances, for he has insisted on more than belts and bonnets as signs of love. In both "Per boa fé, meu amigo" and "Foi-s'ora daqui sanhud[o]" (Nunes, *Cantigas de Amigo*, 171-72 and 175-76) the troubadour's name is revealed because his amorous liaison with the girl has terminated, so that there is no more reason to keep the rule of *celar*. In the expression "o que chufam Guilhade" (i.e., "the one who is mockingly called Guilhade"), found in the final stanza of the latter *cantiga*, Elsa Gonçalves has discerned an allusion to the name's etymology, from the French *guille*, meaning betrayal or deceit (Gonçalves 41). And the betrayal may refer both to Guilhade's relationship with another girl and to the breaking of love's secrecy, as we find in "Diss'ai, amigas, don Jam Garcia" and "Veestes-me, amigas, rogar" (Nunes, *Cantigas de Amigo*, 167-68, 177-78). In both texts, the girl not only declares that her relationship with Guilhade is finished, she gets revenge by broadcasting his name.

The only other *cantiga de amigo* that mentions the name of the beloved man and that was not written by Joam Garcia de Guilhade is "Ai amiga, tenh' eu por de bon sen," by Rodrigu' Eanes d' Alvares (Nunes, *Cantigas de Amigo*, 299). This is a strange text whose refrain begins with the verse "Rodrigu' Eanes d' Alvares é tal:" [This is how Rodrigu' Eanes d' Alveres is:], with the strangeness owing mainly to the contrast occurring in the two following verses, the first being the concluding verse to the stanza, the second being the verse that concludes the refrain (e.g., vv. 6-7: "quer-me milhor ca quis om' a molher, / mais nom sabem se me quer ben se mal" [he loves me more than a man ever loved a woman, / but no one knows if he loves me greatly or not at all]). It would seem to be a case of flagrant injustice: to Rodrigu' Eanes's discreet "service" to his female friend, so discreet that no one knows if he loves her or not, she responds with a *cantiga* that reveals the troubadour's love for her and her own cold detachment in relationship to him. We can easily recognize in this topos a parody of the imbalance between the troubadour's duties and benefits vis-à-vis his lady in the *cantiga de amor*.

The satiric *cantigas* and those in praise of Holy Mary involve other kinds of inversion. To explore the motives for breaking the rule of *celar* in the *cantigas de escárnio e maldizer* is somewhat of an absurdity, since many of the compositions belonging to this genre are deliberately designed to break with the conventions of the *cantiga de amor*. Contrary to what we find in the *cantiga de amor* or *cantiga de amigo*, naming is a common procedure and thus fully expected. I will therefore mention just one text illustrating one of the ways in which the *cantiga de maldizer* deals with the *celar* motif. In "Martin jograr, ai, Dona Maria," by Joam Garcia de Guilhade (Lapa 319), the troubadour claims to suffer because the *jogral* "jester, jongleur" in question spends the night with his (the *jogral's*) wife. This text presents two notable inversions: (1) the troubadour aspires to a liaison with a woman of lower social standing, since the object of his desire is the wife of a man on his payroll, and (2) whereas love is usually conceived as occurring outside of matrimonial ties, here the woman "lies" [*pousa*] with her own husband: reasons enough for the transgressors of the rules of courtly love to have their names publicly broadcast.

In another domain of medieval poetry, that of sacred verse, the *cantigas de Santa Maria* are likewise a genre in which naming is more the rule than the exception, though the motive for divulging the name is quite different from what we find in the satiric corpus. In these sacred *cantigas*, the troubadour is not interested in maintaining the identity of his lady a secret; on the contrary, her name should be disseminated and exalted as far and wide as possible. The reason for this antithetical procedure is that Holy Mary is the lady of all people: men and women, young and old. *Trobar a lo divino* implies a total inversion of the rules governing profane lyric poetry. This is easily confirmed by the continual references to Holy Mary at the beginning of each *cantiga* and particularly by prologue B, on account of the theoretical observations it contains:

> E o que quero é dizer loor
> da Virgen, Madre de Nostro Sennor,
> Santa Maria, que ést' a mellor
> cousa que el fez; e por aquest' eu
> quero seer oy mais seu trobador,
> e rogo-lle que me queira por seu
>
> Trobador e que queira meu trobar
> reçeber, ca per el quer' eu mostrar
> dos miragres que ela fez; e ar
> querrei-me leixar de trobar des i
> por outra dona, e cuid' a cobrar
> per esta quant' enas outras perdi.
> (vv. 15-26, Mettmann 54-55)

[And what I want is to praise
the Virgin, Mother of Our Lord,
Holy Mary, who is the best
thing he made, which is why I
want today to be her troubadour,
and I beg her to have me as her

Troubadour and to receive gladly
my songs, through which I want to tell
the miracles she has done; and
I no longer want to sing
for other ladies but hope to have
from this one all I've lost in others.]

These two stanzas bring to a close my brief survey of the
major types of infraction, in Galician-Portuguese poetry, of
the "no name" policy that accords with the rule of amorous
secrecy. It is now time to make some general observations, in
which I will focus on the *cantigas de amor* and *cantigas de
amigo*, leaving aside the satiric and sacred genres, which, as we
have seen, raise problems of another order.

In most of the *cantigas* considered, the revelation of the
lady's (or man's) name is precisely placed in the text so as to
highlight the infraction. Reference to the name is made in the
very first line of the cantigas "Pois non ei de dona 'lvira," by
Martim Soares, "Se eu ousass' a Mayor Gil dizer," by Vasco
Rodrigues de Calvelo, and in "Diss' ai, amigas, don Jam
Garcia," by Joam Garcia de Guilhade. Sometimes the
reference in the incipit reappears in other, more or less visible,
places, as in Pero Garcia Burgalês's "Joana, dix' eu, Sancha e
Maria," where it shows up again in the last verse of the first
stanza, or in Pero Velho de Taveirós's "Par Deus, dona Maria,
mia senhor ben-talhada," whose incipit is also the first verse
of the second and last stanzas, or in Roi Paes de Ribela's "Par
Deus, ay dona Leonor," whose incipit is repeated in the
refrain. The refrain, in fact, is another of the "high-profile"
places where onomastic references occur: in "Ora vej'eu que
fiz mui gran folia" (Michaëlis I, 217) and "Ay Deus! que
grave coita de soffrer," by Pero Garcia Burgalês, in
"Preguntou Johan Garcia" and "Pois [que] eu ora morto
for'," by Roi Queimado, in Rodrigu' Eanes d' Alvares's "Ai
amiga, tenh' eu por de bon sen," in Fernam Paes de
Tamalancos's "Gran mal me faz agora 'l rei," and in the

anonymous *cantigas* "A mais fremosa de quantas vejo" and "Pero eu vejo aqui trobadores." Names referred to in the refrain are sometimes echoed elsewhere in the *cantiga*, as in Joam Garcia de Guilhade's "Veestes-me, amigas, rogar," with references made in the refrain as well as in verses 1 and 3 of the second stanza.

Mention of the beloved's name in a given *cantiga* is often just one of several peculiarities. Place names, for instance, which are rare in Galician-Portuguese love poetry, occur in a number of the texts we have examined: in "Pois non ei de dona 'lvira," by Martim Soares (Santa Vaia, v. 5, and the refrain "morarei cabo da Maia, / en Doiro, antr' o Porto e Gaia" [I will live around Maia, / in Douro, between Oporto and Gaia]), in Joam Soares Somesso's "Ogan' en Müimenta" (toponymical reference in the first line of each stanza), in the anonymous *cantigas* "A mais fremosa de quantas vejo" and "Pero eu vejo aqui trobadores" (both making mention of Santarém and surrounding localities), and also in Pero Viviaes's "A Lobatom quero eu ir" (reference made in the incipit).

In terms of rhyme and meter (cf. Tavani, *Repertorio metrico della lirica galego-portoghese*), Pero Garcia Burgalês's "Que alongad' eu ando d' u iria" is the only *cantiga* with an *ababbab* rhyme scheme, a characteristic underscored by the use of *coblas unissonans* (same rhyme scheme for all stanzas). "Joana, dix' eu, Sancha e Maria," by the same author and also composed of *coblas unissonans*, is built on a series of intrastrophic and interstrophic lexical repetitions in rhyme position. A less elaborate but likewise uncommon use of repetition occurs in "Ora vej' eu que fiz mui gran folia," with the presence of "word-rhyme" (end word repeated in same position in two or more stanzas) according to an alternating scheme, in the first and third stanzas and in the second and fourth, while the *cantiga* "Ay Deus! que grave coita de soffrer!" presents a parallelistic variation in v. 2 and v. 5. Joam Soares Somesso's "Ogan' en Müimenta" and Joam Garcia de Guilhade's "Per boa fé, meu amigo" are exceptional for having rhyme schemes (#96 and #136 in Tavani, *Repertorio*) shared, in both cases, by just one other *cantiga*. The aforementioned compositions of Pero Viviaes and Rodrigu' Eanes de Álvares, on the other hand, have unique rhyme schemes (#251 and #98). Although not exhibiting unusual characteristics besides the breaking of the *celar* rule, it is interesting to note that a significant group of these *cantigas* employ rhyme scheme #19 (*aaabbb*), reminiscent of the *zajal*: Martim Soares's "Pois non ei de don 'lvira," Roi Queimado's "Preguntou Johan Garcia," Pero Velho de Taveirós's "Par Deus, dona Maria, mia senhor bentalhada," Roi Paes de Ribela's "Par Deus, ay dona Leonor," and the anonymous *cantiga* "A mais fremosa de quantas vejo."

From the generally prominent place accorded to the onomastic infraction in these *cantigas*, from the simultaneous occurrence of uncommon rhyme and metrical features, and from the occasional appearance of other ingredients likewise unusual in Galician-Portuguese troubadour poetry, it is apparent that the troubadours, when they broke the rule of *celar*, had the intention of making compositions that were unconventional in more than one aspect. We are therefore led to conclude that aesthetic reasons were the main motive for the composition of a good many of these *cantigas*. These authors, in other words, composed songs more for their love of composing than for love of a lady, who was incorporeal because nonexistent, and the common names to which they allude would seem to support Tavani's view that in Galician-Portuguese poetry "the Provençal song of love is reduced to a purely stylistic game and rhetorical exercise" (*A poesia lírica galego-portuguesa*, 110). This game is patent in the way reference is made to the beloved person's name in certain satirical compositions, in the *cantigas de Santa Maria* and in the *cantigas de amigo*, which parody the conventions governing the *cantiga de amor*, but not even in this last genre does the breaking of *celar* always represent a zero degree of the breaking of love's secrecy. The fact is that *cantigas* by authors such as Pero Garcia Burgalês also seem to be parodying this convention, taking the Provençal *canso* as their point of reference. Instead of protecting the woman's identity by using a substitute name, this troubadour claims to include it in an onomastic trio that supposedly conceals his love.

The stylistic exercise mentioned by Tavani is apparently favored by the use of first names, without a patronymic or toponymic complement. In Provençal poetry, once the pseudonym is discovered the secret breaks completely down; in Galician-Portuguese poetry, however, by employing only the first name, the *cantigas* resort to the same basic principle used by Pero Garcia Burgalês. Who, for instance, is the *Joana* mentioned by Pero Viviaes? A glance at the index of the Count Dom Pedro's *Livro de Linhagens* quickly shows that names such as these were extremely common in medieval Portugal. But the matter is not so simple as all that, for the troubadours' listeners did not always need the complete reference—Guiomar Afonso Gata or Orraca Abril, for example—to identify the referent. The simple mention of Elvira in Martim Soares's *cantiga* was enough for the public to recognize that the allusion was to Elvira Anes da Maia. In this case and others, the first name did not need to be accompanied by the patronymic or a nickname for the secret to be broken. The key question is: *in how many other cases?* The recent archival study undertaken by Resende de Oliveira (1994) contends that there were various centers—namely private courts—that sponsored troubadour activity, a view that conflicts with the traditional thesis of a single hub. Tavani's interpretation, according to which the *cantiga de amor* lacks specific references and is a purely stylistic game precisely because there was only one center of activity, can no longer be accepted unrestrictedly. From all that has been said, it would seem that the amount of creative play in the *cantiga de amor* relative to its actual basis in reality still needs to be determined. This determination is a task belonging to disciplines such as history and philology rather than other fields, for revisionism with respect to this subject matter and in these two areas of knowledge is, more than anything else, the carrying on of a venerable tradition of studies that has always endeavored to reconsider problems in the light of well-founded research.

Works Cited

Beltrami, Piero G. "Pero Viviaez e l'amore per udita." *Studi mediolatini e volgari*. Vol. 22, 43-65. Pisa: Pacini Editore, 1974.

Blasco, Pierre. *Les chansons de Pero Garcia Burgalês, troubadour galicien-portugais du XIIIe siècle*. Paris: Fondation Calouste Gulbenkian, 1984.

Boutière, J., and A. H. Schutz. *Biographies des troubadours. Textes provençaux des XIIIe et XIVe siècles*. 2nd ed. revised and enlarged, with a glossary of troubadour terminology and French translations of the Provençal texts. Paris: A. G. Nizet, 1973.

Gonçalves, Elsa. "Apresentação crítica." *A lírica galego-portuguesa (textos escolhidos)*. Ed. Gonçalves and Maria Ana Ramos. 1983. Lisbon: Comunicação, 1985.

16 ◆ JOÃO DIONÍSIO

Köhler, Erich. *Sociologia della fin' amor. Saggi trobadorici.* Ed. Mario Mancini. 1976. Padua: Liviana Editrice, 1987.

Lapa, M. Rodrigues. *Cantigas d' escarnho e de mal dizer dos cancioneiros medievais galego-portugueses,* 2nd ed. revised and enlarged. Vigo: Galaxia, 1970.

Mattoso, José. *Livro de linhagens do conde D. Pedro.* Vol 2/1, critical edition. Lisbon: Academia das Ciências, 1980.

Mettmann, Walter, ed. Alfonso X, el Sabio. *Cantigas de Santa Maria (Cantigas 1 a 100).* Madrid: Castalia, 1986.

Michaëlis de Vasconcelos, Carolina. *Cancioneiro da Ajuda,* reprinted from Halle, 1904 edition, enlarged with a preface by Ivo Castro and a glossary. Vol. 1. Lisbon: Imprensa Nacional-Casa da Moeda, 1990.

_____. *Cancioneiro da Ajuda,* reprinted from Halle, 1904 edition. Vol. 2. Lisbon: Imprensa Nacional-Casa da Moeda, 1990.

Monson, Don A. "The Troubadour's Lady Reconsidered Again." *Speculum: A Journal of Medieval Studies* 70.2 (April 1995): 255-74.

Nunes, José Joaquim. *Cantigas d'Amigo dos trovadores galego-portugueses.* Lisbon: Centro do Livro Brasileiro, 1973.

_____. *Cantigas d'Amor dos trovadores galego-portugueses.* Vol. 2. Lisbon: Centro do Livro Brasileiro, 1972.

Oliveira, António Resende de. *Depois do espectáculo trovadoresco: A estrutura dos cancioneiros peninsulares e as recolhas dos sécs. XIII e XIV.* Lisbon: Edições Colibri, 1994.

Roubaud, Jacques. *La fleur inverse. L'art des troubadours.* 2nd ed. revised and enlarged. Paris: Les Belles Lettres, 1994.

Spina, Segismundo. *Apresentação da lírica trovadoresca (introdução, antologia crítica, glossário).* Rio de Janeiro: Livraria Acadêmica, 1956.

Stegagno-Picchio, Luciana. "Motifs de la tradition juive dans l'ancienne lyrique péninsulaire: les poésies d'amour de Vidal, juif d'Elvas." *La méthode philologique. Écrits sur la littérature portugaise,* preface by Roman Jakobson. Vol. 1, 63-90, *La Poésie.* Paris: Fundação Calouste Gulbenkian, 1982.

Tavani, Giuseppe. *A poesia lírica galego-portuguesa.* Lisbon: Editorial Comunicação, 1990.

_____. *Repertorio metrico della lirica galego-portoghese.* Rome: Edizioni dell'Ateneo, 1967.

Vilhena, Maria da Conceição. "A amada das cantigas de amor: casada ou solteira?" *Estudos Portugueses. Homenagem a Luciana Stegagno-Picchio,* 209-21. Lisbon: Difel, 1981.

Chapter 2

Belief in History

Teresa Amado

Most of the Portuguese prose written in the Middle Ages aimed, one way or another, at making History. This affirmation might at first glance seem overly speculative, since the literature contains numerous references to medieval texts that have not come down to us, but it is a conclusion we are authorized to make from those texts that have survived. The first signs of a differentiated, *historical* treatment include, on the one hand, a greater reliance on translation and on preexisting models in the romances of chivalry and in hagiography, and, on the other hand, the changes in rhythm and content that invariably occurred in the rewriting of narratives (whether originally in Portuguese, Spanish or other languages) valued for their historical importance, as well as the utter novelty that often characterized writing of this sort. I will argue that what I call the "genre of historical discourse" responds, in this case, to an epistemological preference.

Justification of this epistemological preference would clearly guarantee the pertinence of the genre of historical discourse, which at this point has only the above observations to recommend it. If we tentatively admit that there was such a preference, we may inquire into the motives that gave rise to it: taste, interest or necessity. These possibilities need not be mutually exclusive.

It should be noted that we are dealing with secular authors, who in the late thirteenth century took over a most important historiographical work, which included the translation of Arab texts or short accounts of isolated episodes in the *livros de linhagens* "genealogical records," an extensive and repeatedly revised *History of the Iberian Peninsula* "from the beginning," and also—throughout the fifteenth century—the national chronicles that recounted the successive reigns or told the lives of heroes.

Although Christian morals and theology continued to provide the value system that visibly or invisibly sustained the discourse, there were some fundamental differences with respect to prior texts, written in Latin by monks between the eleventh and thirteenth centuries. Two factors were crucial to this evolution. First of all, the clerical point of view was replaced by that of the nobility or of the monarchy and even, in the sole but remarkable case of the chronicler Fernão Lopes, by that of the people at large (meaning the various nonaristocratic groups), leading to changes in the underlying motives and intentions, in the topics considered, in the character portrayals, and—throughout all aspects of the narrative enterprise—in the meanings projected on the events. Secondly, the scribes' monastery as the centripetal spatial unit gives way to the kingdom conceived as a social and territorial whole defined in opposition to neighboring territories and in relation to its own past history.

This second development, accompanied by a growth in de facto royal power and in the symbolic importance of the king, only gained real momentum in the mid-fourteenth century, receiving a strong impetus from the victory against Castile in the war over the Portuguese throne that was fought in the century's final two decades and that brought the second dynasty to power. It was precisely this dynasty's first king and his first son and successor that undertook to systematically recover the history of prior reigns, considering this to be an important instrument for political affirmation and cultural consolidation. The nobility, meanwhile, maintained the horizontal ties of solidarity that had always sustained it, as evidenced particularly in the works of Pedro of Barcelos, a bastard son of King Dinis.

In the *Crónica Geral de Espanha de 1344* (the History of the Iberian Peninsula mentioned above) and in the *Livro de Linhagens*, the author not only endeavored to trace all the way back to the generation of Adam the "feats of Spain" (with "Spain" still signifying the whole of the Peninsula) in the former work, and the ancestry of the Navarran and Aragonese kings and of the "noble lords of Castile and Portugal and Galicia" in the latter, but also took on the double role, in the *Livro*, of representing and defending the nobility, distancing himself from the crown's authority and interests.

The nobility referred to here was a vast, transnational class of individuals linked, on the one hand, by an intricate network of family ties placing them in unequal but interdependent relation and, on the other hand, by the blood and inherited renown of common ancestors, particularly those ancestors who conquered land from the Moors. Although there was no explicit link with pre-Christian historical figures and families of the Mediterranean and of Brittany, nor even with the Visigothic kings who governed in the Peninsula, the long enumeration of their names creates the impression of a right to participation in the memory of power and heroism that assured them (as it assured the post-Islamic Christians) a place in history.

The noble contemporaries of Dom Pedro, for whom he wrote, were thus firmly fixed in the whole of time and space, taking their place in a continuum that is the history of mankind. This typically medieval concept, derived from the cosmological image produced by the Old Testament, did not inspire other historiographical projects. Nor would the nobility as a collective body be the subject of any more compilations or narratives; from then on, texts of this nature would be organized around the king and his kingdom or around individual heroes. The *livros de linhagens* contain isolated narrative episodes for which the genealogies serve both as context and pretext. The generational role call (A married B and they had the sons C, D and E; C married Y and they had the sons F and G; D married Z, etc.) is suddenly interrupted by a vignette in which one of the last persons named becomes a protagonist. The vignette ends as suddenly as it began, though it is generally complete within its circumscribed limits and thus constitutes an intelligible piece of the biography of the person in question. There is a surprise effect, the transformation of a name—when unexpectedly brought into relief from a theoretically interminable list of names representing so many links in the reproductive chain of a status and a patrimony—into the identifying label of a man or woman with a body, an existential contingency, a way of occupying a place in a field of interests and affections. In other words, a personal history emerges. In the text as we know it today, completed by a fragment from a hundred years earlier, the *Livro de Linhagens* of Count Dom Pedro is the product of three phases of writing separated by two periods of about twenty years each.

The passage I will analyze belongs to the second phase and alludes to the text containing the original version of the story: *Diz o Conde dom Pedro em seu livro.* The anonymous continuer, therefore, explicitly recognizes the conditions of his work and, after citing his predecessor's version, goes on to present his own version as the truth hidden by the earlier one, now exposed as a slanderous invention. In the investigative procedures that lead him to affirm a legitimate relationship where a birth out of wedlock had previously been indicated, we can identify some of the fundamental mechanisms of historical discourse. I will attempt to describe them and to situate them with respect to this text's particular kind of relationship to reality.

The subject of the passage is Vasco Pimentel, a member of an illustrious fourteenth-century family. According to the text cited by the second author and attributed by him to Dom Pedro, Pimentel was the son of Sancha Martins, who

> made him in the days [during the lifetime] of Dom Gonçalo Rodrigues de Nomães, her husband, with a knight of Riba d'Avizela by the name of Martim Fernandez de Novaes.

This kind of information is never omitted by medieval historical discourse unless it wants to make the opposite seem true, that is, that the marriage vow was respected and that there is therefore no impure blood. Illegitimacy is in fact an irreplaceable signifier for a certain modality of nobility, potentially disdained but also potentially favored, since whatever a bastard achieves might well be counted double in virtue of the handicap he started with.

The author of the cited affirmation does not offer any proofs or even claims to have any, but that very simplicity and a certain mode of certainty suggest that there were no doubts about the matter. An identical impression is caused by the considerable precision with which the names of all those concerned are given (as occurs with the narrative's many other figures). It is fair to say that a documented proper name serves as a historical warranty of what has been attributed to the person in question, such that only a refutation backed up by very persuasive arguments will be able to annul its truth-value. This power of the name seems, in this case, to have been the only weapon at the historian's disposal for winning acceptance of his version of the matter, but he evidently considered it sufficient to achieve his objective.

And we did much, in our time, to know the truth of this matter, if it happened as herein written.

The insistence of the successive writer in verifying the truth of Dom Pedro's words can therefore only be explained by reasons of another order, extraneous to the hermeneutic convention established by the identifying-representative nature of the name. On the other hand, such an attitude is only possible in fairly recent texts, whose author has still not gained the status of an irrefutable authority that time confers. The case, then, is reopened.

There is an obvious similarity in the method employed by history, "investigation of the past," and by judicial activity whenever—as here—the historical work aims to solve a concrete riddle: "we did much . . . to know the truth of this matter." The phrase accentuates the judicial tenor of the motive for the action undertaken. And even more apparent is the judicial character of the means employed, resorting to a form of "investigation" that history-writing since its emergence has employed in order to fulfill its ambition to become credible.

And we learned from noblemen [the names of five noblemen] . . . that this was a slanderous insertion, for they heard from their parents and many others who were from that time and witnessed this matter . . . that it happened this way.

The direct testimony of one who was there is the most totalizing source of information, particularly when the informers are duly identified. The writer clearly assumes that the reader will trust the veracity of words supposedly uttered by eyewitnesses. As we shall see, the hazy line separating what is said by those *who were there* from general *report* or *hearsay*, which everyone knows offers no such guarantees, does not justify this assumption.

Let us go back a little to try to elucidate the circumstances that gave rise to such an ardent effort to confirm or refute what was originally written. There are two passages that might apply. The first (A) concludes Dom Pedro's narrative and is reproduced by the second author

> [t]hey went and pleaded with Dom Martim Gonçalves de Nomães, brother of this Vasco Martins Pimentel, as they had the same mother, to receive him as a brother and not put his mother to shame. And he heard their plea, receiving him as a brother, on the condition that neither he nor any of his descendants would ever have any rights whatsoever over the free land of Palmeira.

immediately before declaring what he has to say (previous quote). The second relevant passage (B) comes at the end of a short biographical digression that follows the second version of the Vasco Pimentel story:

> This Dom Vasco Martins Pimentel married Dona Maria Anes . . . and by her made . . . Dona Orraca Vasquez, who married Dom Gonçalo Pereira, father of the Archbishop Gonçalo Pereira.

That Vasco Martins was an ancestor of the Pereiras, possible sponsors of the *Livro*'s continuation, might have been reason enough to call for a name-cleansing operation, eliminating the black mark of an extramarital generation.

In light of the first passage, it is possible that conflicts over land rights between the legitimate and illegitimate descendants of Vasco Pimentel's mother also made the investigation necessary. Hereditary interests were almost always mixed in with the greater or lesser hostility directed against illegitimate offspring and with the sometimes aggressive way that such offspring defended themselves. By recounting this episode of the Pimentels' story, even while immediately discrediting the only circumstance that would justify it, the anonymous second writer seems to be indicating a relationship between the two instances that transcends mere sequentiality (the only relationship expressed by the copulative "And we did much

. . .". In fact, he suggests that what in the second version is the investigation is the consequence of what precedes it in the text—i.e., of the final episode of the first version. In other words: the harm suffered by Vasco Pimentel (and his descendants) would be incommutable if things happened as Dom Pedro said, but not if the truth of the facts were proved to have been different. The seriousness of the situation justified the search for the truth.

The hereditary issue resurfaces precisely at the beginning of the second version:

> Dom Gonçalo Rodriguez de Nomães treated this Martim Fernandez de Novaes very badly, disinheriting him of his properties . . . . And . . . Dom Gonçalo Rodriguez died, and Martim Fernandez, because he was deprived of his properties, which Dona Sancha Martins had taken from him, harassed her in every way he could. And then the prior of Nandim arrived and made peace between them, so that Dona Sancha Martins gave him his properties.

Although we cannot directly link the two instances, both deal with the question of rights over lands that will belong to Vasco Pimentel, through maternal or paternal inheritance. The text does not warrant us to make elaborate conjectures, but the patronymic influence suggested by text B seems at least plausible.

Text A can, however, be read in another way. The legitimate son's reluctance to recognize his brother, which apparently only the most delicate of arguments—that he "not put his mother to shame"—was able to overcome, brings the force of necessity into the story. Where could Martim de Nomães go to find support and reinforcement for such intransigence— reflected again in the severe conditions he imposed for accepting the brother—if not in the irrefutable assurance, for himself and those involved, that the brother was illegitimate? The story rests on its own evidence, and the text has no chinks. But only a partial story is told; too many causes and links have been omitted. The alternative that will be presented does not erase all doubts, nor will it offer any certain proof, but it will at least fill in lacunae and offer explanations, including an explanation of how the version it replaces came into being.

What we have here, in fact, are two different ways of making History. The text does not explicitly decide which way is better, for neither of the narratives strikes the reader as entirely conclusive. But in the second narrator's discourse there is an implicit belief in the superiority of his own method, and the reader's agreement on this point will determine whether or not he or she adheres to the second version. In other words, the first version, with its perfect internal coherence, will be rejected only if the text that follows it succeeds in convincing the reader that the two authors have different procedural methods and that the method used by Dom Pedro is inferior. I do not wish to explore this last point.

On the other hand, I believe this text offers us a rare opportunity to observe a "historian in action" unveiling his method firsthand and comparing his work with that of a contemporary colleague.

The series of expressions describing the procedures of the two authors reveals a notable semantic difference: "*Diz* o conde C. Pedro" [Count Dom Pedro *says*]; "a fama, a qual *achou* o Conde e feze-a escrever" [the report, which the Count *learned of* and wrote about]. Followed by: "E nós *fezemos* muito" [And we *did* much]; "E *achamos* per fidalgos . . . porque eles *ouviram dizer*" [And we *found out* from noblemen . . . for they *heard*]; "mais *ouvimos dizer*" [we *heard* further].

The form *fezemos* (a verb of action used generically and anaphorically), applied to the first-person speaker, stands out immediately. With it he establishes the transition from Dom Pedro's style (and history) to his own, from an unfounded *dizer* (credulous or ill-intentioned?) to an effort to verify and to determine based on one of the most recommended methods of research—the gathering of eyewitness accounts. The forms *ouviram dizer* and *ouvimos dizer* precede citations from testimonies obtained by this method; as occurs with the first of these terms (examined above), likewise the second term (which comes earlier on in the text) refers to a series of duly named noblemen "who were very true knights, who accompanied Dom Vasco in all the toils he had in Castile," that is, who were with him in the last period of his life and therefore heard from his own mouth what the text reproduces. The verb *achar* is used by the two historians but has rather different meanings, as determined by its different objects. When the second historian says *achamos*, he is announcing with satisfaction that he found what he was looking for, a different version of the story of Vasco Pimentel, guaranteed by the transmission—via just one intermediary—of eyewitness accounts. What the Count of Barcelos *achou*, on the other hand, was no more than *fama*, that is, hearsay evidence.

Let us return to the text of the second version. The aforementioned passage in which the widow Sancha Martins is reconciled with her husband's former enemy, Martim Fernandes de Novais, thanks to the prior of Nandim, leads, somewhat unexpectedly, to

and the knight [Martim] served her and she grew fond of him.

This development comes as a surprise only to those who have not read the earlier version; those who have may wonder why it took so long to appear in this latter version. Here there is no adultery or bastard son. Even so, care has been taken to give the knight the initiative in sentimental matters, Sancha Martins having become attracted to him only after he had "served" her. The emergence of sentimental feeling in the discourse favors the image of the future mother, led by one man (now lost forever) to another (who would enable her to have a future) by the respectable path of chivalrous love, in full accord with the social rules of passion. There is no hint whatsoever of any adulterous relationship as intimated by Dom Pedro's narrative, with the latent suggestion of licentious behavior.

This new relationship continues. Seven months after the death of Gonçalo Rodrigues, a marriage is celebrated before two witnesses. It is kept secret, however, until the full year of mourning stipulated for widows to be able to remarry has passed, and also for fear that the lady might be censured for marrying a man whose blood is less noble.

And this Dom Vasco was made in this period.

Dom Pedro's successor deems that he has discovered the truth he set out to find: a truth which, with specific regard to the time in which Vasco Pimentel "was made," is now known to have been kept a secret known to very few. From the narrator's point of view, this secret acts as a powerful instrument for conferring verisimilitude to the existence of the two versions (essential for the second version to gain adherents), to the doubts that supposedly persisted for many years among certain people, and on the limited access to the truth, only now at this late date made public. From the woman's point of view, on the other hand, the two versions taken together reveal a biting irony of what might be termed destiny. To protect herself against two accusations of what are after all trivial, merely social crimes (disrespect of the customary mourning period and of class distinction) that would, however, "put her mother to shame," Sancha Martins let herself bear the onerous charge of adultery and obliged her son to bear the ignominy of a wrongful birth.

The second narrator recognizes that the assured and peremptory tone used by Dom Pedro to relate his story—with its implications about the mother and son that virtually contradict what the *truth* shows—prompts some questions that need to be answered: Who invented this story? For what purpose? How was it propagated? And he proceeds to address them.

> And after a time . . . there were two young noble brothers of the Marinho family who envied him, and one day in the palace they had words with this Dom Vasco, telling him he was of wrongful birth for having been made in the time of Dom Gonçalo Rodriguez. And this made him very ashamed . . . and he told them they were lying and gave one of them a punch so hard it poked out an eye, and he wrestled with the other, falling with him out of a window of the palace. And the young nobleman Marinho broke a leg and four ribs, and Dom Vasco was so badly wounded he was thought to be dead. For his action he was much praised, and the king promptly awarded him a sum of maravedis.

It is the story of an affront, duly avenged and publicly redressed, with the king's gesture providing for a peaceful, conciliatory end. There is ample detail elucidating the story's various aspects: actions, motives and reactions. The narrator speaks through the words attributed to Vasco Pimentel —"they were lying"—and the entire passage is a gloss on that affirmation, relying for its effect on the exhibition of the lie and its refutation. The vehement rightness of the refutation is reflected in the violence applied to the slanderers, the degree of avenged truth being proportional to the fight's devastating effects, indelible marks on the body of the aggressors and the risk of death for the slandered, whose life would have been worthless had he not upheld his honor.

This scene provides the confirmation of what was reported a little earlier—that the birth was legitimate. The confirmation is necessary for the reader, though superfluous for many others, including the king, to judge by his praise.

Let us not forget that the entire second version depends on the transitive announcement "that it happened this way," according to what those "who were there" told noblemen of the next generation, who later reported the information to the second version's anonymous author. This line of transmission, supposedly immune to subjective interferences, is nonetheless punctuated by two instances of transformation (even before it is transformed into a written account): one that converts what happened into words, and another that states the words that were heard.

The text continues:

> And then, much later, some who did not wish him well, because of his enmity towards them, repeated in his absence the words that the young noblemen had said in the king's palace, and from this grew the report that the Count heard and wrote down in his book.

The historian writing about recent events which he nevertheless did not witness and for which he can find no firsthand witnesses is often constrained to base his information on mere report, or rumor, passed from one person to the next. But the historian writing about a distant past based exclusively on written sources is no less immune to the contigencies of this precarious form of memory, for it was by this means that some of the authors he depends on likewise got their information. Fernão Lopes, a historian of the latter sort, tried to guard himself against the errors that dependence on this kind of information can produce when he wrote such phrases as "they said . . . but I don't know if it's true," or "they said . . . but perhaps because they were friends/enemies of . . . ." However, if a report has circulated widely and for a long time without any challenge to its authenticity, he accepts this as proof that it contains at least a partial truth, particularly if it is presupposed by the logic of subsequent events.

It is disturbing and at the same time reassuringly illuminating to realize, in the text from Count Dom Pedro's

Livro de Linhagens under analysis, that it is not always easy to distinguish between what is mere report and what is not, since oral communication from person to person also permeates, almost inevitably, apparently more trustworthy sources of the so-called truth. (Among the texts that have come down to us, there are very few examples of the extreme case in which the historian tells what he himself saw.)

Within this generalized indefinition, the individualization preferably through a name—of the orally transmitted eyewitness account—seems to be decisive for establishing credibility. In the case of written information, the possibility of attributing it to an author (even when anonymous) carries an identical weight, since writings are in general automatically accorded authority after a certain amount of time has lapsed. As we have seen, the written version of an event that can still be superseded by a plausible version of an eyewitness account does not enjoy this same privilege.

Let us return to the text one last time to consider yet another heuristically motivated episode, the end of the narrative, in which Vasco Pimentel wreaks vengeance on his detractors. This time it is the narrator himself who heard the description of the events: "we heard further" (cited above). And he recounts that Dom Vasco, meeting up with the fellow whose eye he had poked out, now threw him into a well, and it took many men to pull the fellow out.

> And for this cause the king was furious with Dom Vasco and ordered him arrested . . . and later . . . released and thrown out of his household.

This may serve to validate the declaration, several lines down in a separate biographical passage on Vasco Pimentel, that "because the king was unjustly angry with him, he went to Castile." But if that is its purpose, it accentuates rather than attenuates our bewilderment over the motives of the king's action, so contrary to his response to the first physical altercation involving the same persons. There is an obvious attempt (since the king acted "unjustly") to preserve Dom Vasco's honor, both personal and as a liege. But the reader is apt to feel a certain empathy with the king, whose patience was perhaps exhausted by what he considered, in the offended nobleman, to be an exaggerated sense of honor. In the same way, the author's exaggerated eagerness to marshall evidence prompts him to append this episode, which only detracts from the reputation he wishes to defend. It is as if, at a certain point, knowing that doubt can never be eradicated and that his readers also know this, he had lost control of his discourse, which becomes openly argumentative.

We do not know what considerations Dom Pedro had in mind when he wrote his account, how he obtained it, and how rigorously he tested it. But we can be sure that he believed in it, either because he was satisfied by the evidence offered to support the facts that were presented to him, or because it seemed to be compatible with contemporarry rules and expectations.

From the historian's point of view, history is the past in which he believes. This belief comprises not only facts but also values, interests, interpretations, present consequences and future expectations. He would perhaps like all of this to coincide with the truth, but truth is only attainable through faith, whose proper domain is precisely that of the ineffable. History remains, therefore, an amalgam of truth, belief and desire. The necessity of this impurity, of the simultaneous presence of these three components, seems to me to explain the medieval preference—among the various prose genres available—for historical discourse.

Work Cited

Livro de Linhagens do conde D. Pedro. 2 vols. Ed. José Mattoso. Lisbon: Academia das Ciências de Lisboa, 1980.

Chapter 3

The Songs of Melancholy: Aspects of Mannerism in Camões

Vítor Aguiar e Silva

From the time of Greek medicine and philosophy up to the Renaissance and then Mannerism, melancholy has played a prominent role in Western thought and art. Its history—as a nosological and psychological phenomenon and as a philosophical, anthropological and aesthetic category—is nowadays well known, thanks to the research work of eminent specialists.[1] I do not intend to summarize this history, but for the benefit of less-informed readers and to facilitate the comprehension of the present study's objectives, I would like to look briefly at how reflection on melancholy and the symbolic, iconographic and poetic uses of melancholy acquired new and deeper significance in the Renaissance and in Mannerism, becoming crucial elements for understanding the cultural and aesthetic phenomenology of these historical periods.

In the most celebrated of his *Problems* (XXX, 1),[2] Aristotle conferred an anthropological aspect on melancholy that goes beyond the strictly physiological, nosological and medical meaning evident in the etymological composition of the word: *melankholia* is the black bile, the *melaina khole* , one of the four humors which, according to the Hippocratic doctrine, constitute man's corporal and psychological systems. At the very beginning of this text, Aristotle affirms that "all who have been outstanding [*perittoi*] in philosophy, politics, poetry and the arts were manifestly melancholy." Among the more recent illustrious examples, Aristotles cites Empedocles, Plato and Socrates. Depending on how it is combined with the other humors—blood, yellow bile and phlegm—melancholy can, like wine, generate highly diverse effects in humans. "Those in whom black bile is abundant and cold become lazy and stupid," we are told, whereas those in whom "it is superabundant and hot get excited, are full of verve, prone to love, and open to emotions as well as lust, with some of them becoming rather talkative." If in some people melancholy is merely a disease of the body and mind (epilepsy, apoplexy, paralysis, choler, cowardice and lassitude are all *melancholy* diseases), in others a preponderance of this humor, making them *melancholy* by nature (*melankholikoi dia phusin*), endows them with a natural eminence, a singular *ethos*, which distinguishes them from normal people, that is, the "majority of men" (*hoi polloi*).

Aristotle's authoritative considerations—cited and corroborated by Cicero (*Tusculanae disputationes*, I, 80) and by Seneca (*De tranquilitate*, 17: 10-12)—were decisive for fomenting the notion that all intelligent, ingenious and exceptional people, inhabited by the "divine furor," are melancholy. Aulus Gellius, with a touch of irony, writes in his *Noctes atticae* (XVIII, 7, 4) that "this species of intemperance known as *melancholia* does not occur in mediocre and common spirits; on the contrary, *this affectation is almost heroic* and very often expresses truths with power, but *irrespective of the right moment or proportion*."

Whether as a physiological and medical phenomenon or as a characteristic of the *psykhe*, the relationship of melancholy to the life, condition and genius of poets finds eloquent expression toward the end of the Middle Ages and the dawning of the Renaissance.

Dante, who in one of the sonnets from his *Rime* evoked the visitation he received from Melancholy through the use of a prosopopoeic allegory—"Un dí si vene a me Malinconia / e disse: 'Io voglio un poco stare teco'; / e parve a me ch'ella menasse seco / Dolore e Ira per sua compagnia" [One day Melancholy came to me / and said: "I want to spend some time with you"; / and it seemed to me that he brought along / Sorrow and Wrath for his company] (79)—was portrayed by Boccaccio, in the *Trattatello in laude di Dante*, as having the following traits: "il colore era bruno, e i capelli spessi, neri e crespi, e sempre nella faccia malinconico e pensoso" [he had a dark complexion, thick and curly black hair, and a forever pensive and melancholy expression] (608).

Petrarch, in whose *Canzoniere* the word *malinconia* never occurs, portrayed himself in the incipit of sonnet XXXV with one of the words used by Boccaccio to characterize Dante: "Solo e pensoso i piú deserti campi." According to various commentators and exegetes of Petrarch's work, it is highly probable that the genesis of the famous verse is indebted to the Homeric vision of Bellerophon, who in the *Iliad* (6.200-202) is described as a solitary wanderer on a barren plain, forsaken by the gods, inwardly tormented and fleeing from human company.[3] Bellerophon, significantly enough, is one of the mythic figures, along with Hercules and Ajax, evoked by Aristotle in *Problem* XXX, 1, as a paradigm of the *homo melancholicus*. As he dramatically reveals in Book II of his *Secretum*, Petrarch was conscious that he suffered from the pernicious disease of the soul known as *aegritudo* by the ancients and called *acedia* in more modern times: "in hac autem tristitia et aspera et misera et horrenda omnia, apertaque semper ad desperationem via et quicquid infelices animas urget in interitum" (590-92).[4] It is this "solo e pensoso" Petrarch, steeped in sadness and solitude, that Tasso will place among the great melancholy wanderers.[5]

But it was in the domain of Florentine Neo-Platonism that reflection on melancholy attained a depth and dissemination sufficient to transform—in the Renaissance and Mannerist periods—the *morbus melancholicus* into a definite psychological, anthropological and aesthetic category. Marsilio Ficino, the leading figure of Florentine Neo-Platonism and himself a *homo melancholicus*, characterized the man of genius as a melancholy man and considered melancholy to be a "unique and divine gift" bestowed by Saturn, the mightiest and noblest planet. Saturn, *planetarum altissimus*, endows those under its influence with an understanding of the loftiest and most secret things and guides them in the path of "divine contemplation," though this planet can also exert a malign and dangerous influence.[6] It was thanks to Marsilio Ficino and the artistic centers of the Italian Renaissance, particularly Venice, that artists stopped being associated with Hermes or Mercury, to be seen instead as depending on Saturn, that ambivalent god who is cruel and sinister yet also the bestower of ennobling creative energies.[7]

In accord with the basic precepts of humanist thought, Ficino was concerned to teach *literati*, the men of genius, that "they must navigate, as it were, between Scylla and Charybdis," in order to avoid the perils and ill effects of melancholy, as indicated in the title to the first book of his treatise *De vita triplici: De studiosorum sanitate tuenda, sive eorum, qui litteris operam navant, bona valetudine conservanda*. Saturn, like Mars, is a dangerous planet for common men but propitious for "contemplative spirits," for the *literarum studiosi*, for artists.

At the root of Ficino's melancholy there is a sense of primordial *loss*, the loss of an original unity, asserted over and over in *De Amore*, the treatise by Ficino that exercised an especially wide and profound influence on the Renaissance's cultured milieus, particularly in Italy and France.[8] This original loss is a separation from the Father, from the plenitude of the One. Saturn is the god of time and therefore of differentiation and separation, but he is also the god of nostalgic desire, of the desire to return to the original unity. For this reason the Saturn-ruled melancholy of *uncommon* men is a state of mind and spirit that evinces man's nobility and dignity in all its splendor. It is the consciousness of the limits of the human condition, the memory of the lost plenitude and the recognition of the present degeneration and fragmentation, but it is also the drive, the dynamic impulse, the *protentio* to recover the original well-being, to return to the Father, in a movement of *epistrophe* that is essential to Renaissance Neo-Platonism. Ficino's melancholy, then, accords with an optimistic and heroic anthropology, for the loss therein contained is not irrevocable, nor does man sink into a gloomy sadness or agonize in a hopeless state of guilt.

When the anthropological ideal of the Renaissance began to show the first signs of erosion (at the end of the first quarter of the sixteenth century, according to the general consensus of specialists), a new notion of melancholy gradually replaced Ficino's concept, and this was to become one of the most deep-rooted and troublesome notions of Mannerism. As Klaniczay has written: "Certain aspects of Renaissance Platonism ceased to make sense once Mannerism arrived, for they were inextricably linked to the apogee of optimism and harmony of the initial period" (63-64).[9] The words may have been the same, but the meanings they conveyed and disseminated were different and even antagonistic.

With its complexity and secret symbolism, Dürer's *Melencolia I*, dated 1514, represents an idea of melancholy very different from Ficino's notions and the eudemonist ideals of the Renaissance. According to Panofsky's interpretation, Dürer's Melancholy is a man of genius who lapses into despair and depression because of his superabundant intelligence and imagination, for he recognizes in his own genius his limits vis-à-vis the riddle of the universe. His inertia and paralysis of will express the resignation of one who knows that science's secrets and instruments are useless and that all activity is vain.[10]

The literature and art of Mannerism abound with examples of artists and *fictae personae* dominated by neuroses and depressions, steeped in an anxiety without respite, wracked by dilemmas and uncertainties, now driven by an aggressive urge, now prisoners of a unhealthy inertia. The melancholy of Mannerism, unlike the "generous" and "heroic" melancholy of Renaissance Humanism, is a disease, a pathology of the body and soul, a morbid state of mind in which genius and the exceptionality of the creative faculties are allied to suffering, anguish and insanity. No *ficta persona* better exemplifies the *homo melancholicus* of Mannerism than Hamlet. No poet, in his life or work, incarnates and expresses more profoundly this *homo melancholicus* than Torquato Tasso, a pilgrim wanderer fleeing from others and from his own self, prisoner in the hospital of Sant'Anna, divested of his home and name, crushed in body and spirit by what he himself called *soverchia maninconia*, a Hydra he classified as a *nuova pazzia*, for it was a *maninconia per infermità* and a *maninconia per natura* (18-19).[11] For Tasso, as for many theologians, moralists, doctors, philosophers and other sixteenth-century thinkers, melancholy could lead to the heights of genius as well as the depths of insanity.[12]

In the lyric poetry of Camões, if my noncomputerized reading is not mistaken, there is not a single occurrence of *melancolia, melancólico* or any other form of these words, which appear rather frequently in texts from the fourteenth to sixteenth centuries.[13] In *Os Lusíadas* we find the adjective *merencório*, with the meaning of vexed, wrathful, in the first canto, stanza 36, when the narrator describes Mars's intervention on behalf of the Portuguese in the council of the gods: "Merencório no gesto parecia" [He was wrathful in appearance]. In his *Auto dos Enfatriões* the noun *manencória* occurs twice, once in the mouth of Jupiter and once in the mouth of Almena. And yet the words *melancolia* and *melancólico* were already well known and regularly used in the time of Camões. To take just one example, we may cite a work that was definitely known to Camões, Garcia da Orta's *Colóquios dos simples e drogas e cousas medicinais da Índia* (1563). These "colloquies"—for which Camões wrote his first published text, the ode "Aquele único exemplar"—use the word *melancolia* a number of times, with the technical meaning it had in the medicine of the period.[14]

The semantic field of *melancholy* is filled with lexemes in the Latin and vernacular languages of the fifteenth and sixteenth centuries. In a note written in 1989 for the French edition of *Saturn and Melancholy*, Klibansky informs us of a highly interesting list of equivalent Latin terms for *melancholy* appearing in the *Vocabolario italiano-latino* elaborated by the Italian humanist Nicodemo Tranchedini between 1450 and 1460 and conserved in manuscript form in the Biblioteca Riccardiana of Florence: "Melanconia / anxietas / egritudo / animi egritudo / afflictio / solicitudo / meror / mesticia / amaritudo / mestitudo / dolor / angor / cura / molestia / turbatio / perturbatio / calamitas / languor / procella / difficultas / tristitia / confusio / pena / scrupulum / supplicium / stimulus / miseria."

Of the various equivalents indicated by the Italian humanist, one stands out—both in Latin and in the various vernacular tongues—for its frequent usage, for its literary tradition, and for its semantic complexity (which frequent usage gradually trivialized): the term *tristitia*. It is not by chance that one of the most famous chapters of Montaigne's *Essais* is entitled "De la tristesse."[15] In Portuguese and Castilian poetry of the fifteenth and sixteenth centuries, the words *triste* and *tristeza* are extremely frequent and often constitute—from both the semantic and the formal points of view—the core element around which a poem is built. A reading of Garcia de Resende's *Cancioneiro Geral* readily shows how important those words were for the Peninsula's poetic language in the second half of the fifteenth century and the beginning of the sixteenth. In the *Rimas* of Camões, whether in the traditional-style or Italian-style verses, the words *triste* and *tristeza* (or *tristura*) often appear and have an exceptional semantic resonance. Ovid-inspired Camões no doubt found in them a poetic aura not offered by *melancolia*, a more technical word, metrically inconvenient on account of its length, even when anonymous, in lines that employ Italian meter.

As has been repeatedly shown by analysts of the etiology and phenomenology of melancholy, from Freud (2092 ff.) to Julia Kristeva (22 ff.), at the root of melancholy is the loss of a beloved object, the loss of the *Thing*, to use the term employed by Kristeva—the *Thing* that is the principle and pulse of life.

This sense of dissipation and loss of a good, of a beloved object, of the beloved *thing*, is obsessively expressed in Camões's ninth and tenth *canções* [songs]. In the latter *canção*, the poet designates this lost good as the *cousa amada, e tão amada!* [beloved thing, and so beloved!].[16] The references to the *cousa amada* are always in the past: "claros olhos que já vi" [clear eyes that I have seen]; "as orelhas angélicas . . . / daquela em cujo riso já vivi" [the angelic ears . . . / of her in whose smile I once lived]; "a fermosura, os olhos, a brandura, / a graça, a mansidão, a cortesia, / a sincera amizade, que desvia / toda a baixa tenção, terrena, impura, / como a qual outra algua não vi mais . . ." [the beauty, the eyes, the softness, / the grace, gentleness, courtesy, / the sincere friendship, which transforms / every mean, earthly, impure intention, / like no other I ever again saw . . .]. In the ninth *canção*, this lost good is situated in a past that lives on, through memory, in a dead present. The expression of the life of that past is interesting from the formal, rhetorical-stylistic point of view, for it is founded on the verbal form *vi* "I saw"—the sense of sight being the vehicle by which the *espíritos*, the *luz* and the *lume* "flame" of love circulate—and on its phonic duplication in the first person singular of the preterite tense of the verb *viver*:

> trazendo-me à memória
> algua já passada e breve glória,
> que eu já no mundo vi, quando vivi.

> [bringing to my memory
> some brief and bygone glory
> I once saw in the world, when I lived.]

This past mixes and merges with birth itself, having a primarily existential rather than chronological significance. Symbolically speaking, the loss is *original*, meaning that it was always there. The third stanza of the tenth *canção*, suppressed in the 1595 edition of the *Rimas* and published for the first time in the 1598 edition, situates the beginning of the remembered tragedy at the threshold of life itself:

Quando vim da materna sepultura
de novo ao mundo, logo me fizeram
Estrelas infelices obrigado;
com ter livre alvedrio, mo não deram,
que eu conheci mil vezes na ventura
o milhor, e pior segui, forçado.
E, para que o tormento conformado
me dessem com a idade, quando abrisse
inda minino, os olhos, brandamente,
manda que, diligente,
um Minino sem olhos me ferisse.
As lágrimas da infância já manavam
com ua saüdade namorada;
o som dos gritos, que no berço dava,
já como de suspiros me soava.
Co a idade e Fado estava concertado;
porque quando, por caso, me embalavam,
se versos de Amor tristes me cantavam,
logo m'adormecia a natureza,
que tão conforme estava co a tristeza.

[When from the maternal womb
I first came into the world, already
I was ruled by unlucky Stars;
though I had free will, I was forbidden
a thousand times from choosing what was
best, being forced to follow the worst.
And in order that I would be accorded
the right torment with age, as soon as
I gently opened my still infant eyes
a Child without eyes was ordered
to injure me with all diligence.
My childhood tears already flowed
with an impassioned nostalgia;
the cries I made in my crib
already sounded to me like sighs.
I was in harmony with my age and Fate;

for whenever they rocked me,
if they sang sad verses of love,
I naturally fell right to sleep,
so resigned was I to sadness.]

This narrative stanza should not be interpreted in strictly autobiographical terms as meaning that the birth of the poet led to his mother's death. In Faria e Sousa's commentaries to this *canção*, readers and exegetes of Camões's lyric poetry can find hermeneutic and intertextual information that contributes substantially to a *poetic* reading of these verses, drawing us away from the temptation to indulge in fanciful biographical interpretations. As Agostinho de Campos recommends, "look here for more *Dichtung* than *Wahrheit*, more poetry than biography" (in Camões 265).

Birth, according to the Neo-Platonic concepts of the universe and of life, is the threshold of an exile and of ontological degradation. The maternal womb is a "materna sepultura," that is, an enclosed space, without light. In the elegy "Que novas tristes são, que novo dano," Camões makes a reference to the "materno, escuro ninho." According to Marsilio Ficino, obscurity and want of light characterize *Penia*, or Indigence, the female and maternal principle (209). The downplaying of motherhood that occurred in Neo-Platonic Renaissance thought is unequivocally borne out by the chapter of *De Amore* in which Ficino, taking up ideas from Plato and Pausanias, explains that heavenly Venus, the intelligence of the sovereign God, was born without a mother, since *the mother is matter*, and between the supreme intelligence and matter there can be no commerce: "Venus prima, quae in mente est, celo nata sine matre dicitur, quoniam mater apud Physicos materia est. Mens autem illa a materie corporalis consortio est aliena" (154). The day of birth is one of suffering and disgrace, often marked by fateful and dreadful signs and about which poets, following a long tradition going back to the *Book of Job*, utter curses and imprecations. The *fera humana* "human beast" mentioned in the fourth stanza of the tenth *canção*—be it a wild animal such as the "tigre Hircana" at whose breast the poet, when a "fraco infante," would like to have been raised, as we read in the elegy "O Poeta Simónides, falando," be it an unloving step-mother, or be it (as Faria e Sousa proposes) a lascivious whore, like those "lobas isentas, que amor vendem" [wolves in the wild, who sell their love] of the last stanza of the fourth ode[17]—is in any case a metaphor or symbol of birth's cruelty and suffering.

Indigence, obscurity and the indistinct nature of the feminine and maternal principle do, however, receive seeds of light, splendor and energy from the masculine and paternal principle, symbolized in the divine lightning bolt. According to Ficino, the masculine principle, "like the seed, contains the reasons for all things." From the dawning moment of conception, from the painful hour of birth, love manifests itself as an anamnestic longing to regain the lost unity, to redeem the original loss, commented on at length by Ficino in the first chapter of *De Amore*. Exceptional, melancholy persons know love from the cradle and drink the *amorous poison* from the tenderest age, being ruled by *ill-fortuned stars* and condemned to torments, madness and griefs. This theme of Neo-Platonic and Petrarchan poetry from the sixteenth century is well expressed in the following sonnet of Boscán:

> Aún bien no fuy salido de la cuna,
> ni de l'ama la leche uve dexado,
> cuando el amor me tuvo condenado
> a ser de los que siguen su fortuna.
>
> Diome luego miserias d' una en una
> por hazerme costumbre en su cuydado;
> después en mí d' un golpe ha descargado
> cuanto mal hay debaxo de la luna.
>
> En dolor fuy criado y fuy nacido,
> dando d' un triste passo en otro amargo,
> tanto que, si hay passo, es de la muerte.
>
> ¡O coraçón! que siempre has padecido,
> dime: tan fuerte mal, ¿cómo es tan largo?
> Y mal tan largo -di-, ¿cómo es tan fuerte? (239)

Both in the ninth and tenth *canções*, the beloved woman—always evoked and described by Neo-Platonic and Petrarchan topoi in a symbiosis of human and divine traits—is absent, distant and lost. The loss of the *cousa amada* reveals the limitations and contradictions of human love, inextricably interwoven with impulses and longings for spiritual elevation as well as with madness, griefs and guilt. In Camões, as in other Mannerist poets, love is shrouded by a tragic shadow. In both *canções*, love and the lyric persona's story of love are dominated by an obsessively invoked entity: the blind force of destiny. Freedom, one of the fundaments of the *dignitas hominum* exalted by Renaissance humanism, is denied and crushed by an obscure, cruel and inescapable power that the poet denounces and accuses: "fera ventura" [brutal luck]; "soberba Fortuna; / soberba, inexorável e importuna" [haughty Fortune; / haughty, inexorable and vexatious]; "o Destino nunca manso" [Destiny never gentle]; "as Estrelas e o Fado sempre fero" [the Stars and forever harsh Fate]; "o inexorável e contrário / Destino, surdo a lágrimas e a rogo" [inexorable and hostile / Destiny, deaf to tears and supplication]; "Estrelas infelices" [unlucky Stars]; "Fortuna injusta" [unjust Fortune]; "Fortuna flutuosa" [fickle Fortune].

In perfect accord with the diagnosis formulated by Freud in "Mourning and Melancholy," the loss of the *cousa amada* results in a dramatic accumulation of psychic erotic tension in the poet. Thought, memory, nostalgia, complaint, envy, wrath and passion consume his soul, body and life. The two *canções* form a somber semiological picture of the obsessions, anxieties and depressive reactions generated by the erotic psychic tension of the melancholy man. Claude-Gilbert Dubois, who considers melancholy to be one of the Mannerist period's distinguishing themes, writes, with reference to Hamlet, that for the Mannerists

> to be is a perpetual dying, but death is not death. "To die, to sleep": perchance to dream, and the dream recaptures all the images of life. Of *this* life that is a death. A living death and a dying life. The antithesis becomes an oxymoron and the dissociated elements of the concept reunite in a tragically lived complex, which expresses itself through a verbal complex whose elements reinforce instead of cancelling each other. Melancholy is the complex result of this opposition of complements. (200-01)

The dilemmas and contradictions that wreck the sensibility, the will and the intelligence are expressed in the antitheses, oxymorons and paradoxes so frequently found in Mannerist literature. In the *envoi* of *canção* IX, Camões invokes an antithesis and paradox with one of the longest traditions in love poetry, running from the Middle Ages to the baroque period:

> Assi vivo; e se alguém te perguntasse,
> Canção, como não mouro,
> podes-lhe responder que porque mouro.

> [Thus I live; and if anyone asks you,
> Song, why I don't die,
> you can say it is because I die.]

The equation of life to death found ample expression in the *dolce stil novo* poets, in Petrarch, in fifteenth-century Peninsular poetry, and in the neo-Petrarchans of the sixteenth and seventeenth centuries. The following *letrilla* from a fifteenth-century Spanish love song, glossed *a lo divino* by St. Theresa of Avila and St. John of the Cross, became very popular:

> Vivo sin vivir en mí
> Y de tal manera espero
> Que muero porque no muero.[18]

The death of love as a theme, besides expressing the mortal suffering of the lover, can also represent—on the plane of divine as well as human love—love's consummation, the climax of the amorous union, so that both the troubadour-lover and the mystic-lover long for that supreme moment and *die because they do not die*. Camões, however, diametrically inverts the fifteenth-century *letrilla* and the glosses of the two sixteenth-century mystic saints, saying "I do not die because I die, and therefore I live." This paradox is explained in the light of the Neo-Platonic concept of love. As Marsilio Ficino wrote, "he who loves is dead in himself," but the lover lives in his beloved, is transformed into his beloved, and therefore—dying of love in himself—does not die, because he lives in his beloved lady.

Melancholy is expressed in Camões as the consciousness and anguished feeling of life's dispersion in space. The theme of errancy, of wandering without respite, hyperbolized by Tasso as a symptom of his *soverchia maninconia*, is dramatically represented in the ninth and tenth *canções*. The theme of the *locus horrendus* that opens *canção* IX, with its impressive accumulation of dysphoric adjectives, is a vehicle for expressing this other theme of errancy around the world:

Aqui, nesta remota, áspera e dura
parte do mundo, quis [minha fera ventura] que a vida breve
também de si deixasse um breve espaço,
porque ficasse a vida
pelo mundo em pedaços repartida.

[Here, in this remote, harsh and rough
part of the world, [my brutal luck] wanted fleeting life
to occupy a likewise fleeting space,
causing my life to be strewn
around the world in pieces.]

The theme of geographical wandering acquires an unusual existential breadth and depth in the lyric voice of Camões, due to his life and experiences as a Portuguese man of the mid-sixteenth century, battling as a soldier in north Africa, braving the fierce oceans, and fighting in the lands of the Orient:

Destarte a vida noutra fui trocando;
eu não, mas o destino fero, irado,
que eu ainda assi por outra não trocara.
Fez-me deixar o pátrio ninho amado,
passando o longo mar, que ameaçando
tantas vezes me esteve a vida cara.
Agora, experimentando a fúria rara
de Marte, que cos olhos quis que logo
visse e tocasse o acerbo fruto seu
(e neste escudo meu
a pintura verão do infesto fogo);
agora, peregrino vago e errante,
vendo nações, linguages e costumes,
Céus vários, qualidades diferentes,

só por seguir com passos diligentes
a ti, Fortuna injusta, que consumes
as idades, levando-lhe diante
ua esperança em vista de diamante,
mas quando das mãos cai se conhece
que é frágil vidro aquilo que aparece.

[Thus I exchanged my life for another;
not I but savage, wrathful destiny,
for I myself wouldn't have exchanged it.
Destiny made me leave my beloved native nest
and cross the wide seas, which often
put my dear life in danger.
Now, enduring the matchless fury of Mars,
who early on wanted me to see and touch
with my own eyes his bitter fruit
(and in my shield others can see
the picture of the hostile fire);
now, an aimless and wandering pilgrim,
I see nations, languages, customs,
various Skies and diverse qualities,
merely to follow with diligent steps
you, unjust Fortune, who consumes
the ages, dangling before them a hope
that looks like a diamond
but, when it falls from the hand,
turns out to be fragile glass.]

Geographical wandering, a hostile change imposed by Fortune, is seen by the poet as antithetical to the peace, tranquility and security of the *pátrio ninho amado*, a symbol that recurs, in slightly different form, two other times in the work of Camões. The epic song of *Os Lusíadas*, inspired by a high patriotic love, is a "pregão do ninho meu paterno" [cry from my paternal nest] (I, 10), and Monçaide addresses the Portuguese navigators with these words: "Ó gente, que a Natura / vizinha fez de meu paterno ninho" [O people, whom Nature / has made neighbor to my paternal nest] (VII, 30). The presence of the possessive pronoun in these phrases underscores the speaker's strong emotional attachment to his native land, *the land of my father*. The expression *materno ninho*, which occurs in the elegy "Que novas tristes são, que novo dano," has a dysphoric force, deriving from its usage in combination with the adjective *escuro*, placed between *materno* and *ninho*, and from the context in which the phrase is used: the women bared their bellies to the frightened Persians, yelling at them with rage and scorn to hide "outra vez no materno escuro ninho." The *ninho materno* is the mother's belly or womb, a dark and enclosed space, like a tomb. The *ninho paterno* (or *pátrio*) is a space that embodies love, that symbolizes man's identity, continuance and unity. The pathetic image of "vida / pelo mundo em pedaços repartida," evoking a bloody corpse torn to pieces, expresses dispersion, fragmentation and discontinuity—the opposite of the values symbolized by *pátrio ninho*.

Incessant wandering over furious seas and through strange and inhospitable lands is the outer manifestation of a constant inner agitation. Even more cruel and destructive than the harsh natural elements—"o sol ardente e águas frias, / os ares grossos, férvidos e feios" [the burning sun and cold waters, / the thick, sweltering and harsh air]—are the thoughts that continually wreck the poet's captive soul, allegorically represented as a torn-up body, covered with gaping wounds, surrounded by torments and exposed to the blows of Fortune:

> Chagada toda, estava em carne viva,
> de dores rodeada e de pesares,
> desamparada e descoberta aos tiros
>   da soberba Fortuna:
> soberba, inexorável e importuna.

> [Covered by sores, its raw flesh burning,
> surrounded by griefs and sorrows,
> forsaken and exposed to the blows
>   of haughty Fortune:
> haughty, inexorable and vexatious.]

Using words spoken by Jesus in the Gospel of Saint Matthew ("nowhere to lay his head," 8:20), an intertextual relationship that cosmically hyperbolizes the suffering of the lyric *persona*, the poet dramatically emphasizes his agitation and his despair by metaphorically adding on a spiritual and psychic complement not found in the Gospel:

Não tinha parte onde se deitasse,
nem esperança algua onde a cabeça
um pouco reclinasse, por descanso.

[He had nowhere to lay down,
nor any hope on which his head
might lean a little and rest.]

This modification of the evangelical subtext expresses the extreme sensation of abandonment and the radical solitude of those who have no place on earth where they can rest their head nor a shred of hope to which they might cling. In a world in turmoil, man vainly searches for rationality among things and events—"dar às coisas que via outro sentido, / e pera tudo, enfim, buscar razões; / mas eram muitas mais as sem-razões" [to give another meaning to the things I saw, / and to seek reasons for everything; / there was, however, much more unreason]—but discovers that he is helpless and impotent before the ruthless, wrathful and even sadistic powers that rule the world:

Somente o Céu severo,
as Estrelas e o Fado sempre fero,
com meu perpétuo dano se recreiam,
mostrando-se potentes e indignados
contra um corpo terreno,
bicho da terra vil e tão pequeno.

[Only stern Heaven,
the Stars and forever harsh Fate,
took delight in my perpetual suffering,
showing themselves mighty and indignant
gainst an earthly body,
a paltry worm of the vile earth.]

In these verses man, divested of spiritual dignity, is no longer a creature formed from the dust of the earth in the image and likeness of God. Forsaken by an indifferent Creator, he becomes merely a "corpo terreno," a "bicho da terra vil e tão pequeno."

Over and against this tortured wandering through space, the melancholy man obsessively looks back at a past time—the time when he knew the *cousa amada*. The poet, through his memory, lives in the past, recalling the lost age, reliving in his imagination the gentleness and grace of the beloved woman, wishing he could reverse time:

> Que se possível fosse, que tornasse
> o tempo para trás, como a memória,
> pelos vestígios da primeira idade,
> e de novo tecendo a antiga história
> de meus doces errores, me levasse
> pelas flores que vi da mocidade;
> e a lembrança da longa saudade
> então fosse maior contentamento,
> vendo a conversação leda e suave,
> onde ua e outra chave
> esteve de meu novo pensamento . . .

> [If only it were possible for time
> to go back, like memory,
> to the vestiges of my first years,
> spinning once more the old history
> of my sweet roamings, taking me
> past the flowers of youth I once saw,
> so that my nostalgia's remembrance
> would be a greater joy,
> seeing the soft and fair conversation,
> that held one and another key
> to my youthful way of thinking . . .]

The *cousa amada* is (re)constituted in memory and by memory, and so this poem of melancholy is presented as the *history* of a lost time, the *history* of a loss, a dissipation, an absence. Only an ingenuous or strictly biographical reading could interpret this history as an autobiographical record of actual events. It is a history inscribed in the lyrical poetry model that held sway in Europe from the fifteenth to the seventeenth century—the Petrarchan model—and its poetic, anthropological and metaphysical significance must be construed in light of its Neo-Platonic and Petrarchan context. The poetry of Camões, like that of Petrarch or Herrera, is the *poetic construction* of an autobiography in which fiction and reality, literary memory and experiential memory, figments of the imagination and actual facts are woven and fused together. Poetry and the poetic *fictio*, therefore, are what form— according to the model of Petrarch and his followers—the "history" of the narrated and confessed love; it is not the *res gestae* of a biography that give rise to the confession and narration of the history and generate, in consequence, the poem.[19] In melancholy souls, the *cousa amada* can be an erotic phantasm, an obsessively elaborated inward image, disassembled and reassembled by the *spiritus phantasticus*, by the lover's tireless meditation that gives body to the incorporeal and makes what is corporeal bodiless.[20] Camões continually emphasizes this work of his imagination and his meditations: "aqui estiv'eu co estes pensamentos / gastando o tempo e a vida" [here I was with these thoughts / wiling away time and life], "aqui o imaginar se convertia / num súbito chorar" [here imagination transformed / into sudden weeping], "em vos afigurando o pensamento, / foge todo o trabalho e toda a pena" [when my thought is fixed on you, all toil and grief disappear], "aqui, sombras fantásticas, trazidas / de alguas temerárias esperanças" [here, fantastic shadows, called up / by rash hopes], "mas a dor do desprezo recebido, / que a fantasia me desatinava, / estes enganos punha em desconcerto" [but the pain of the disdain I received, / rendering my fantasy wild, / turned these illusions against each other], "as águas que então bebo, e o pão que como, / lágrimas tristes são, que eu nunca domo / senão com fabricar na fantasia / fantásticas pinturas de alegria" [the waters I drink and the bread I eat / are sad tears, which I can never master/ except by fabricating in my fantasy / fantastic pictures of joy]. The *cousa amada* does not necessarily refer to an actual woman but may be a fictional entity metaphorically standing for the original unity, plenitude and purity that are God—the God in whom man, beset by misery and agony, must place his faith, so as not to founder inexorably in a tragic world reduced to nothing, as happened to the giant Adamastor, one of Camões's most eloquent expressions of melancholy.[21]

The melancholy man, in his anxiety and agitation, often exhibits an almost pathological verbosity (but like a two-faced Janus he has another, taciturn side), as we find in a poet such as Tasso and in a *ficta persona* such as Hamlet. Melancholy in Camões—a mixture of pain and ire, nostalgia and desire—

vents itself in shouts, in weeping, in rhetorical questions, and, above all, in poetic discourse committed to paper, "meu tão certo secretário" [my faithful secretary], but written like a confused confession blurted out before a cosmic audience that includes God, the world, humanity and the wind, and that is directed in particular to the *desesperados*, whose trials and sufferings make them the poet's ideal listeners:

> Chegai, desesperados, para ouvir-me,
> e fujam os que vivem de esperança
> ou aqueles que nela se imaginam,
> porque Amor e Fortuna determinam
> de lhe darem poder para entenderem,
> à medida dos males que tiverem.

> [Come and hear me, whoever despairs,
> and flee from those who live by hope
> or those who think they have it,
> for Love and Fortune have given you
> the wherewithal to understand
> in proportion to the wrong you've suffered.]

The first two stanzas of *canção X* expound the model of writing employed by the poem: a dramatic enunciation in which the subject summons *paper*, his *faithful secretary*, in order to shout out—in writing—his grief, his tears, and the "suspiros infinitos" [infinite sighs] which inhabit his soul and through which he will subsequently appeal to his ideal listeners, the "desesperados."[22] The confession must be shouted, so intense is the grief consuming the poet, but the human voice is too weak to express the violence of this grief, which will therefore always be imperfectly communicated. Using an audacious metaphor in verses of extraordinarily dramatic force, Camões desires and entreats that his song be transformed into a tremendous, unprecedented fire of human grief: "acenda-se com gritos um tormento / que a todas as memórias seja estranho" [let a torment blaze with shouts, / a torment unknown to human memory].

This torrentially confessional writing, composed of shouts, complaints, imprecations, memories and desires, regains a metaphorical dimension in the envoi, when the subject, as if exhausted from so much confession, shouting and complaining, becomes aware of the verbosity—so symptomatic of the melancholy person's agitation and anxiety—that has dominated the poem:

Nô mais, Canção, nô mais; qu'irei falando
sem o sentir, mil anos. E se acaso
te culparem de larga e de pesada,
não pode ser (lhe dize) limitada
a água do mar em tão pequeno vaso.
Nem eu delicadezas vou cantando
co gosto do louvor, mas explicando
puras verdades já por mim passadas.
Oxalá foram fábulas sonhadas!

[No more, Song, no more, or I'll talk on
in a daze for a thousand years. And if
they complain you're long and heavy,
reply that the sea's water will not fit
in such a small vessel.
And I will not sing of niceties
to bring myself praise but tell
stark truths I have experienced.
Would they were mere dreams!]

This envoi finds an intertextual echo in the *commiato* of Boscán's song "Quiero hablar un poco," where we read: "Canción: si de muy larga te culparen, / respóndeles que sufran con paciencia; / que un gran dolor de todo da licencia" [Song: if they complain that you're too long, / tell them to endure with patience, / for an overwhelming grief gives licence]. And it probably also echoes, as noted by Faria e Sousa, the beginning of the fourth book of the *Tristia*, where Ovid explains the possible defects of his books through his poetry's profound and direct relationship to the wrongs and sufferings he has known as an exile. These intertextual memories demonstrate that Camões knew how to literarily forge his autobiography. The Petrarchan poetics of poetry as *imitatio vitae* produce the effect of reality and justify the poem's formal excesses and imbalances.

In their anxiety and affliction, obsessed by their doubts, meditations and phantasms, the artists and *fictae personae* ruled by Mannerist melancholy are aware of being persecuted by an implacable force, and they withstand their suffering in solitude, without finding relief or compassion. Paradoxically, the melancholy wanderer, in his "curso contino de tristeza" [ongoing journey of sadness], in his "passos tão vãmente espalhados" [so uselessly scattered steps], walking "sem ver por onde" [without knowing where to], roaming across so many lands and seas, has nowhere to place his feet, no air to breathe, no time nor even any world of his own to live:

> A piedade humana me faltava,
> a gente amiga já contrária via,
> no primeiro perigo; e, no segundo,
> terra em que pôr os pés me falecia,
> ar para respirar se me negava,
> e faltavam-me, enfim, o tempo e o mundo.
> Que segredo tão árduo e tão profundo:
> nascer para viver, e para a vida
> faltar-me quanto o mundo tem para ela!

> [In the first danger I faced, I found
> no human pity, and friendly folk
> spurned me; in the second,
> there was no earth on which to place
> my feet, no air to breathe,
> nor even time and the world.
> What a deep and terrible secret:
> to be born to live while lacking
> all that the world has for life.]

Ruled by the tyranny of their own phantasms, melancholy men, as Burton explained, citing "the philosopher of Conimbra" (vol. I, 308), are incapable of coping with normal, daily life, for the fear and intensity of their meditations make them prisoners of their own suffering, inhibiting all action.[23] Camões expresses the melancholy man's inability to have a normal life and activity in this way:

> que inda agora a Fortuna flutuosa
> a tamanhas misérias me compele,
> que de dar um só passo tenho medo.

[for even now fickle Fortune
afflicts me with such misfortunes
that I'm afraid to take a single step.]

Without land, air, time or a world, without the compassion of other men, and forsaken or forgotten by God, the melancholy man of Camões turns inward, transforming his misfortune into a "gosto de ser triste" [fondness for being sad], beholding himself in an inward mirror, like a distraught Narcissus who, through poetic confession, shouts to the heavens and to men, telling the extravagance of his suffering, his love and his destiny. The Saturnian melancholy of Mannerist artists found an emblematic figure in a neurotic Narcissus[24] that can embody an extraordinary tension of psychic and fantastical libidinal energy and whose furious, irrepressible desire continually reopens the wounds of his devastated, melancholy heart, as we read in the verses preceding the envoi of *Canção IX*:

mas o Desejo ardente, que detença
nunca sofreu, sem tento
m'abre as chagas de novo ao sofrimento.

[but ardent Desire, which never
delays, heedlessly
reopens my wounds to suffering.]

In the agitated, labyrinthine, ambiguous, dilemmatic and cruel world of Mannerism, before which reason not only wavers[25] but founders, narcissistic melancholy—by introducing into the ego a mental fixation on the lost *cousa amada*, the lost object of desire—tragically incorporates Eros and Thanatos. Like the torment that afflicts the eternally damned in the Greek myths that so obsessed Camões, desire— far from being able to restore and re-create the original unity, as Marsilio Ficino had hoped—incessantly reopens the wounds that symbolize the physical, moral and spiritual misery of man. The Saturn of Mannerism, as depicted by Camões in his second eclogue, is a somber and cruel divinity who kills and devours his children and whose turning of the wheel of time only aggravates human misery. It is a misery that can only be alleviated when the Father, in an act of pure

love made possible by divine grace, receives the son in the
paterno ninho. After the shipwreck of reason, Camões places
his faith in a return to the law of the Father.

Notes

1. The most important studies on melancholy, in its various facets and
manifestations, are: Klibansky et al.; Wittkower; Jackson; Préaud; Brilli;
Schleiner; Schiesari; Enterline; Lambotte; Panofsky; Carchia; Kristeva.
There are several particularly relevant studies concerned with
manifestations of melancholy in specific authors: see Screech; Pot;
Starobinski; Chambers; Dolfi; Pensky.

2. The Greek text of this *Problem*, edited in 1988 by Raymond
Klibanksy and accompanied by a French translation and excellent
notations, is found in Klibansky et al. 52-75. Another French translation
of this *Problem* is found in Aristotle. There is considerable doubt about the
the Aristotelian authorship of this text.

3. The Homeric vision is taken up by Cicero in the *Tusculanae
disputationes*, 3: 26: "Qui miser in campis maerens errabat Aleis,—ipse
suum cor edens, hominum uestigia uitans."

4. On the *acedia* of Petrarch, see: Wenzel 155-63, 185-86; Rico 197 ff.
On *acedia*, or *accidia*, see the cogent study by Agamben 5-35.

5. In his dialogue *Il Messagiero*, Tasso, when evoking the melancholy
wandering of Bellerophon, does not quote the aforecited verses of Homer
but the first quatrain of Petrarch's sonnet "Solo e pensoso i piú deserti
campi," thus implicitly including Petrarch in the lineage of the great
melancholy souls (cf. Tasso 18-19).

6. Ficino's main work on melancholy is his treatise *De vita triplici* (in
Opera omnia, vol. 1, Basileae: 1576), recently issued in a facsimile edition
as *De vita libri tres*. There are two editions of the work with an English
translation: *The Book of Life*, ed. and trans. Charles Boer (Irving, Texas:
Spring Publications, 1980), and *Three Books on Life*, ed. and trans. Carol
Kaske and John R. Clarck (Binghamton: Medieval Texts and Studies—
Renaissance Society of America, 1989). On Ficino's ideas regarding
melancholy and his Saturnian conception of genius, see: Chastel;
Klibansky et al. 389 ff; Schiesari 112 ff.

7. On this point see Wittkower.

8. Ficino wrote his treatise *In Convivium Platonis sive de Amore* in
1468-69, revising and enlarging the text various times until arriving at
what may be regarded as the definitive version in 1482, when the
philosopher dedicated his translation of Plato to Lorenzo di Medici. Ficino
himself made an Italian translation of the Latin text of his treatise some
time before 1474. From 1484, the date of the first edition of his translation
of Plato's works, until 1602, there were at least twenty-three editions of *De
Amore*. For a modern, authoritative edition of Ficino's treatise, see Marsile

Ficin, *Commentaire sur le Banquet de Platon* (full reference under Works Cited). A Spanish translation of the treatise was recently published: Marsilio Ficino, *De Amore: Comentario a "El Banquete" de Platón*, translated, with a critical introduction, by Rocío de la Villa Ardura (Madrid: Tecnos, 1986). For commentary on the treatise, see Martins 1: 383-404.

9. Excellent analyses and interpretations of melancholy, anxiety and anguish as guiding notions of the Mannerist vision of the world can be found in Hauser, and in Hocke.

10. See also chapter 4 of Klibanksy.

11. On Tasso's melancholy, see Schiesari, especially chapter 4, and Basile.

12. Cf. Screech 37.

13. See Machado 2: 1535-36.

14. For one such usage, see Orta 2: 137: ". . . e pollo pulso dizem se tem febre ou não, e se está fraco ou rijo, e qual he o humor que peca, se he sangue ou colera, ou fleima, ou melamcolia: dam bom remedio para as opilações" [. . .] and from the pulse they can tell if one has a fever, and if he is feeble or hale, and which of the humors is at fault, whether blood or choler, or phlegm, or melancholy; they have a good remedy for obstructions].

15. Defaux points out that *tristesse* is a semantically highly charged term for Montaigne: "if it also means, as Montaigne indicated after 1580, 'maliciousness' and 'malice' in Italian, it is very close, in its Latin meanings, to what in French we understand not only by 'tristesse' but also by 'mélancolie,' 'désespoir,' or 'accablement,' moral or physical 'dépression'" (5).

16. All citations from Camões's lyric poetry are taken from Costa Pimpão's edition of the *Rimas*. There can be no doubt as to Camões's authorship of the ninth and tenth *canções*. The phrase *cousa amada*, which also occurs in the incipit of the famous Camões sonnet "Transforma-se o amador na cousa amada," has a long genealogy, having already appeared, for example, in the eighteenth canto of *Purgatorio* in *The Divine Comedy*, when Virgil explains the nature of love:

> Poi, come 'l foco movesi in altura
>   per la sua forma ch'è nata a salire
>   la dove piú in sua matera dura,
> cosí l'animo preso entra in disire,
> ch'è moto spirituale, e mai non posa
> fin che la cosa amata il fa gioire.

The phrase *cosa amata* also occurs in one of the most widely read books of the sixteenth century, *Il libro del cortegiano*, by Baldassare Castiglione (Castiglione 39).

17. Prostitutes are *lobas isentas*, in accord with Morais's *Dicionário*, because free of affections and distinctions.

18. For a discussion of St. Theresa's and St. John of the Cross's glosses *a lo divino* of this *letrilla*, see Hatzfeld 167 ff. See also Dias 78-79.

19. I have analyzed these issues, of fundamental importance for interpreting Camões's lyric poetry, in the essay "Aspectos petrarquistas da lírica de Camões." As concerns Petrarch, a number of important studies on this subject have been written, including Santagata. The problem of poetic fiction vs. autobiography in the work of Herrera has been superbly analyzed by Cuevas.

20. See Agamben 28 ff.

21. The giant's love story is a tragic tale of deceit, illusion and loss of the *cousa amada*. Led on by the cruel dictates of "Fado imigo" [enemy Fate], the giant, when he hugs and kisses the naked body of Thetis, loses "the Ocean's most beautiful" nymph and is horrified to find himself converted into hard earth and rocks.

22. This model of enunciation recalls the discourse of the sonnet "O dia em que eu nasci moura e pereça," whose authorship, however, cannot with certainty be attributed to Camões, as I have demonstrated in "Inquirições sobre o soneto *O dia em que nasci moura e pereça.*"

23. Burton writes: "Why students and lovers are so often melancholy and mad, the philosopher of Conimbra assigns this reason, *because, by a vehement and continual meditation of that wherewith they are affected, they fetch up the spirits into the brain; and, with the heat brought with them, they incend it beyond measure; and the cells of the inner senses dissolve their temperature; which being dissolved, they cannot perform their offices as they ought.*" This "philosopher of Conimbra" is obviously not Camões, contrary to what Marie-Claude Lambotte writes (Lambotte 51). Burton cites the author of the celebrated *Comentarii Collegii Conimbricensis Societatis Iesu in quattuor libros de Coello Aristotelis Stagiritae* (Lisbon: S. Lopes, 1593), published as a collective work.

24. Mathieu-Castellani 351-64, and Enterline. On the relationship of narcissism to melancholy in *canção X*, see the interesting essay by Earle.

25. Cf. Eduardo Lourenço's splendid essay.

Works Cited

Agamben, Giorgio. *Stanze. La parola e il fantasma nella cultura occidentale.* Turin: Einaudi, 1977.

Aristote. *L'homme de génie et la mélancolie.* Paris: Éditions Rivages, 1988.

Basile, Bruno. *Poëta melancholicus: Tradizione classica e follia nell'ultimo Tasso.* Pisa: Pacini Editore, 1984.

Boccaccio, Giovanni. *Opere in versi, Corbaccio, Trattatello, prose latine, epistole.* Milan: Ricciardi, 1965.

Boscán, Juan. *Obras.* Ed. Carlos Clavería. Barcelona: Promociones y Publicaciones Universitarias, 1991.

Brilli, Attilio, ed. *La malinconia nel Medio Evo e nel Rinascimento.* Urbino: Quattro Venti, 1982.

Burton, Richard. *The Anatomy of Melancholy.* London: G. Bell, 1904.

Camões, Luís de. *Camões lírico*. Ed. Agostinho de Campos. Vol. 5, *Canções*. Lisbon: Livraria Bertrand, undated.

Carchia, Gianni. "Spirito e malinconia." *Aut aut* 251 (1992): 75-93.

Castiglione, Baldassare. *Il libro del cortegiano*. Ed. Ettore Bonora. Milan: Mursia, 1972.

Chambers, Ross. *Mélancolie et opposition: Les débuts du modernisme en France*. Paris: Corti, 1987.

Chastel, André. *Marsile Ficin et l'art*. 2nd ed. Geneva: Droz, 1975.

Cuevas, Cristóbal. "Introducción." Fernando de Herrera. *Poesía castellana original completa*. Madrid: Ediciones Cátedra, 1985.

Dante Alighieri. *Rime*. Ed. Gianfranco Contini. Turin: Einaudi, 1973.

Defaux, Gérard. "Montaigne et la rhétorique de l'indicible: l'exemple 'De la tristesse' (I, 2)." *Bibliothèque d'Humanisme et Renaissance*, 55. 1, 1993, 5-24.

Dias, Aida Fernanda. *O "Cancioneiro Geral" e a poesia peninsular de Quatrocentos (contactos e sobrevidência)*. Coimbra: Livraria Almedina, 1978.

Dolfi, Anna, ed. *Malinconia, malattia malinconica e letteratura moderna*. Rome: Bulzoni 1991.

Dubois, Claude-Gilbert. *Le maniérisme*. Paris: PUF, 1979.

Earle, T. F. "Autobiografia e retórica numa canção de Camões." *Arquivos do Centro Cultural Português* 23 (1987), 507-19.

Enterline, Lynn. *The Tears of Narcissus: Melancholia and Masculinity in Early Modern Writing*. Stanford: Stanford University Press, 1995.

Ficin, Marsile. *Commentaire sur le Banquet de Platon*. Ed. and trans. Raymond Marcel. Paris: Société d'Édition "Les Belles Lettres," 1956.

Ficino, Marsilio. *De vita libri tres*. Ed. Martin Plessner. Hildesheim: Georg Olms Verlag, 1978.

Freud, Sigmund. "Duelo y melancolia." *Obras completas*. Vol. 2. 3rd ed. Madrid: Biblioteca Nueva, 1973.

Hatzfeld, Helmut. *Estudios literarios sobre mística española*. 2nd ed. Madrid: Gredos, 1968.

Hauser, Arnold. *El Manierismo: La crisis del Renacimiento y los orígenes del arte moderno*. Madrid: Ediciones Guadarrama, 1965.

Hocke, Gustav René. *El mundo como laberinto. I. El Manierismo en el arte europeo de 1520 a 1650 y en el actual*. Madrid: Ediciones Guadarrama, 1961.

Jackson, Stanley W. *Melancholy and Depression from Hippocratic Times to Modern Times*. New Haven: Yale University Press, 1986.

Klaniczay, Tibor. *La crisi del Rinascimento e il Manierismo*. Rome: Bulzoni, 1973.

Klibansky, Raymond, Erwin Panofsky, and Fritz Saxl. *Saturne et la mélancolie. Études historiques et philosophiques: Nature, religion, médecine et art*. Paris: Gallimard, 1989 [original edition: *Saturn and Melancholy. Studies of Natural Philosophy, Religion and Art* (New York: Thomas Nelson & Sons, 1964)].

Kristeva, Julia. *Soleil noir. Dépression et mélancolie.* Paris: Gallimard, 1987.

Lambotte, Marie-Claude. *Esthétique de la mélancolie.* Paris: Aubier, 1984.

Lourenço, Eduardo. "Camões e o tempo ou a razão oscilante." *Poesia e metafísica: Camões, Antero e Pessoa*, 31-49. Lisbon: Sá da Costa Editora, 1983.

Machado, José Pedro. *Dicionário etimológico da língua portuguesa.* 2nd ed. Lisbon: Ed. Confluência-Livros Horizonte, 1967.

Martins, José V. de Pina. *Humanisme et Renaissance de l'Italie au Portugal: Les deux regards de Janus.* Lisbon-Paris: Calouste Gulbenkian Foundation, 1989.

Mathieu-Castellani, Gisèle. "Narcisse maniériste?" Ed. Daniella Dalla Valle. *Manierismo e letteratura.* Turin: Albert Meynier, 1986.

Orta, Garcia da. *Colóquios dos simples e drogas da Índia.* Facsimile of the 1895 edition "coordinated and annotated by the Count of Ficalho." Lisbon: Imprensa Nacional Casa da Moeda, 1987.

Panofsky, Erwin. *The Life and Art of Albrecht Dürer.* Princeton: Princeton University Press, 1971.

Pensky, Max. *Melancholy Dialectics: Walter Benjamin and the Play of Mourning.* Amherst: University of Massachusetts Press, 1993.

Petrarca, Francesco. *Opere.* 4th ed. Ed. Emilio Bigi. Milan: Mursia, 1968.

Pot, Olivier. *Inspiration et mélancolie: L'épistémologie poétique dans les "Amours" de Ronsard.* Geneva: Droz, 1990.

Préaud, Maxime. *Mélancolies.* Paris: Herscher, 1982.

Rico, Francesco. *Vida e obra de Petrarca. I. Lettura del Secretum.* Padua: Antenore, 1974.

Santagata, Marco. *I frammenti dell'anima: Storia e racconto nel Canzoniere di Petrarca.* Bologna: Il Mulino, 1992.

Schiesari, Juliana. *The Gendering of Melancholia: Feminism, Psychoanalysis, and the Symbolics of Loss in Renaissance Literature.* Ithaca: Cornell University Press, 1992.

Schleiner, Winfried. *Melancholy, Genius, and Utopia in the Renaissance.* Wiesbaden: Otto Harrassowitz, 1991.

Screech, M. A. *Montaigne and Melancholy—The Wisdom of the "Essays."* London: Duckworth, 1983.

Silva, Vítor Manuel de Aguiar e. "Aspectos petrarquistas da lírica de Camões." *Cuatro lecciones sobre Camoens*, 99-116. Madrid: Fundación Juan March/Cátedra, 1981.

_____. "Inquirições sobre o soneto *O dia em que nasci moura e pereça.*" *Camões: Labirintos e fascínios*, 191-207. Lisbon: Cotovia, 1994.

Starobinski, Jean. *La mélancolie au miroir: Trois lectures de Baudelaire.* Paris: Julliard, 1989.

Tasso, Torquato. *Prose.* Milão: Ricciardi, 1959.

Wenzel, S. *The Sin of Sloth: "Acedia" in Medieval Thought and Literature.* Chapel Hill: University of North Carolina Press, 1967.

Wittkower, Rudolf, and Margo Wittkower. *Born under Saturn: The Character and Conduct of Artists: A Documented History from Antiquity to the French Revolution.* London: Weidenfeld, 1963.

◆ **Chapter 4**

Baroque Literature Revised and Revisited

Margarida Vieira Mendes

The Baroque in Portugal (1600-1750): Under Mercury's Wing

Of all the concepts invented to describe and understand literary orders or periods, that of the baroque is no doubt the most fantastical. The notion, forged in the twentieth rather than in the seventeenth century, is both illegitimate in the field of literature, and overcharged with controversial meaning, or simply overused. Perhaps it would be more salutary for literary criticism to eliminate this epithet altogether, which is as short on precision as it is long on fantasy, and to deal directly with the literary production of the time. The truth remains, however, that without the baroque as a guiding notion we would be without glasses to see, without an image, without a form, without a whole. It is, furthermore, a concept that does not hinder monographic studies, editions of texts from the "baroque period," and other pertinent scholarship, and it has a heuristic value, being useful for comparative studies and as a mediator of dialogue between artistic systems. To ban the concept would bring no benefit to history or to criticism, but to define it as an autonomous entity would be a waste of time. It is still possible, moreover, to speak of the Portuguese literature produced between 1600 and 1750 without characterizing it as baroque.[1]

The fact is that the fondness for the baroque prompted the discovery, the appreciation, and many renewed interpretations of literature from the seventeenth century, largely neglected until it was visited by the twentieth. The founders of Luso-Brazilian baroque literary studies, divisible into two generations, are well known and need only be briefly mentioned here. The pioneering *discoverers*, to use a conventional metaphor, were Maria de Lourdes Belchior in Portugal, under the influence of Dámaso Alonso's stylistic criticism, and Afrânio Coutinho in Brazil, in the field of the theory of literary history. These critics, working in the 1950-60s, began to study and reassess writers and styles from the period in question, considering them in the context of an international artistic category and not merely as a part of Portuguese and Brazilian literary history. The second generation, which may be called that of the *constructors*, was active in the 1970s and includes Vítor M. Aguiar e Silva, whose seminal work, based on a study of themes and stylistic devices from seventeenth-century Portuguese poetry, distinguished the baroque from Mannerism, and Aníbal Pinto de Castro, who traced the evolution of the treatises on oratory during the baroque period in Portugal. The primary bibliography assembled by these scholars is still one of the best instruments of study for researchers. They all worked directly with manuscripts and/or rare editions that had been forgotten in libraries around the country, and they were instrumental in having some of these texts published or reprinted.

Moving forward to the last quarter of our own century, we may observe that the mode of recognition for the baroque is no longer according to style or historical period and that the focus has shifted to individual authors and texts, viewed in light of a given problem or theoretical perspective; at the same time, efforts are being made to edit and provide access to texts. I would call particular attention to António J. Saraiva's essays on the inventive writing of Padre António Vieira and the doctrines of the *concept*, within the theoretical framework opened up by Foucault's notion of *discourse*, and to Maria Lucília Pires's studies on Father Manuel Bernardes (concerning problems of intertextuality) and on seventeenth-century poetic theory and criticism. In the past ten years the baroque has become a star attraction, accompanying speculations on modernism, postmodernism, the media and cultural studies as well as the surge in the description and classification of Portugal's artistic patrimony with exhaustive exhibitions and official support of inventory work having assumed an unprecedented importance in the last decade.[2] With one of its main promoters being José A. Freitas de Carvalho, attention has also been showered on the Portuguese baroque in relationship to the culture of Iberia, Europe and the areas around the world that were explored and/or settled by the Portuguese, and in relationship to scholarly studies in areas such as spiritual literature.[3] Ana Hatherly, guided by the artistic affinities of her own visual poetic creation, has called attention to the poetic genres that intersect with the visual arts (labyrinths, portraits, lipograms) and has promoted studies and editions of novellas and rare works, particularly of Sóror Maria do Céu and of the late baroque, under King John V. In 1988 she founded an important journal of baroque literature and art, *Claro Escuro*.[4] In Brazil João Hansen, in his study of the Bahia poet Gregório de Matos, has introduced a vision of literary production linked to the institutional context and cultural models, being interested as well in *preceptismo* and the doctrines of decorum. There are also recent studies on religious oratory, viewed ideologically (João Marques), in terms of baroque rhetoric and aesthetics (Margarida Vieira Mendes), and from a political and theological perspective (Alcir Pécora), these last two being concerned with the sermons of Padre António Vieira.[5]

With respect to the concept of the baroque that emerges from Portuguese literature, I will here try to sum up my own hypotheses—delineated in previous studies—on a baroque model of signification.[6] I focus on three distinct, but overlapping, aspects of literary communication: (1) the discursive context, (2) the figurative thematic composition, (3) the reference. In much of the poetry, religious oratory and historiography of the time, the creative force of form derives from a baroque expressivity in which the technical means of celebratory rhetoric attain the refinement achieved by Mannerist poetic language. The result was a highly nuanced and artificial and, at the same time, narcissistic and ancestral relationship between man, language and the world.

The discursive context was that of the special occasion or circumstance, informed by an elocutionary archetype that might be the *laudatio* (as a literary strategy of service and offering), or the satire (as a literary strategy of imprecation), or the complaint, as well as the slander, or indeed any kind of speech. When an author uses the epideictic or demonstrative genre, he shows off as an *hacedor*, and we have then ostentation or performative self-representation (the writer/orator *erecting* a metaphor or concept to offer it to someone). In this context, the relationship of language to reality is not substitutive and metaphorical, as is often thought about the baroque language, for metaphor cannot reveal or make known any reality. Rather, the aim seems to be to impress the reader by means of clever devices or *jogadas* (see Ávila). In Jerónimo Baía's sonnet to a parrot in the palace, similes such as *Primavera com pés* [Spring with feet], *jardim alado* [winged garden] or *ramalhete de plumas com sentido* [meaningful/sentient bouquet of feathers] do not make us see better or hear better a talkative and indiscreet parrot; they merely call attention to the language and to the performer, the cultured and conceptualist writer, whose skill allows him to use eccentric concepts. He displays his verbal wares to negotiate with someone—no doubt the bird's owner, the recipient of the composition. That is why the crystal chandelier of the Duchess of Savoy is attributed the properties of *Alpe luzido, luminar nevado* [Lustrous Alp, snowy luminary] among many others, and also why unorthodox metaphors are applied to Saint Peter in a sermon of Padre António Vieira.

Poetic language naturally tends to flatter in a courtly setting, which is where baroque communication in Portuguese literature took place. A parrot, a butterfly, a chandelier, a saint or a monarch, when lauded with a poetic or oratorical edifice of *concetti*, acquires an added facet of existence, and this existential accretion, which was apparently lacking, is a simulacrum predicated on the verbal edifice itself. And so writers created pretentious verbal artifacts that circulated in a market so closed and so long-enduring that it ultimately became worthless and finally extinguished in the course of the eighteenth century.

This simulacrum became complex due to the figural density of textual composition, achieved through tropes of argumentative and persuasive discourse. The predominant form of composition may be called prophetic, for it is based on repetition and mirroring, through recourse to figures, dreams, portraits and paintings—that is, to prophecies. The metaphorical mode of composition is complicated by a series of reversible analogical fictions that, just like prophecy, serve as proof and rely on the medieval technique of allegorical figurativism, placed now at the service of the panegyric, both sacred and profane. Within the chain of painted images or figures that reflect each other, with scenes on top of scenes— as in the sonnet of Sóror Madalena da Glória (1672-?) *a uma caveira pintada em um painel que foi retrato* [to a skull painted on a panel that used to be a portrait]—each figure can as easily be prior, contemporaneous, or subsequent to another, since time is abolished. There is only a kind of childlike presentness. As Vieira says, the copies come before the originals, and the originals are also copies. This prophetic reversibility has aesthetic consequences, for it shapes the form or the structure of texts. The name *Sebastião*, as it amphibologically designates the saint and the Portuguese king, decisively affects the ambivalent composition of Vieira's entire "Sermon on St. Sebastian" (1634). The poem "Ao Menino Jesus em metáfora de doce" ["To Baby Jesus through metaphors of desserts"][7] is also strategically based on the meeting of two motifs: that of religious worship and that of desserts. The euphoria is overwhelming, for everything is enhanced and exalted: Baby Jesus and His theological significance; Portuguese sweets and their vocabulary; poetry and its *techne*; the author and the one to whom his or her text is addressed. This exuberance, aroused by the high-charged linguistic discourse, goes beyond the art of textual composition to construct an equally repetitive order for life itself. And so the critic Manuel Severim de Faria, to exalt Camões, asserted that he had been messianically prophesied by the Sibyl of Cumae in Virgil's fourth eclogue, where she speaks of the poet who would sing the history of the second Argonauts.[8]

The figurative reversibility that takes place in texts also occurs in relation to reality, that is, to the subject of reference. The zealous strategy of flattering the mimetic instruments themselves seems to have operated quite independently of an anemic and misprized world that the most serious and realistic literary historians usually consider frivolous and insignificant (parrots, saints, birthdays, small feet, hunts and bleedings). But this does not imply, at least in the Portuguese baroque, an ultimate failure of intentions. Whatever the thematic scenario and its object, the real intention was almost always different from the theme, being situated in the contiguous present of the communicative situation centered on the speaker and on the language, that is, in the *deixis*. In baroque epideictic discourse, the reference runs through the analogical series of figurative mediations but is pragmatically aimed at a concrete reality, contemporary and contiguous to what is being said. It is an oblique and deferred realism, which is sometimes able to mobilize various types of art and create dialogue among them, resulting in chains of emblems and effigies. We have, for example, the various *ekphrasis* by Academy members on paintings of Bento Coelho,[9] or the drawing that was commissioned and commented on by Dom Francisco Manuel de Melo as an emblem of his concept of history, with the meaning of each allegorical figure leading ultimately to the author and the one he addresses (the Duke of Bragança), both of whom are quite real.[10]

The realism of Portuguese baroque literature does not rely only on this type of reference but is founded as well on a conception and usage of language that excludes both mimesis and worldly knowledge. What matters instead is the force of the discourse. The meaning is in the *energy* of the argument and the proof, with passion and emotion playing a vital role, for the word is meant to act on things. Such a pragmatic stance is evident in the festive poetry, sermons, apologies and moral satires—in that part of literature, in other words, that participated in the rituals of community life as a ceremonial gesture, a quasi-athletic performative act, a commentary and effective transformation of the world's realities. What we have here is a pragmatical and performative, nonmimetic realism. It was this baroque model of signification that allowed for the literary impregnation of the political *pathos*, an essential characteristic of the Portuguese literature of the time.

Two Baroques: Conceived as Two Ellipses

The architectural plans of certain churches (e.g., Providência Divina, drawn for Lisbon by Guarino Guarini) intersected ellipses with polygons. Portuguese baroque literature is likewise marked by regional, chronological and authorial variations that belong to the very definition of baroque. Chronologically speaking, there are at least two baroques. But cutting across time there is another, geographical paradigm that would distinguish between a Portuguese, a Brazilian, and a Luso-Brazilian baroque. Can we identify a literary baroque that is specifically Brazilian? Or that is present in Brazil? Is there a baroque unique to Bahia? To Minas Gerais? Keeping these questions in parentheses, I will propose a dual-centered sketch or *caprice* for both the first and second periods.

The first, early baroque period covers the seventeenth century, especially from the reign of Phillip III (IV of Spain) on (1621), and had its most fruitful years immediately following the Portuguese Restoration (1640-68). Dominated by nationalist fervor and by sacred oratory, the literature still depended on Spanish models and was by and large bilingual.

The second, late baroque, situated in the first half of the eighteenth century, orbited around King John V, the Magnanimous (1706-51), and was dominated by courtly celebration and ostentation, the conventual catechism, the triumph of the Academies, and the forging of a national patrimony.

Both periods have a Luso-Brazilian component, since important authors were born or died in Brazil (Vieira, Gregório de Matos, Manuel Botelho de Oliveira, António J. da Silva). Their texts, furthermore, allude to specific New World realities and address themes whose origins are not confined to the cultural reality of the Lisbon court or Portugal's academies, convents and colleges. And indeed how could they be? The circumstantiality of baroque literary communication brings into literature the singular, local realities of its time and place.[11]

Both periods are also marked by an unequal distribution of better authors among the various genres. This clearly contrasts with the preceding period, the Golden Century of Portuguese literature,[12] in which talent was more evenly apportioned, with excellence in courtly theater (Gil Vicente), the novella (*Menina e Moça*), the epic (*Os Lusíadas*), lyric poetry (Camões and Sá de Miranda), historiography (João de Barros), travel accounts (*Peregrinação*), philosophical dialogue (Frei Heitor Pinto), and tragedy (*Castro*).

Early baroque literary production was bicephalous and imbalanced. It may be described as an ellipse, with two rather different focal points. One focus is sacred oratory with its discursive satellites and its "star" author, Padre António Vieira (1608-97), who wrote and preached in Portugal, Rome and Brazil. The other focal point was summed up in a single but versatile and masterful writer, Dom Francisco Manuel de Melo (1608-66). These foci stand for artistic quality in the religious and secular aspects of baroque conceptualism. Both participated in the realist and politically conformist dimension of early baroque literature and referentiality.

The aesthetic case of Vieira is obsessive and one-sided. His oral, written and political texts (thirteen volumes of sermons, political commentary, letters, and prophetic apologies on the Fifth Empire) derive from the discursive matrix of religious oratory, whose potentialities they systematically exploit, and they are imbued with a sacramental aspect sustained by the medieval figurative-allegorical method. The sermons were much read and glossed, particularly in subsequent poetry and in *jogos florais* [poetical and literary contests]. Even the Mexican writer Sor Juana Inés de la Cruz commented on a sermon of Vieira in her *Crisis*, giving rise to a controversy that for her had tragic consequences.

Dom Francisco, a bilingual writer, was a moralist who experimented with the various discursive forms of the literature of the day. With one of the most acerbic and sententious styles of all Portuguese literature, this author, who aspired to be *libertine* and open-minded, undertook a critical revision of various elements of the society, culture and customs of the time, employing a number of genres: treatises (on the Kabbalah, marriage, military policy, poetry, history), works in verse, personal letters, biography, hagiography, compilations of sayings, the novella, comedy, moral apology and historiography.

I am convinced that the knowledge and the inclusion of these two authors in the canon of European baroque literature will contribute to a renewal of the very notion of the baroque. Vieira's works, in particular, seem to me to be fundamental for a proper understanding of the aesthetic, linguistic and historical category known as the baroque.[13]

The late baroque is likewise centered on two literary figures, one in the religious sphere and the other in the world of theater (*óperas de bonecos* "puppet operas"): Padre Manuel Bernardes (1644-1710) and António José da Silva (1705-39). As with Vieira and Dom Francisco, this pair likewise exemplifies the kind of literature that prevailed at the time: the asceticism of an ingenuous and limited conventual catechism, on the one hand, and showy, operatic entertainment on the other. Bernardes naturalized the rhetorical devices of public speaking, creating an effect of simplicity that combined well with his expertise in the art of the exemplum. The nine comedies of António José da Silva were written for a kind of puppet theater that already parodied opera, with sung parts and props. The themes were mythological, the plots labyrinthine and the dialogues witty, depending greatly on the "reparteeist" sort of character, on puns, and on quid pro quos. The niceties of love, metamorphoses, and mistaken identities were served by witty and piquant sayings.

Many other poets and erudite writers proliferated in these two ellipses. With the refinement and regularization of poetic language brought about by the Mannerists at the end of the Golden Century, poetry came to be one of the most popular and practiced arts among the general public, but it also became a minor art, giving rise to countless poetic parodies. A good deal of Portuguese baroque poetry still exists only in manuscript form, and for the time being I dare mention only the works of Sóror Violante do Céu (1607-93), António Barbosa Bacelar (1610-63), Jerónimo Baía (?-1688), Gregório de Matos (1633-96), Manuel Botelho de Oliveira (1636-1711) and Francisco de Vasconcelos Coutinho (1665-1723). These, together with the four top-ranking authors mentioned above, were undoubtedly the creators of the Portuguese and Luso-Brazilian literary baroque. Little more art is likely to turn up.

I should also mention the poetry, prose and theater produced by women, which was a novelty of the time. The writers were usually, though not always, cloistered nuns. Besides the early baroque Sóror Violante do Céu, there was also the late baroque Sóror Maria do Céu (c. 1658-1752), whose edifying literature based on *a lo divino* allegory and on the books containing emblems of Christian piety has been gaining increasing attention.

Another popular baroque genre was the novella. Some novellas were "exemplary," others were byzantine in character—by authors such as Gaspar Pires Rebelo (?-1684), Frei António (Gerardo) de Escobar (1616-81), Frei Lucas de Santa Catarina (1660-c. 1740)—and others still were meant for Christian edification, such as those written by Padre Mateus Ribeiro (c. 1618-c. 1693). There were also novellas written in Brazil, such as the one by Nuno Marques Pereira (1728).[14]

In the area of poetics, the *Nova arte de conceitos* (1718-21), by Francisco Leitão Ferreira (1667-1735), is a theory of elocution and metaphor well deserving of publication. In the *preceptista* mode, a study still needs to be made of the complete work of Manuel Pires de Almeida (1597-1655), most of which remains unpublished and in a fragmentary state.[15] The work of both authors was carried out in the ambit of the Academies, the institutions where the greater part of literary life took place. In addition to theory, literary criticism in Portugal is a baroque invention: in the Academies, in Dom Francisco Manuel de Melo's *Hospital das Letras* (c. 1657), and in the studies of those who edited and commented on Camões, beginning with the first prologue to the *Rimas*, by Fernão Rodrigues Lobo Soropita (1595), and with Manuel Correia's edition of *Os Lusíadas* (1613), followed by an intense critical, apologetic and philological labor throughout the rest of the seventeenth century.[16] Finally, it may be said that the baroque includes, as one of its fundamental components, the establishment of a published, comprehensive literary memory, in the dictionaries and "libraries" of Portuguese authors.

Hospitals and Libraries: The Telling of a History

The most tedious aspect of the Portuguese baroque may have been the most useful: the formation of a library of writers. It was a huge undertaking that involved several men of letters, several generations and several institutions. These same men of letters (Manuel Severim de Faria, Manuel Pires de Almeida, João Franco Barreto, João Soares de Brito, Manuel Faria e Sousa, Dom Francisco Manuel de Melo), who maintained close intellectual contact through various channels, produced criticism, polemical texts, and literary satire. All this happened in the Academies, in book prefaces, and in apologies and satires.

Always under the banner of demonstrative rhetoric and national fervor, the realizations in this area (gathering, cataloguing, summarizing and praising) belong to the age of baroque literary art and therefore enter into its description. But the previous century had opened up the process on two fronts, which makes Portuguese baroque literature seem like the last hurrah of the Manueline humanist Renaissance and narrows the gap between the gold tribute money from the Orient that had poured in during the 1500s and the gold that would arrive from Brazil in the 1700s.

The first front was that of nationalist ideology. Beginning with the reign of King Manuel I (1495-1521)—who patronized all arts that symbolized the imperial character of Portuguese royal power—humanist erudition, rhetoric and a whole eulogistics concerning the sovereign[17] converged on behalf of national propaganda, and these were later joined by the militant and triumphant programs and practices of the Jesuits, the royal panegyric, and the erudite fantasies of the antiquarians (such as André de Resende and Francisco de Holanda). This activity generated an enormous amount of data that served the *inventio* of seventeenth-century writers and of the prevailing panegyrical mode of communication (Hesiod reminds us that the Muses were the daughters of Memory). Consider the Portuguese legends such as that of Inês and Pedro, a pair of heroes who, since the time of Fernão Lopes, Garcia de Resende and Anrique da Mota, were seen as the Lusitanian reincarnation of the Greek and Latin lovers of Ovidian extraction. Consider as well André de Resende's ancient inscriptions from Évora or Lusitania,[18] the personified etymologies such as Lisibeia in Gil Vicente's *Auto de Lusitânia*, the myths of national origins such as the Battle of Ourique, the founding heroes such as Clarimundo, Ulysses and Tubal, and the holy warriors such as the Condestável. In short, a private Olympus of the Portuguese is reclaimed for identity purposes out of the territory of the great Greek, Latin and biblical narratives. *Os Lusíadas* (1572) was the literary enshrinement of this vast project, and Frei Bernardo de Brito's monumental historical and geographical compilation, *Monarquia Lusitana* (1st vol. 1598, 8th vol. 1727) extended it to a fanciful universal history. The intellectual attitude of imitating the Romans led to the promotion and promulgation of Portugal's *excelências*, colored by the nationalist pathos, as in the fourth of Frei Amador Arrais's *Diálogos*, "Da glória e triunfo dos lusitanos" (1589).[19] It was this movement to exhaustively record national origins and apologetic fictions that inaugurated the formation of the patrimonial corpus of Portuguese literature.

The second front has to do with the Renaissance love of discovery, description and study of the country's physical characteristics, such as its cities, its capital, the rivers and hills, the people and the agriculture, but, first and foremost, its language. The *Gramáticas* of Fernão de Oliveira and of João de Barros date from 1536 and 1540, and the first attempts to standardize spelling, by Pero de Magalhães Gândavo and by Duarte Nunes de Leão, are from 1574 and 1576,[20] preceding by more than a century João Franco Barreto's *Ortografia da língua portuguesa* (1671). Dictionaries and lexicography represent the first concerted effort to search and record a memory with respect to the language. Jerónimo Cardoso's dictionary dates from 1562,[21] followed in the next century by Agostinho Barbosa's dictionaries (1611) and by the linguistic studies of the Jesuit Bento Pereira (1605-81).[22] The culminating result of these preliminary efforts was Rafael Bluteau's grandiose *Vocabulário Portuguez e Latino* (1712-28), a baroque literary summa.[23]

In other parts of Europe, "General Libraries" began to be compiled and sometimes published in book form as early as the sixteenth century, according to Barbosa Machado's own words in the prologue of his *Biblioteca lusitana* (1741). But it was only in the seventeenth century that a similar effort got under way to systematically catalogue the heroes, religious orders and nobility of Portugal, by means of "Temples," "Mirrors," "Gardens" and "Theaters" of remembered saints, women and illustrious men, without any poetic or epic pretext, just encyclopedic oratorical purposes. Examples include Frei Luís dos Anjos's *Jardim de Portugal, em que se dá notícia de algumas santas e outras mulheres ilustres em virtude* [Garden of Portugal, in which are recorded some female saints and other women famed for their virtue] (1626), António de Sousa de Macedo's *Flores de España. Excelencias de Portugal* [Flowers of Spain. Excellencies of Portugal] (1632), or Jorge Cardoso's *Agiólogo lusitano de santos e varões ilustres em virtude do reino de Portugal* [Lusitanian hagiologium of saints and men famed for their virtue in the kingdom of Portugal] (3 vols., 1652-66).[24] A similar intent would inspire the "Theaters" or "Libraries" of the heroes of letters, that is, writers, as well as the "Parnassuses" or poetic anthologies, such as *Fénix Renascida*, or *obras poéticas dos melhores engenhos portugueses* (5 vols., 1716-28), and, in the previous century, the collections resulting from the poetic contests in the *Academias dos Singulares*.[25] These anthologies gave disproportionate importance to modern writers, which accords with the character of baroque realism. All of this labor occurred outside of schools and the university, being undertaken by courtly literary circles, by convents, by printers and booksellers, and by the various Academies.

Another genre that praised by way of compilation is that of the "Viagens ao Parnaso" or "Templos de Apolo," of Italian origin and almost always satirical, with Cervantes having set the example in *Viaje del Parnaso* (1614). In his *Laurel de Apolo* (1630) Lope de Vega devoted the third *silva* to Lisbon, eulogizing various contemporary authors (from the previous century he singled out only Sá de Miranda, Camões and Jorge de Montemor). Jacinto Cordeiro tried to fill out the list in his *Elogio de poetas lusitanos* (1631), likewise written in verse. António Figueira Durão, in *Laurus Parnassea*, has Fame praise contemporary Portuguese poets (mentioning only Sá de Miranda and Camões from the past),[26] and in an epithalamic poem to the Duke of Bragança, *Templo da memoria* (1635), Manuel de Galhego apostrophizes thirty-three *engenhos* "inventive, talented people" of Portugal, all of them active poets. The "Viagem ao Parnaso" genre gave rise to significant parodies of baroque epideictic communication, with the literary institution itself serving as the theme. The unpolished Diogo de Sousa Camacho, for example, satirized the intellectual milieu in his *Jornada às Cortes do Parnaso* (1614-21?). And one of the interlocutors in the dialogue *Hospital das Letras*, discussed below, was Boccalini's *Ragguagli di Parnaso*.

There was also a specifically baroque way of conceiving and making books, with a number of prefatory Latin and vernacular poems that eulogized the author and the work he was publishing. It was the names of living poets that mattered, and the same names appeared over and over, as if the publishers themselves were the promoters of academies and poetic contests. It was the kind of attention that had been enjoyed by Garcia de Resende in the court of King Manuel, around 1500, and that would again occur with Castilho in the third quarter of the nineteenth century.

Even a book that seems to be of literary criticism can take the form of an onomastic "Parnassus" or library of authors. Such was the case with Dom Francisco Manuel de Melo's highly felicitous dialogue, *Hospital das letras* (1650-54, not published until 1721). So as to undertake its survey in an amusing way, needling by means of moral and aesthetic satire, this dialogue between four appraisers proceeds to a minute *shelf-by-shelf* critical inspection of the library of Portuguese authors. This kind of inspection presupposes the physical existence of such a library. In fact various large libraries besides Dom Francisco's had been formed (that of Severim de Faria, for example, or of the Marquis of Nisa). This was very much within the spirit of collecting that grew out of the humanist Renaissance but that bore fruit especially in the seventeenth century. (An example of an ardent collector of Portuguese art is Vicente Nogueira, who lived in Rome.)

The *Hospital* reveals a concern to group Portuguese authors in general categories that nevertheless overstep the boundaries of what we now call literature and that would better fit in a wide concept of "Belles Lettres," on the condition that political works and treatises could be included. Although this apologetic dialogue remained unfinished, the literature section visited by the interlocutors offers us a systematic grouping of books and manuscripts by poets, critics (of Camões, for example, called *camoístas*), politicians, historians and preachers. It is one of the first classifications of Portuguese literature, different from the one that Dom Francisco himself set forth in his Letter no. 414 and that Machado's *Biblioteca Lusitana* adopted in its indices almost a century later.

Another aspect that stands out is the oratorical structure underlying this dialogue, typical of the "Paralelo" genre and marking a departure from the allegorical narratives previously employed in certain poetic works, to ridicule the poetic practices of the time through fictions, such as Soropita's *Descobrimento das ilhas da poesia,*[27] where the allegory of the *enfermarias da ilha* first appeared. In the *Hospital*, the Portuguese writers are appraised in groups right after the most famous foreigners. In fact the character of the author—or rather, of his book, since it is the book that speaks—is the only Portuguese interlocutor and repeatedly shows a bias for writers of his own country. (The other interlocutors are critical works by Justus Lipsius, Boccalini and Quevedo.) Also conspicuous is the high appreciation shown for contemporary writers, an inclination that stimulated the development of baroque literary studies.

In addition to evaluating books, Dom Francisco Manuel de Melo was also concerned to catalogue authors. In a circular letter to *Varões doctos* "Learned Gentlemen," he asked for information on "Portuguese writers, ancient and modern," for a "Catalogue of all the writers of this Kingdom, in every science, art, faculty and discipline." The ideal entry would be accurate and laudatory, with as much information as possible "about the work as well as the author, the year and place he wrote it, to whom he dedicated it, what qualities he possessed, in what language he wrote and if he wrote on other subjects, what acclaim he had"—whatever would be "useful for making him known and lauded" (Melo, Letter no. 558, 533-34).

Dom Francisco was also one of the first to conceive an editorial project of works by "our poets from the past," which was aimed at adorning and improving the Republic of Letters and for which he formulated a coherent set of editorial principles and criteria for transcription (Melo, Letter no. 579, 548-50). And in a letter from 1650, repeating the old sixteenth-century commonplace that the Portuguese, unlike other nationalities, do not appreciate what belongs to them, he proposed to celebrate the best modern writers, whom he enumerated and divided into subject areas, which Barbosa Machado called Faculties: scriptural exegesis, philosophy, rhetoric and letters, moral theology, Latin, vernacular poetry, mathematics, medicine and surgery, politics, history and epitomizing, apologies, genealogy, mystical theology, morals, music, law, and canons. Such was the order "of this literary edifice erected against mortality" (Melo, Letter no. 409, 422). In his *Diálogo em defensão da língua portuguesa* (1574), Pero de Magalhães Gândavo had already traced the first outline of a canon of Portuguese literature, having named the following authors from among his contemporaries, along with some of their works: Sá de Miranda, the "foremost" (in "comedies and verses"), followed by João de Barros's *Ásia*, Frei Heitor Pinto's *Imagem da vida cristã*, Lourenço de Cáceres, Francisco de Morais, Jorge Ferreira de Vasconcelos and António Pinto—all of these in prose—and by Camões, Diogo Bernardes and António Ferreira in poetry, plus André de Resende's *Livro da antiguidade de Évora*.[28] In the seventeenth century this list was reduced to Sá de Miranda and Camões, thus making more room for the exhaustive inclusion of the coterie of living writers, as the goal was no longer to single out quality but merely to fill up the totality of a field.

The most important baroque project of Portuguese literature was to "put into print an entire library,"[29] a collective undertaking that lasted a century, as Diogo Barbosa Machado explains in the prologue to his *Biblioteca Lusitana*. In our own century, Rui Vieira Nery has called this grandiose

enterprise the "gestation cycle for the Portuguese Library."
The cycle began with Francisco Galvão de Mendanha (?-
1627), the first known compiler, with a list of 677 authors.
Manuel de Faria e Sousa listed 823 names,[30] and João Soares
de Brito elaborated a *Theatrum lusitaniae litterarium* . . . ,
ready for publication in 1655, with 876 authors and
appreciations of each. I have already mentioned Dom
Francisco Manuel de Melo's contribution in this domain.
Next came João Franco Barreto's *Biblioteca lusitana: autores
portugueses*, with six volumes written in 1662-65. In
manuscript form, it contains posthumous addenda and is
incomplete.[31] There were yet other efforts (by Padre Francisco
da Cruz and by Dom Francisco de Almeida, not mentioned by
Barbosa Machado), and crowning them all was the work of
Diogo Barbosa Machado himself, who gathered everything
together and undertook to organize, complete and publish—
between 1741 and 1759—the *Biblioteca lusitana, histórica,
crítica e cronológica. Na qual se compreende a notícia dos
autores portugueses e das obras que compuseram desde o
tempo da promulgação da Lei da Graça até o tempo presente*
(4 vols.). The author revealed that he also used catalogues
from the *Histórias* of religious orders, as well as Jorge
Cardoso's *Agiólogo* and António dos Reis's *Enthusiasmus
poeticus* (1731).

The baroque Academies were the institution where the
libraries of authors got started, the first such Academy being
the *Sertória* of Évora, founded in 1615, followed by the
Singulares (1628) and the *Generosos* (1663), both of these in
Lisbon.[32] All were dedicated to the humanities, but they did
not receive the systematic support of sovereigns until the
eighteenth century, when their sphere of activity had shifted to
the fields of history and the physical sciences. It was a new
and different age. But a Portuguese philology had already
been formed, without which it would not have been possible to
write about baroque literature.

Notes

1. Teófilo Braga, in 1896, used the designation *Os culteranistas*
(preceded by *Os quinhentistas* and followed by *Os árcades*), and in 1916 the
term *Os seiscentistas* (the title of the volume following *A renascença*).
Titles of other authors include Mendes dos Remédios's *Escola gongórica ou*

seiscentista (2nd ed. 1902) and Fidelino Figueiredo's *Literatura clássica, 2ª época 1580-1756* (1918). In their *História ilustrada das grandes literaturas* (1966), O. Lopes and A. J. Saraiva used the term "Seiscentismo," but in the eighth edition of their *História da Literatura Portuguesa* (1975), they changed the section titled "Restauração e época joanina" [Restoration and Reign of King João V] to "Época barroca."

2. There have been numerous exhibitions accompanied by carefully produced descriptive and illustrated catalogues, and a *Dicionário da arte barroca em Portugal* (Lisbon: 1989) was recently published. Various international conferences on the visual arts have also been held: *I Congresso internacional do Barroco* (University of Oporto, 1989; proceedings published, 1991) on the concept of the baroque; *Le baroque littéraire, théorie et pratiques* (Gulbenkian Center in Paris, 1989; proceedings published, 1990); the conferences sponsored by the Fundação das Casas de Fronteira e Alorna (Lisbon, 1994); and *Struggle for Synthesis: The Total Work of Art in the 17th and the 18th Centuries* (Nogueira da Silva Museum and Tibães Monastery, Braga, 1996).

3. A testimony of this intellectual sphere is the first issue of the new series of *Vértice* (1988), which opens with an uncontrolled, explosive text by Paulo Varela Gomes, in the spirit of O. Calabrese's *The Neobaroque Age* (1987). J. A. Freitas de Carvalho was the editor of *Bibliografia cronológica da literatura de espiritualidade em Portugal* and of the journal *Via spiritus*.

4. Seven issues were published between 1988 and 1991. See other works by Hatherly in Works Cited.

5. For a classic study on Vieira's sermons see Cantel.

6. See Mendes "Mimesis," "Autoportrait," "Apport," "Ledice."

7. Cf. the poems by Jerónimo Baia and Sóror Madalena da Glória.

8. *Discursos varios políticos* (Evora: 1624), folio 124r, as cited in Pires, *Crítica*, 66. Padre António Vieira, in veiled self-praise, would later apply the same prophecy to himself as a chronicler of the future (at the beginning of *História do Futuro*, 1718), in a performative self-portrait that represented the book he was writing as the ship *Argos*, and himself—the author—as the helmsman Tiphys.

9. See Teixeira; Sobral (which includes the Academy members' texts).

10. The illustration is printed in *D. Teodósio II* 48, and reproduces the drawing from codex CIII-II-16 of the Library of Évora. It was explained by Dom Francisco Manuel himself in his letter of 10 May 1649 to António Luís de Azevedo (no. 227 of *Cartas familiares*).

11. On the other hand, the history of Brazilian literature elaborated in the second half of the twentieth century has applied the category of the baroque to authors of the colonial period who now form part of Brazil's canon and tradition.

12. I have borrowed this auspicious epithet for the sixteenth century of Portuguese literature from Mateus (10).

13. My arguments for these points are found in *"Viera, Velazquez: questões de mimesis"; "L'apport de Viera"; " L'autoportrait baroque"* and *"Ledice e esforço."*

14. Teresa Margarida da Silva Horta's *Aventuras de Diófanes* (1752), an important work of maxims in the form of a novella, is already on the threshold of Enlightenment literature.

15. See Amora, which contains a list of his writings, many of them unfinished. See also Maria Lucília Pires, "Inéditos de Manuel Pires de Almeida," in *Xadrez* 27-39.

16. Critical edition by Jean Colomès, *Le Dialogue "Hospital das Letras" de D. Francisco Manuel de Melo* (Paris: 1970); *Lusiadas de Luís de Camões . . . comentados por Manuel de Faria e Sousa* (Madrid: 1639, 2 vols.; facsimile, Lisbon: IN-CM, 1972); *Rimas varias de Luís de Camões . . . comentadas por Manuel de Faria e Sousa,* (Lisbon: 1685, 4 vols.; facsimile, Lisbon: IN-CM, 1972). Other editors and commentators include Manuel Correia (1613), João Franco Barreto (1663, 1666, 1669) and Dom Marcos Lourenço (ms.). See Pires, *Crítica.*

17. See the diplomatic language in the prayers of obedience to the new popes recorded in *Orações de obediência: séculos XV a XVII* (Lisbon: Inapa, 1988).

18. *De antiquitatibus Lusitaniae* (1593?).

19. Several years before, Fernão de Oliveira had left manuscript fragments of the same sort in his *Livro da antiguidade, Nobreza, liberdade e imunidade do reino de Portugal,* conserved in Paris and dated with certainty to 1581. See Teyssier.

20. *Regras que ensinam a maneira de escrever e ortografia da língua portuguesa* and *Ortografia da língua portuguesa,* respectively.

21. *Dictionarium ex lusitanico in latinum sermonem.* António Luís left a *Tratado da língua portuguesa* (1565) in manuscript form, and Manuel Barata published his *Arte de escrever* in Lisbon in 1572.

22. *Prosodia in Vocabularium . . . Latinum et Lusitanum* and *Tesouro da língua portuguesa* (1634). See also Verdelho.

23. The title is indicative: *Vocabulário português e latino, áulico, anatómico, arquitectónico, bélico, botânico, brasílico, cómico, crítico, chímico, dogmático, dialético, dendrológico, eclesiástico, etimológico, económico, florífero, forense, frutífero, geográfico, geométrico, gnomónico, hidrográfico, homonímico, hierológico, ictiológico, índico, isagógico, lacónico, litúrgico, litológico, médico, músico, meteorológico, náutico, numérico, neotérico, ortográfico, óptico, ornitológico, poético, filológico, farmacéutico, quiditativo, qualitativo, quantitativo, retórico, rústico, romano, simbólico, sinonímico, silábico, teológico, terapêutico, tecnológico, uranológico, xenofónico, zoológico, autorizado com exemplos dos melhores escritores portugueses e latinos e oferecido a el rei de Portugal D. João V.*

24. It is interesting to note the feminine presence in these frescoes. See also *Portugal ilustrado pelo sexo feminino. Notícia histórica de muitas heroínas portuguesas que floresceram em virtude, letras e armas . . .* (1734), by Manuel Tavares, and *Teatro heroíno, abecedário histórico e catálogo das mulheres ilustres em armas, letras, acções heróicas e artes liberais* (1740), by Damião de Frois Perim (Frei João de São Pedro).

25. The first edition is from 1665, 1668 (2 vols.), and the second from 1692, 1696. Padre António dos Reis compiled eight volumes of poetry in Latin under the title *Corpus illustrorum poetarum* (1745-48).

26. The text corresponds to *Ramus II* of *Lararium Apollinis*, in *Opera omnia* (Lisbon: 1635).

27. Fernão Rodrigues Lobo Soropita, in *Cancioneiro Fernandes Tomás, fac-simile do exemplar único* (ms.) (Lisbon: 1971), folios 89-95.

28. Gândavo 61-63.

29. The expression is from João Manuel de Melo's prefatory poem in Diogo Barbosa Machado, *Biblioteca Lusitana*, vol. I (Lisbon: 1741).

30. In the *Catálogo* or *Aparato de los Escritores portugueses* (Ajuda Library, ms. 51-II-68, autograph); a shorter version of the list was published in the *Epítome de las historias portuguesas* (1628), Part IV, 689-96.

31. The manuscript of the Cadaval Library (in Muge) has been photocopied by the National Library of Lisbon.

32. The Academia Portuguesa (founded 1717) of Dom Francisco Xavier de Meneses was philological; among other activities, it promoted illustrious women and men. Its bylaws contained a chapter establishing a research project whose results were meant to be published. Entitled "On the works of the Academy," the chapter gave priority to a Dictionary, and then the "apparata for the composition of a Portuguese orthography, grammar, rhetoric and poetry. And work will also be done on a Critical History of the Language, on a History of its poetry, on two treatises, one dealing with Prosody, another with versification, and on Dictionaries of Poetics, of Rhymes and of the terms used in the Liberal and Mechanical Arts." In another article, where it is recommended that Academy members pass critical judgment on texts and authors so as to determine their worth and authority as examples of "purity in the use of the Portuguese language," it is also suggested that these evaluations be "accompanied by a brief note on the author's life, all of which will serve as a great resource for a Critical Library of Portuguese Authors and for a Literary History of Portugal, works to be undertaken by the Academy." Perhaps it is worth mentioning that in Brazil, the Academia dos Renascidos da Bahia would only adopt the project of making a history (natural, military, ecclesiastical and political) of Portuguese America—in Latin and with prefatory summaries in Portuguese—in the time of King Dom José (first session held in 1759). Cf. Matias 358-59.

Works Cited

Amora, António A. Soares. *Manuel Pires de Almeida—um crítico inédito de Camões*. São Paulo: FFCL, 1955.

Ávila, Afonso. *O lúdico e as projecções do mundo barroco*. São Paulo: Perspectiva, 1980.

Belchior, Maria de Lourdes. *Frei António das Chagas, um homem e um estilo do séc. XVII* Lisbon: 1953.

Cantel, Raymond. *Les sermons de Vieira—étude du style.* Paris: Ed. Hispano-Americanas, 1959.

Carvalho, J. A. Freitas de. *Bibliografia cronológica da literatura de espiritualidade em Portugal.* Oporto: Fac. Letras, 1988.

Castro, Aníbal Pinto de. *Retórica e teorização literária em Portugal: do humanismo ao neoclassicismo.* Coimbra: 1973.

Coutinho, Afrânio. *Aspectos da literatura barroca.* Rio de Janeiro: 1950.

_____. *D. Teodósio II* . Oporto: Civilização, 1944.

Gândavo, Pero de Magalhães. *Regras que ensinam a maneira de escrever e ortografia da língua portuguesa, com um Diálogo que adiante se segue em defensão da mesma língua*(1574); facsimile ed. Lisbon: Biblioteca Nacional, 1981.

Gomes, Paulo Varela. "O anjo e o robot." *Vértice* 1, 1988.

Hansen, João. *A sátira e o engenho—Gregório de Matos e a Bahia do séc. XVII.* São Paulo: Companhia das Letras, 1989.

Hatherly, Ana. *A casa das Musas.* Lisboa: Estampa, 1995.

_____. *A experiência do prodígio.* Lisbon: INCM, 1983.

Maria do Céu, Soror. *Triunfo do Rosário.* Ed. A. Hatherly. Lisbon: Quimera, 1992.

Marques, João. *A parenética portuguesa e a Restauração. 1640-1668.* 2 vols. Oporto: INIC, 1989.

Mateus, Osório. "Livro das obras." *Vicente.* Lisbon: Quimera, 1993.

Matias, Elze M. H. Vonk .*As Academias literárias portuguesas dos séculos XVII e XVIII.* Thesis presented to the Faculty of Letters. Lisbon: Lisbon University, 1988.

Melo, Francisco Manuel de. *Cartas familiares.* Lisbon: INCM, 1981.

Mendes, Margarida Vieira. *A oratória barroca de Vieira.* Lisbon: Caminho, 1989.

_____. "L'apport de Vieira au baroque: perdre le référent, gagner le réel." *Le baroque littéraire, théorie et pratiques*, 75-83. Paris: Fondation Calouste Gulbenkian, 1990.

_____. "L'autoportrait baroque: littérature et arts plastiques." *Os estudos literários: (entre) ciência e hermenêutica. Actes du I congrès de l'APLC*, 2 vols. 2: 145-52. Lisbon: 1990. (Published in a revised, expanded Portuguese version in *Estudos portugueses e africanos*, no. 17, 17-26) 1991, Instituto de Estudos da Linguagem, Universidade Estadual de Campinas.

_____. "Ledice e esforço, o visionarismo barroco em relatos do milagre de Ourique." *Românica. Revista de Literatura* 1-2 (1993): 183-95.

_____. "Vieira, Velazquez: questões de mimesis," [Various authors], *Afecto às Letras. Homenagem da literatura portuguesa contemporânea a Jacinto do Prado Coelho,* 410-17. Lisbon: INCM, 1984.

Nery, Rui Vieira. *A música no ciclo da "Bibliotheca Lusitana."* Lisbon: Gulbenkian, 1984.

78 ◆ MARGARIDA VIEIRA MENDES

Pécora, Alcir. *Teatro do Sacramento, a unidade teológico-retórico-política dos sermões de António Vieira*. São Paulo: EDUSP, 1994.
Pires, Maria Lucília Gonçalves. *A crítica camoniana no séc. XVII*. Lisbon: ICALP, 1982.
_____. *Para uma leitura intertextual de "Exercícios espirituais."* Lisbon: INIC, 1980.
_____. *Xadrez de palavras, estudos de literatura barroca*. Lisbon: Cosmos, 1996.
Saraiva, António José. *O discurso engenhoso*. São Paulo: Perspectiva, 1980.
Silva, Vítor Manuel de Aguiar e. *Maneirismo e barroco na poesia lírica portuguesa*. Coimbra: Centro de Estudos Românticos, 1971.
Sobral, Luís de Moura. *Pintura e poesia na época barroca-A homenagem da Academia dos Singulares a Bento Coelho da Silveira*. Lisbon: Estampa, 1994.
Sousa, Diogo de. *Jornada às Cortes de Parnaso*. Ed. V. Tocco. Bari: Adriatica, 1996.
Teixeira, Heitor Gomes. *As tábuas do painel dum auto (António Serrão de Castro)*. Lisbon: 1977.
Teyssier, Paul. "L'História de Portugal de Fernando de Oliveira . . . ." *Actas do III Colóquio internacional de estudos luso-brasileiros*. 1: 359-79. Lisbon: 1957.
Verdelho, Telmo Verdelho. *As origens da gramaticografia e da lexicografia Latino-Portuguesas*. Aveiro: INIC. 1995.
Violante do Céu, Soror. *A Preciosa*. Ed. A. Hatherly. Lisbon: INIC, 1990.

◆   Chapter 5

Portuguese Poetics in the Eighteenth Century

Maria de Lourdes A. Ferraz

According to the commonly accepted (but not on that account erroneous) view, the eighteenth century in Portugal can be divided into two moments: a baroque period that endures without too many hitches until the 1750s, when the death of King John V—the main patron of this movement that had already characterized the previous century—symbolically marks its end, and a second period, lasting until the end of the century and dominated by an academic neoclassicism that flourished under the rationalism of the Marquis of Pombal, prime minister of the next king, Joseph I. This latter period also had its symbolic event: the Lisbon earthquake of 1755, which made it possible to implant over the ruined lower town—like a synecdoche for a new Portugal—the so-called "baixa pombalina" [Pombaline lower town], which reflected not only the genius of its architects but the new rationality that its architecture represented. It was indeed a new Portugal that woke up first to enlightened despotism, then to liberalism at the beginning of the nineteenth century, and finally— undergirded by these two political-cultural movements—to a romanticism that was not firmly established until after the first quarter of the nineteenth century.

This schematic characterization also serves for literary chronologies, for it was in 1756-57 that neoclassicism was officially inaugurated with the foundation of the Arcádia

Olissiponense (or Lusitana) [Lisbon (or Lusitanian) Arcadia], under the not surprising auspices of the Marquis of Pombal, thus historically closing the baroque period.

However, this division between a baroque first half of the century and a neoclassical second half is far from being clear-cut, for there were practices we regard as typically baroque that continued to flourish within the so-called neoclassical poetics. Such is the case, for example, with visualism ["to impose the described object on the reader's vision," "to visualize what is read" (Pires, *Poetas do Período Barroco*, 28)] and of its related fondness for extravagant detail, rightly considered to be basic to baroque poetry.[1] Visualism, though it gave rise to many refinements at the formal level, betokened the predominance of an elaborate conceptual[2] process that would endure as the outward evidence of an irreversible mentality, albeit with a different finality and a different descriptive function within the ambit of neoclassical rationality, which ardently reinvoked a poetics of imitation and verisimilitude to replace the baroque predilection for the unusual and the eccentric.

That the differences in this visuality cannot be identified on a strictly chronological basis was recently demonstrated by a critical appreciation of an eyewitness account of the festivities held to celebrate the unveiling, in June of 1775, of the equestrian statue of King José I, a grandiose event that crowned (sculpturally, in the literal sense) the ideals of enlightened absolutism defended by the king's prime minister. The author of the appreciation (Canaveira) considers the visualism of the account[3] to be a manifestation of baroque exuberance, which is debatable, since the source text criticizes precisely the excessive character of the event with a very detailed but by no means *recherché* narration of the preparations and related expenses. The scrupulous description of the statue's materials and manufacture and of the system used to transport it (not forgetting the secrecy that surrounded it) to the *Terreiro do Paço* "Palace Square" does not seem to be marked by a baroque style of writing, except for brief passages when excessive language is used to adequately portray the excessive food offerings at the Public Tables. On the whole, however, the copious details and information are meant to relate the idea of grandeur and power underlying the event (with the concomitant abuses suffered by the common people). The result is a description of festive exuberance, to be sure, but already displaying concerns and a perspective which belong to another ideological and literary order.

It may be said that visuality—the ensemble of "discovered" techniques for appealing to the reader's senses—predominated from then on as the preferred descriptive mode. Although this makes it difficult to establish the boundaries and common denominators of the eighteenth century's various tendencies, at the general level of poetics it enables us to trace a literary shift that gradually arrives at the tenets and procedures we identify with twentieth-century modernism. And when we arrive at this point, we must admit that the focus on a kind of constructive self-reflection is reminiscent of the baroque with its inordinate, palpable pleasure in the materiality of language.

Even if we are led to conclude that the visualist sentiment is not *per se* baroque, the notion nevertheless helps us to understand two distinct facets of eighteenth-century Portuguese poetics, both of which seem to appear simultaneously: (1) the reconfirmation of a Horatian tradition (of imitation and accommodation) that will endure—in spite of transformations—as a now visible-now invisible bulwark until the late ninetenth century, thereby hindering a full-fledged romantic movement, and (2) the gradual but inexorable demise of the classical mode with respect to literary forms—patent in the sheer variety and combinations of themes and meters, in the vocabularies employed, and in the semantic universe represented—and the increasingly obsessive presence of an authorial subject. This may help explain the kind of literary identity crisis which was felt as late as the mid-nineteenth century, after it became obvious that Portuguese romanticism had not lived up to its claims of innovation and originality and when, on a theoretical level, it became difficult to justify all these differences and articulate them in a literary history. Only in the last quarter of that century was a veritable literary history established.[4]

Perhaps none of this should come as a surprise, since something similar was occurring in the rest of Europe. Fortini, with respect to the first half of the nineteenth century, writes, "While in schools and universities literature was still faithful to the humanist and classicist canons, editions aimed at the larger public obeyed the new civic and educational canons that found support in the national and liberal politics then prevalent in European countries" (179). In very general terms, Portugal was no exception, but its literary development came later, perhaps due in part to the upheavals generated by the civil war between royalists and liberals. The war itself lasted from 1832 to 1836 but it was brewing as far back as 1820 or even earlier, at the time of the Napoleonic invasions.

We need to take a look at the vast literary panorama of the eighteenth century—with a special focus on the tension created between a rich classical tradition and a timid, innovative romanticism—to understand the avatars that have marked the various cyclical crises in nineteenth-century Portuguese literature, when literary antagonisms brought into focus acute social, regional and political differences among authors. These were to persist without letup almost to our own times, in which there is an obvious effort to subdue tensions such as has not occurred in at least two hundred years.

Let us begin with the paradigmatic publication, in 1704, of Frei Lucas de Santa Catarina's *Serão Político*. Written in 1695 under one of the pseudonyms of the Dominican friar and member of the Academia de História, the text is a baroque deconstruction of abuses attributed precisely to baroque excessiveness. The subtitle, *abuso emendado* "corrected abuse," is in keeping with the rhetorical procedures by which the author "corrects"—in a precious, conceptualist style—the abuses resulting, he believes, from a kind of linguistic libertinism without ground rules. The author, who proves to be keenly aware of accepted conventions, seems to advocate the rules of an erudite tradition over and against mundane curiosities which, because they are mundane, do not merit serious attention. From the text's opening dedication, marked by the ambiguity of an act of flattery that he would like to avoid but recognizes as an inevitable circumstance—for the deer "that antiquity described as a symbol of flattery was also a symbol of life. That is how ancient or ingrained in man is flattery for living one's life"—the author's work is ultimately a sophisticatedly "cultured" version of the same kind of linguistic exercise. And so the occasion for this correcting is at the same time literary and mundane in a way that only seems to be innocuous, for it is in fact full of moral symbolism. Taking advantage of the three days of carnival, a time of libertine merrymaking, a group of friends decides in the good tradition of Boccaccio to make an intellectual retreat to a country estate outside of Lisbon, where they will discuss and experience things that symbolize the ideal at stake: a painstaking style that eschews all gratuituous excesses and thus resembles true love, which is also painstaking insofar as it modestly and patiently pursues the object of its desire.

One of the most interesting aspects of the baroque prolongation into the eighteenth century has to do precisely with the baroque language employed by certain writers who condemn the lack of restraint in this literary style. This is patent not only in a novella such as *Serão Político* but in other works of fiction by the same author (see Pires, *Xadrez de Palavras. Estudos de Literatura Barroca*) and even in the opinions he writes in his capacity as a royal censor. Such is the case of the long Opinion he submitted in 1719 on Manuel de Andrade Figueiredo's *Nova Escola para aprender a ler, escrever e contar*, whose content the Dominican friar finds so meritorious that he passes "precisely to praise from censorship," calling the author a "Phoenix whose feathers will be venerated by posterity." Even more to the point is his Opinion (1727) on *Prosas Portuguesas*, by Padre Rafael Bluteau, whom he characterized in this way: "the boldness of a Pericles, the gentleness of an Isocrates, an Antiphon in his precepts, a Cephalus the Athenian in his cadences and, finally, a Licinius Crassus in his skill at combining and uniting the profound with the florid, the praiseworthy with the harsh, the ponderous with the festive, it being possible, through these Sacred and Human, Theological and Political, discursive and informative fecundities, to recognize in the Author the torrents of gold that Tullius found in the rhetorical works of Aristotle." With regard to the peculiar grammatical inversion of passing from censorship to praise, in the first instance, and the glut of epithets in the second, it is worth citing Pires's remark that "it is not excess or exaggeration that defines hyperbole, but the incompatibility between that excess and the nature of the subject to which it is attributed" (*Poetas do Período Barroco*, 26).

This same Padre Rafael Bluteau, much appreciated for his *Vocabulário Português e Latino* (1712-27), is another author who condemned baroque excesses in a kind of writing that displayed those very excesses. In his opening remarks to a group of "Conferências Eruditas,"[5] which he classifies as "colloquies of Wit, courts of elegance, and Assemblies of discretion," the word *word* is personified as a "clear and resonant interpreter of the understanding," which in memory becomes "an epitaph of itself, the voice's shadow and speech's cadaver, until it finally achieves another life and, roused from remembrance, issues once more from the mouth or from the pen of Writers and, successively linked to other words in a thread of discourse, shares with the doctrine of the wise—in works of eloquence, in the narratives of History, and in the explanations of every branch of the Sciences—a glorious and ever admirable immortality."

With stylistic excesses such as these, any critique of previously committed excesses differs only in the author's obvious awareness of what he's doing and in the naming of erudite authorities who ought to be remembered, though not necessarily followed or imitated. Invoking classical models and resuming—through a highly elaborate reading—the grammatical and rhetorical work of linguistic purity undertaken by certain Portuguese writers of the sixteenth century, what these neoclassicists defended was the legitimacy of a laborious prose provided it was rooted in an erudite tradition. To appreciate this we must look closely at the "corrections" that raised questions of authority, with models being invoked that gradually, as the century wore on, enshrined not only Horace and Aristotle but also Camões, Sá de Miranda, António Ferreira, a few contemporaries (e.g., Garção, Diniz), and the most respected of the *preceptistas* (e.g., Boileau, Dacieux, Luzán).

But other principles were promulgated in the search for a naturalness of expression to accord with a rationalism whose semantic universe of reference was the literature of science. This is apparent in the poetry of António Ribeiro dos Santos (whose Arcadian pseudonym was Elpino Duriense). In the book of poems published in 1818, the year of his death, he writes to Almeno, asking him to sing "coisas dignas d'alta estima" [things worthy of high esteem]:

> Do sábio Locke que a razão aclara,
> Do douto Malebranche que descobre
> As nossas prevenções, os nossos erros
>
> .   .   .   .   .   .
>
> O excelso Newton que a Natura alcança!
> Pôs nela os olhos d'alto lume acesos,
> E a noite escura, que a cobria, abisma
> E faz raiar a clara luz do dia.

Estes Almeno são os que merecem
Um eterno padrão de jaspe e bronze,
uma estátua sublime que honre a praça,
um nobre quadro do famoso Apeles.

[Of wise Locke who enlightens reason,
Of learned Malebranche who discovers
Our preconceptions, our errors

.   .   .   .   .

The lofty Newton who fathoms Nature!
He looked at her with heavenly lit eyes,
Routed the dark night that veiled her,
And made the clear light of day shine.
These, Almeno, are the ones who deserve
An eternal pillar of jasper and bronze,
a sublime statue honoring the square,
a noble painting of the famous Apelles.]

Elsewhere the same author wrote that does not live alone or in solitude "quem vive ledo" [whoever lives gladly],

De Lucrécio, d'Horácio, de Virgílio,
De Sá, e de Ferreira acompanhado,
Quem conversa Camões, Menezes, Castro
E outros vates ilustres d'alta Lysia
Aos Romanos iguais, iguais aos Gregos.

[With Lucretius, Horace and Virgil,
Accompanied by Sá and by Ferreira,
Whose talk is Camões, Menezes, Castro
And other illustrious bards of lofty Lycia,
Equal to the Romans, equal to the Greeks]

To this list he adds Bernardes, Rodrigues Lobo, Garção and Diniz.

The invocation of authorities as a means of correction is obviously related to matters of taste. Whether authors rail against excesses, "mere bagatelles" and "inferior subjects of unwarranted flattery" or, on the contrary, recommend other subjects "d'alta estima," it is always in the name of taste that they correct, counsel and promulgate.

How to appraise or vouch for this taste? There is an unstated but powerful note of authority in the writer himself, deriving from the implication that he can do better than those he criticizes (without their names necessarily being mentioned, as if it were obvious who was being talked about) and, secondly, from his eminent social position, as evidenced by his relationship to the king or another powerful lord. That he can express gratitude to this lofty authority seems to act as a sufficient guarantee of the aesthetic worth of literary practices in transition. The dedication in which the study was offered to the consideration of a high dignitary gradually, almost imperceptibly, turned into a dedication that was itself a guarantor of the worthwhileness of what was being presented, as if it were self-evident that taste was metonymically a function of the political realm, or of power, and thus an accommodation to a new, not necessarily literary, model of authority.

This transformation, one of the most remarkable to accompany the new supremacy of "enlightened" ideals, was one of the signs that marked important differences in a literature that outwardly preserved existing conventions. In addition to the altered function of general dedications (and of some of the censors' opinions), we find dedications serving as titles to individual poems, which in itself seems to suggest new modes of reading. This occurs, for example, in the work of the aforementioned António Ribeiro dos Santos, for when he dedicates to a friend a poem that is in fact a commentary on the right models to use, on the state of the language, on terms that can be legitimately employed, or on any meta-literary matter, then the figure of the reader is distinctly altered. He or she goes from being an extrinsic figure (very much present in the epistolary tradition and now incorporated as the addressee of other literary forms) to an instrinsic receiver. It is this figure of the reader that will become common, in the latter nineteenth century, as the recipient of romantic texts, not only as the author's chosen confidant who can theoretically understand what the author wants to communicate, but also as an ideal reader, a necessary prop to replace all the other props that gradually fell into disuse—that is, the punctilious precepts for literary genres, particularly the countless subgenres of the eighteenth century.

And so here, as in other countries, a debate naturally arose (even if only implicitly) not only around the issue of conventions or models but around the very concept of literature as an activity reserved for an intellectual (rational!) elite at the helm of society (Reiss 174). To be sure, there was always an elite in literature as in the other arts, and it naturally addressed its output to those in power (Pires, *Poetas do Período Barroco*, 23). But the new elite was different in the way it appropriated literature (in the widest sense, without emphasizing its artistic character) as a linguistic practice that would allow it—through poetic, philosophical, political and ethical involvement and expression—to give direction to a society undergoing radical change in terms of the social distribution of institutional powers. We could say that literature, in the eighteenth century, serves to instruct, while in the nineteenth century, with the romantic movement, instruction will serve literature, as, with the changes brought about by romanticism, to receive instruction as soon as one begins to learn reading and writing will be a prerequisite for arriving at literature, thus transformed into life experience.

With respect to the eighteenth century, the changes in the learned elite became more pronounced as the decades wore on. If the author of *Nova Escola para aprender a ler, escrever e a contar*, in his dedication to King John V, aimed to "organize harmonically the body of any piece of writing, so that the feats of Your Majesty will fill everyone's soul," in 1756 the Academia Olissiponense was formed directly under the auspices of the King and his Minister the Marquis of Pombal (as well as the Virgin Mary, a by-no-means-negligible detail). But in 1765 and again in 1781, Pedro José da Fonseca, in *Elementos da Poética Tirados de Aristóteles, de Horácio e dos mais célebres Modernos*, affirmed that "Poetry . . . also has as its goal to be useful, by its very nature as well as by the fundamental subordination that all art should have to Politics, whose overall goal is the public good."

But there were also changes of another order. The ranks of the learned, which had been mainly occupied by aristocrats and clergy, became increasingly filled by the bourgeoisie. Poets not only had other, less "noble" kinds of occupations, as they also boasted of their business dealings in poetry, with Nicolau Tolentino—always in need of financial backers—

being a typical example. Others, such as Tavares Gamboa, boasted of their ability to poetize without art or, like Bocage, emphasized only their passion and spontaneity. These changes are corroborated by the criticisms they earned. In an *Invectiva contra os maus poetas* (1785), Verissimo Lusitano (the pen name of Pedro José da Fonseca) scoffed those who thought it was possible to write poetry without considerable study:

> Ser poeta, não é cousa comum.
> É dom divino, que um génio apoucado
> Nunca pode alcançar por mais que sue.
>
> Mas este mesmo dom, se não for guiado
> Pelas regras da arte, ao princípio
> Corre como cavalo desbocado.
>
> Que julgas tu? Que a Arte o seu principio
> Teve em fúteis caprichos? A razão
> É sobre que se firma este Edifício.
>
> .   .   .   .   .
>
> Musas, fazei que a dividir-se
> Chegue o ouro da escória; e que do engano
> Até possa o vulgacho enfim sair-se.
>
> Goze em paz só do título soberano
> De Poeta o que ornou a natureza,
> Do que há mais peregrino e mais ufano.
> Goze da justa glória, e da grandeza
> Um tal espírito, e sejam sepultados
> Os fanáticos loucos na vileza.
>
> Pelas ruas com vaias, e apupados
> Os rapazes lhes tirem dos vestidos,
> Que ou sejam da mania melhorados,
> Ou por fim nas casinhas recolhidos.
>
> [To be a poet is no ordinary thing.
> It's a divine gift that a mean wit,
> However much he sweats, cannot attain.

But this same gift, if not guided
To principles, by the rules of art
Will run like a horse unbridled.

Do you suppose that Art began
With random whims? Its Edifice
Is founded on reason.]

.　　　.　　　.　　　.

[Muses, winnow the chaff
To divide out the gold, and free
Even the masses from deceit.

May only the one who crowned nature
With what is lofty and extraordinary
Enjoy in peace the high title of Poet.

May such a spirit enjoy all due glory
And greatness, and may the mad
Fanatics be buried in wretchedness.

Amid hoots and hisses, may the boys
On the street pull at their clothes
That they be cured of their mania
Or else shut up in homes.]

Notwithstanding this change, expressing how literature's social basis was becoming ever more personalized in the figure of the author (and the end of the previous poem quoted, still under the aegis of the conclusion to Horace's *Ars Poetica*, showed how hard it is for the figure of the author to change!), the essentially imitative function of the art of language remained apparently intact. This even seems to be confirmed by one of the crucial texts of eighteenth-century Portuguese poetics, crucial in part because of when it appeared, in 1748, with a second edition in 1759. Its author, Francisco Joseph Freire, was to become a member of the Arcádia Olissiponense, with the pen name Cândido Lusitano.

Freire's immediate concern was to respond to the criticism made by the author of *Verdadeiro Método de Estudar* (1746),[6] accusing the Portuguese of not having an *ars poetica*, just arts of versification. Freire contends that his art of poetry

is not an art of versification, since poetry is not the
consequence (versified or not) of composition but an act of
representation. But if we note the care he takes in defining
imitation (which would seem to be unnecessary were the term
taken for granted as a presupposition of his exposition) and in
justifying it in a history of poetry going all the way back to
the dawn of humanity, we are once more confronted with the
force of visualism rather than the act of representing. He
affirms that imitation or representation is only possible
because fantasy, a natural quality, is capable of dressing things
with pleasing images. This natural way of proceeding, we are
told, spontaneously makes us see what is being imitated.
"[T]he truths and things represented by the Poet can cause
delight either because they are new and marvelous in
themselves, or because the Poet makes them so with his skill
. . . . These marvelous truths are the soul of poetry and the
origin of delight." (55-56). Can't we already find, in these
lines, observations that will later serve as a transforming force
and impetus for anti-imitative, anti-Aristotelian and
anticlassical conceptions?

In an age when verisimilitude began to be invoked for the
rational ordering of artistic representation, it was only natural
that the classical conception of literature as imitation would be
called in as justification. But there was, at the same time, an
increasing emphasis on an *ethos*, formerly restricted to the
rhetorical dimension and its suitablity to a given discursive
circumstance.

Tragedy and epic poetry, according to Freire, continued to
be unquestionably the most important genres, sanctioned by
their antiquity and canonicity; Freire, nevertheless, also calls
attention to comedy (though remarking on the poor quality—
due to the poor writing—of contemporary comic theater) as
well as to mimetic poetry and tragicomedy. He questions the
inclusion of this last genre in the poetics of some of his
contemporaries. Of greater import are the remarks he makes
after finishing his study on epic poetry, which is what many
authors, including the well-known Luzán, felt should conclude
the study of poetics. Freire, to satisfy the needs and wants of
the beginning poet to whom he addresses his work, states that
he has decided "to discourse on other kinds of poetry"
(258). And only here does he mention lyric poetry, along with
the eclogue and satire, after having deliberated at great length
on numerous subgenres.

Yet it is for lyric poetry—here still hardly given notice—that Portuguese literature of the eighteenth century will be most remembered: not because of the poetic precepts it fiercely defended but because of the greater naturalness it achieved, because of the larger poetic "I" whose world imposed itself on the forms required by reliance on a legitimizing classicism, and because of the lexical and syntactical transformation that made for greater intimacy of expression. It is these factors that altered the concept of poetry for the poet Domingos dos Reis Quita, who wrote in 1781 that poetry had its birth "with Nature," with man who had hardly left his Creator's hands when he "saw the light of the World, was dumbfounded, and marveled at the wondrous spectacle of the Universe." Men gradually joined together their initially inarticulate sounds, "formed ideas from their feelings, examined Nature, sought the great and sublime, invented lofty expressions, and from all this they forged a kind of Poetry, a certain order and harmony . . . ." Poets, in this process, appear as benefactors of humanity.

The century also closed with a symbolic event. The year 1799 marked the birth of Almeida Garrett, not only the founder of romanticism but also the promoter of the very notion of a national literature in Portugal.

Notes

1. There is a vast bibliography on the Portuguese baroque, including two studies by Pires (see Works Cited) and another by Vítor Manuel Aguiar e Silva: *Maneirismo e Barroco* (Coimbra: Centro de Estudos Românicos, 1971).

2. The notion of *concept* presented as characteristic of baroque poetry ("the work of the mind in discovering unusual relationships among things and among words, and the work done on language to make these relationships new and unsuspected") defines a mentally visualist *activity*, not just a style.

3. *A Inauguração da Estátua Equestre de El-Rei D. José I. Narração verídica feita por um Jesuita, testemunha ocular do acontecimento*, ed. Ângelo Pereira. Lisbon: Editorial Labor, 1938.

4. Before c. 1875, the notion of a literary history was at best vague in Portugal, being confounded until the mid-nineteenth century with a history of poetics or with an inventory of Portuguese authors and their literary output or, again, with a history of the various influences affecting

Portuguese literature down through the centuries, from Latin prototypes to Spanish, French and Italian models.

5. The "Conferências Eruditas" were sponsored by Dom Francisco Xavier de Meneses, 4th Count of Ericeira, beginning in 1690. The speech referred to here is reproduced in *Prosas Portuguesas*.

6. By Luís António Verney, but published anonymously.

Works Cited

Bluteau, Rafael. *Prosas Portuguesas recitadas em Diferentes Congressos Académicos* . . . . Lisbon: Oficina de José António da Silva, 1729.

Bocage, Manuel Maria Barbosa du. *Rimas*. Vol. 1. Lisbon: Oficina de Simão Tadeu Ferreira, 1791.

Canaveira, Manuel Filipe. "Sedução dos sentidos. O significado político da festa popular na celebração dos fastos da monarquia." *Revista da Faculdade de Ciências Sociais e Humanas*, 2.8 (1995), 27-42.

Figueiredo, Manuel de Andrade. *Nova Escola para aprender a ler, escrever e contar* . . . . Lisbon: Oficina de Bernardo da Costa Carvalho, undated.

Fonseca, Pedro José da. *Elementos da Poética Tirados de Aristóteles, Horácio, e dos mais célebres Modernos*. Lisbon: Oficina de Miguel Manescal da Costa, 1765.

Fortini, F. "Literatura." *Enciclopédia Einaudi*. Vol. 17. Lisbon: Imprensa Nacional-Casa da Moeda, 1989.

Freire, Francisco José. *Arte Poética ou Regras da Verdadeira Poesia* . . . 2nd ed. vol. 1. Lisbon: Oficina Patriarcal de Francisco Luis Ameno, 1759.

Gamboa, Joaquim Fortunato Valadares. *Obras Poéticas*. Lisbon: Tipografia Rollandiana, 1779.

Pires, Maria Lucília Gonçalves. *Poetas do Período Barroco*. Lisbon: Editorial Comunicação, 1985.

_____. *Xadrez de Palavras. Estudos de Literatura Barroca*. Lisbon: Edições Cosmos, 1996.

Quita, Domingos dos Reis. *Obras de* . . . . Lisbon: Tipografia Rolandiana, 1781.

Reiss, Timothy J. *The Meaning of Literature*. Ithaca: Cornell UP, 1992.

Santa Catarina, Frei Lucas de. *Serão Politico / Abuso Emendado / Dividido em Tres Noites para divertimento dos curiosos* . . . . By Felix da Castanheira Turacem. Lisbon: Valentim da Costa Deslandes, 1704.

Santos, António Ribeiro dos. *Poesias de Elpino Duriense*. Vol. 1. Lisbon: Impressão Régia, 1812.

Silva, Vítor Manuel Aguiar e. *Para uma Interpretação do Classicismo*. Coimbra: Coimbra Editora, 1962.

Tolentino, Nicolau. *Obras Poéticas*. Lisbon: Imprensa Régia, 1801.

◆ Chapter 6

Socio-institutional Literary Practices in Portuguese Romanticism

Helena C. Buescu

Portuguese romanticism was a late bloomer in the panorama of European literature. Almeida Garrett's narrative poems "Camões" and "Dona Branca," published in 1825 and 1826, were more a declaration of intentions than an actual implementation of romantic principles. We must look to the middle of the next decade to find the first literary texts that were clearly indebted to the romantic aesthetic. This was true both for lyric poetry (which will in any case—including that of the founders of Portuguese romanticism, Garrett and Alexandre Herculano—conserve for some time a "mixed" tone, with certain strains of neoclassical diction still evident) and for narrative prose, which in the 1840s would develop above all in the historical mode, while at the same time inventing models for narrating contemporary life. The parallel evolution that took place in dramatic literature, both in the historical and contemporary modes, likewise confirms that the 1830s and 1840s were the period when the romantic aesthetic took root and developed in Portugal.

In political and ideological terms, it is worth noting—as an already specifically *modern* gesture—the deep and widespread involvement of the romantic authors in aesthetic, sociopolitical and ideological tensions and conflicts: not only because in Portugal the entire first third of the century was marked by a generalized social crisis (the French invasions, the English presence in Portugal) leading to a civil war between absolutists and liberals with far-ranging consequences in the short run and beyond, but also because these gave rise to themes whose literary expression was anchored in personal, social and ideological experience (freedom, exile). This involvement took two seemingly opposing forms: revolutionary activity, which in the first romantic generation meant personal participation in the civil war (Garrett and Herculano), and "withdrawal" from the world, frequently associated with an inclination toward solitary contemplation. This latter form, which ultimately translates into an ideologically negative judgment on worldly values, would later be emblematized by Herculano.

The particularly significant presence of historical narrative prose was in full accord with the general tendency of European romantic fiction. If we consider, on the one hand, the weak showing of the novelistic genre in eighteenth-century Portuguese literature (a situation clearly *not* in accord with the rest of Europe), and on the other hand the fact that narrative prose concerned with contemporary life—the other major area in which the modern novel was founded and developed—would not make a strong showing until the late 1840s, then we must conclude that it was up to historical narrative prose to try out models, forms and procedures leading to the institutionalization of the novel in Portuguese romanticism. And in fact Herculano, the "patriarch" of romantic historical narrative in Portugal, began in the early 1840s—in the magazines *O Panorama* and *Revista Universal Lisbonense*—to publish prose texts that would later either constitute some of his historical novels (*O Bobo; O Monge de Cister; Eurico, o Presbitero*) or be included in the volume *Lendas e Narrativas*. Clearly delineated characters, particularly that of the hero, an eminently novelistic structure and plot development, and the use of devices such as description, digression, and the contrast between action and the didactic/ideological "agenda" that Herculano always explicitly brings to his fictional production are the main characteristics of his writing, in which the hero inevitably reflects a personal project as well as a collective, national project with roots that go back to medieval times. Alexandre Herculano is, at the same time, rightly regarded as the founder of modern historiography in Portugal, having carried out projects comparable to those of Guizot and Thierry (*História de Portugal, Portugaliae Monumenta*

Historica). A number of authors followed in his steps: Garrett himself (*O Arco de Sant'Ana*), Rebelo da Silva, Arnaldo Gama and Andrade Corvo.

Literary magazines and journals were of prime importance for the development and institutionalization of the romantic aesthetic and for the still precarious formation of an autonomous literary field, as defined by Pierre Bourdieu. It was the post-civil war period, beginning in the mid-1830s, that saw a marked increase in the number of these publications and in the diversity of their objectives, though they were all clearly concerned to foster a reading public whose composition would embrace heterogeneous interests, among these literature, and they all insisted on the democratization of culture, for which the periodicals themselves would act as fundamental agents. In this context we should mention the serial [*folhetim*], which played a key role in the formation and transformation of the romantic narrative genre. Some of the important writers of serial fiction included António Pedro Lopes de Mendonça, Júlio César Machado and Teixeira de Vasconcelos, but many others wrote sporadically in this subgenre that was already highly attuned to the laws of the market.

Literature in translation, by way of the *feuilleton*, also figured prominently. Portuguese romanticism developed in large measure around the increased activity of translation, which had been modest in Portugal until the mid-eighteenth century (particularly with respect to the literature of the day) but then gained steam, creating a reading public whose expectations coincided with those of the European romantic canon, crystallized around certain paradigmatic figures (the heroes à la Byron, Hugo, Dumas or Scott), as well as diversifying the contacts between Portuguese and other European literatures (though the French model continued to dominate). In this context magazines—including the first publications aimed specifically at women—had a major role in developing and disseminating what would come to be the dominating literary taste.

The serial also had important consequences for the very configuration of the literary system in romanticism. Among other things, it allowed for the emergence of literary forms with no previously determined place in the hierarchy of genres, thus putting into practice the crossing of literary genres defended by the theoreticians of romanticism. There was a proliferation of new forms—ranging from social chronicles and accounts of urban life to travel journals (real or fictional), brief narratives and short stories—whose salient features seem to have been their *brevity of form* and *heterogeneity* (both thematic and formal).

It was in the nineteenth century, and thanks especially to the romantic movement, that the short story form made significant headway in Portuguese literature. Though the short story was occasionally practiced in prior centuries, it was only with the socio-institutional conditions fostered by romanticism (democratized access to the written form through magazines; new institutionalized formats such as the serial, particularly suited to short narratives; and market conditions that partially offset the modern lack of a traditional sponsor or patron) that it could become a potentially important form for one of the most significant developments in the literature of the period: noncompliance with the system of genres deriving from the traditional understanding of Aristotelian theory.

In terms of theme, while the novel generally revolved around a few more or less felicitous stock formulas (with Herculano, Garrett and Camilo Castelo Branco being in the "more" category, followed by countless lesser, epigonic practitioners) such as obsessive and overwhelming passion, travel notes and impressions, or the appearance (especially after 1850) of the man or woman with a heart "of bronze" or "of marble" (in reaction to the notion of sensibility inherited from the eighteenth century), the short story represented a more open genre. The same was true in terms of structure. Even authors whose novels were based on historically situated stereotypes, such as Pinheiro Chagas, practiced the short story in a much freer and generally more interesting way. Herculano's short stories (*Lendas e Narrativas*) continued to present historical scenarios, an example followed by Rebelo da Silva and others. But there were also authors who wrote stories about contemporary life, both in its rural version (Andrade Ferreira, Rodrigo Paganino, Júlio Dinis) and in its urban, mundane version (Júlio César Machado), or even in the fantastic mode (Teófilo de Braga and, above all, Álvaro do Carvalhal).

The theoretical concern with the contemporary, evident in all of the romantic literary manifestations (whether historical, regionalist or urban), began to be reflected in actual practice in the mid-1840s, the paradigmatic work in this regard being

Almeida Garrett's *Viagens na Minha Terra*, published (in book form) in 1846. The other great systematizer of Portuguese romanticism, Alexandre Herculano, though better known for his historical fiction, also produced a small body of highly effective fictional texts devoted to contemporary themes. But it was *Viagens na Minha Terra*, and to a lesser extent António Pedro Lopes Mendonça's novel, *Memórias de um Doido*, that marked the emergence of contemporary life as a theme to be developed in the middle of the century. Besides the numerous aspects that make Garrett's novel both a precursor and an epitome (the descriptive and digressive elements, the character of the protagonist, the choice of the civil war as the political moment when the action takes places, the heteroclite and fragmentary composition), there is another aspect—also found in Lopes de Mendonça's novel—that should be emphasized: the *problem* of novelistic discourse, which is rooted in the formulation of irony and marked by a continual self-reflection, all in keeping with a new world view whose most salient feature was its relativism.

Yet another aspect common to these two novels is the reflection on the conflict between the "small world" of daily life and the huge dimensions of the individual. This conflict may also be considered fundamental to Camilo Castelo Branco's voluminous fictional output, whose sheer size as well as its heterogeneity make any single epithet to characterize it immediately insufficient. "Impassioned" is undoubtedly an appropriate term, given the violence and wide array of obsessive passions that fill his fictional universe, but epithets such as "satirical," "parodic" and "sentimental" also apply.

The case of Camilo leads us to consider an extremely interesting phenomenon with respect to the romantic experience, namely, that of the osmosis that occurred between literature and life. Indeed it is tempting to see this writer's entire biography as yet one more outcome of the imaginary models that guided his literary practice. Orphanhood, the existential centrality of passion, blindness, the madness that surrounded him, and suicide are just some of the circumstances that, combined with others, transformed him into a kind of myth in action, both during his life and afterwards. It is legitimate to say, in fact, that a number of the great romantic writers led lives that *represented*—each in their own way—the directions taken by their literary practice. The social world of Garrett's fiction reflects, in part, his own character with its fundamentally narcissistic bent; the narrative and poetic universe of Herculano comports the same discriminatory exclusions that will lead him to withdraw from public life to Vale de Lobos, an act whose mythic as well as pragmatic efficacy earned him the reputation as the great, unimpeachably *coherent* figure; Camilo, for his part, lived out the same violent and at times demented passions that obsessed his characters; Antero de Quental's poetry elaborated a biographical-fictional trajectory whose resolution was epitomized by his own suicide; Júlio César Machado testified, through his act of suicide, to the impossibility of dealing with the death of his son; Lopes de Mendonça went mad at scarcely 39 years of age; yet other writers such as Soares de Passos, followed somewhat later by António Nobre, succumbed when still young to the disease of the century, tuberculosis, in a kind of poetic irony that would stamp both their literary production and its subsequent reception. All the great names of the Romantic movement seemed to be marked by this imaginary osmosis between biography and fiction.

Particularly poignant in this respect is the case of Camilo, who also stands out for the diversity of forms in which he wrote (comparable, in this regard, only to Herculano and especially Garrett). Camilo was a journalist, poet, playwright, polemicist and literary critic, as well as a fiction writer, though it was this last category that guarantees his place in any vision of Portuguese romanticism. Between 1851, when he published *Anátema*, his first novel (or novella, to be more accurate), and 1890, the year of his death, Camilo produced dozens of fictional works that may be seen as the continual *rewriting* of the same basic story: the impassioned violence of the act of living, centered around amorous passion and the (self-) destructive effects it inevitably generates (e.g., *Amor de Perdição, O Retrato de Ricardina*). This thematic obsession is joined by an obsessive (self-) irony, apparent above all in the transparency of the discursive procedures, which thus reject the conventions of novelistic illusion (see, for example, *Coração, Cabeça e Estômago; Aventuras de Basílio Fernandes Enxertado; Memórias de Guilherme do Amaral*). The rhetorical consciousness of his literary works, and in particular his novels, informs Camilo's perspective and allows him to employ an "author-narrator" who reacts to and comments on the narrated universe, sharing it in this way with the reader. These various characteristics of Camilo's work also make it possible to identify—apart from its patently tragic aspect—another side which accentuates the grotesque and in which criticism is often allied to satire and parody of a scathing violence (c.f. *A Queda de um Anjo* or *A Mulher Fatal*) no less intense than the exacerbated passion found in other novels. And works such as *Novelas do Minho* or *A Brasileira de Prazins* reveal his ambition to examine, in a quasi-analytical fashion, the pathologies of a day-to-day world whose defining characteristics include, still and always, the same violence and emotional intensity.

If the condensation that typifies Camilo's narrative prose is an important characteristic for the fictional discourse of romanticism, so too is the digressive and centrifugal component that informs the novelistic structure, affecting the relationship of the essential plot to the action strictly speaking. This component enables the author to introduce a series of fictional elements not directly dependent on the basic plot, thereby enlarging the figure of the narrator, whose personal feelings, opinions and reflections are thus granted an outlet through which they can be freely aired. The work that inaugurates and establishes this procedure (as it does so many others) is once again Garrett's *Viagens na Minha Terra*, but it was also invoked by feuilletonists such as Lopes de Mendonça and Júlio César Machado, and by novelists such as Camilo, whose works combine emotional concentration with the ongoing commentary of an intrusive narrator who is never outside the fictional universe he presents. Another author to consider from this point of view, though keeping in mind his very different way of telling a story, is Júlio Dinis, who in his novels (*Uma Família Inglesa, As Pupilas do Senhor Reitor, A Morgadinha dos Canaviais* and *Os Fidalgos da Casa Mourisca*) accentuates the analytical dimension of digression, with comment made on the sociohistorical as well as political spheres, whose relationship to the amorous intrigue, which ends happily, is always underscored.

Yet another opportunity for authorial digression was afforded by the generalized use of prefaces, prologues, afterwords and notes, conceived precisely as an opening up of the literary object to paraliterary, aesthetic and even didactic remarks, providing a rich source for studying the romantic tenets (as well as their occasional incongruity with actual practice). The romantic paratext is a privileged place for establishing and explaining the pacts and conventions of reading and should not be overlooked. It was also in these texts that we find a critical formulation that gradually cemented the project of a national literary history, whose romantic roots are clearly evident. And we may also relate these texts to the essay as a genre, of which Herculano is one of Portuguese literature's exemplary practitioners (*História da Origem e Estabelecimento da Inquisição em Portugal*).

Within the overall panorama of Portuguese romantism, dramatic literature played a decisive, albeit ambiguous, role. Perhaps because Garrett and Herculano considered it one of the genres best suited for defining and systematizing a national literature, romantic drama was asked to achieve what few, besides Garrett himself, could realize. And yet there were many who wrote dramatic texts, particularly since the theater as a stage of social representation fulfilled a paradigmatic function in the milieus of romantic society. We must remember that to go to the theater—beyond the immediate objective of seeing a play—was an act invested with symbolic and ideological significance. Since there existed a sociological predisposition and institutional venues for theatrical practice, it is no wonder that dramatic production was stimulated and that the writing of dramatic texts increased sharply, though this was not always accompanied by an increase in quality.

The precepts set forth by Victor Hugo—the mixing of tones, the blurring of the boundaries between genres, and the introduction of the grotesque alongside the sublime—led to the elaboration of so-called romantic drama, which in Portuguese literature finds its highest expression in the work of Garrett (ambiguously enough, since he explicitly maintained aspects of the "tragic" genre that seemed to him ineluctable), particularly in the play *Frei Luís de Sousa*. Treating a theme whose political and ideological implications do not shroud the tragic and mythic dimension, Garrett in this play continued and refined his previous dramatic work (*Um Auto de Gil Vicente* and *O Alfageme de Santarém*). The prefatory texts that accompany *Um Auto de Gil Vicente* and, more importantly, *Frei Luís de Sousa* ("Memória ao Conservatório Real") are still fundamental documents for understanding not only the breadth of Garrett's thinking but also the actual conditions under which this reflection on theatrical art emerged in the middle of the nineteenth century. But Garrett's activity in the area of theater was not limited to dramatic production. In the years immediately following the victory of the constitutional party, it fell to him to reorganize and restructure the national theater, conceiving a plan for making this art into a genuine expression of Portuguese nationality and its relationship to the liberty now formalized by the political-constitutional system.

It was in this context that dramatic literature developed along lines virtually identical to those followed by fiction and by the novel in particular. But if both historical drama and drama about contemporary life—generally based on stereotypical plots marked by sentimentality, sharp ethical polarities, and moralism—underwent the same evolution as the novel, they did not find authors (except for the works already mentioned) capable of carrying out the profound change that was announced.

The same terms characterize the extensive output of romantic poetry, which would seem to have been the preferred mode of expression for writers. Until mid-century, there was a heterogeneity of devices and practices, with certain eighteenth-century techniques still being used, even as medieval structures and meters (which clearly influenced "new" literary forms such as the romantic ballad) were being revived. António Feliciano de Castilho, in this respect, was associated early on with a certain kind of canon that many would imitate without, however, being able to attain its formal refinement. The reclaiming of historical and especially medieval roots should be considered in light of the oral component that was crucial to certain practices, whether in the "popular" and colloquial vein explored by Garrett (*Flores sem Fruto* and especially *Folhas Caídas*), João de Deus and Júlio Dinis with suprisingly positive results, or through a diction that sometimes incorporated an oratorical register and that was used to best effect by poets such as Herculano, Soares de Passos and Antero de Quental, being combined in the first two (Herculano and Soares de Passos) with a rich and carefully wrought, quasi-narrative phraseology.

With respect to the "popular" and colloquial vein, we should mention the first specifically literary reclamation of oral and traditional literature, the initial fruits of which were brought together in Garrett's *Romanceiro* (systematized and enlarged from the middle of the century onward, by Teófilo Braga and others). The transcription and publication of these oral "romances," a process begun by the romantics, denotes a profound change in the literary canon, a change that shapes our notion of the canon even today.

The sometimes "oratorical" diction employed by certain writers, on the other hand, may be related to the unequivocal metaphysical anxiety that began to swell in the late nineteenth century until it was finally embodied, paradigmatically, in the various aporias expressed by Fernando Pessoa and his heteronyms, already well into the twentieth century. The preeminent romantic reference on this point is unquestionably Antero de Quental. The commitment to civic and socio-ideological concerns that in one way or another characterized all of the most representative figures of Portuguese romanticism found its epitome in the figure of Antero, whose biography is itself a testament to the personal and historical tensions typical of romantic thought at its most reflective. Antero, unable to sustain them, committed suicide in 1891. Antero's poetry, of a philosophical and analytical bent not often found in Portuguese literature (though evident in poets such as Camões and Pessoa), expresses these existential tensions now as a revolutionary cry of revolt (*Odes Modernas*), now as the assimilation of a speculative project whose metaphysical, largely Schopenhauerian anxiety is susceptible to Oriental influences (*Sonetos Completos*). Antero's way of making poetry is just that: a *making*, an attitude deriving from his intense mental reflection at both the personal and social levels, so that his poetry depends directly on the success of this reflective activity, which comports—in his case—the awareness of an abiding unhappiness. It is no wonder, therefore, that the pessimistic note becomes predominant, anticipating characteristics that fin-de-siècle movements such as symbolism and decadence (and particularly the poetic practice most typical of Camilo Pessanha) will eagerly explore and systematize as an inheritance passed down to some of the twentieth century's vanguard movements.

Basic Bibliography on Portuguese Romanticism

Cabral, Alexandre. *Dicionário de Camilo*. Lisbon: Caminho, 1989.
Castro, Anibal Pinto de. *Narrador, Tempo e Leitor na Novela Camiliana*. 1976. Vila Nova de Famalicão: Centro de Estudos Camilianos, 1995.

Chaves, Castelo Branco. *O Romance Histórico no Romantismo Português.* Lisbon: ICALP, 1980.

Coelho, Jacinto do Prado. *A Letra e o Leitor.* Lisbon: Portugália, 1969.

_____. *Introdução ao Estudo da Novela Camiliana.* 1946. Lisbon: Imprensa Nacional-Casa da Moeda, 1982.

Ferraz, Maria de Lourdes. *A Ironia Romântica. Estudo de um processo comunicativo.* Lisbon: Imprensa Nacional-Casa da Moeda, 1987.

Ferreira, Alberto. *Perspectiva do Romantismo Português (1834-65).* Lisbon: Edições 70, 1971.

França, José-Augusto. *O Romantismo em Portugal. Estudo de factos sócioculturais.* 1974. Lisbon: Livros Horizonte, 1993.

Lopes, Óscar. *Antero de Quental. Vida e Legado de uma Utopia.* Lisbon: Caminho, 1983.

Lourenço, Eduardo. *Poesia e Metafísica. Camões, Antero, Pessoa.* Lisbon: Sá da Costa, 1983.

Monteiro, Ofélia Paiva. *A Formação de Almeida Garrett. Experiência e Criação.* 2 vols. Coimbra: Author edition 1971.

Nemésio, Vitorino. *A Mocidade de Herculano.* 1934. Lisbon: Bertrand, 1978.

Picchio, Luciana Stegagno. *História do Teatro Português.* Lisbon: Portugália, 1969.

Rebelo, Luís Francisco. *O Teatro Romântico.* Lisbon: ICALP, 1980.

Reis, Carlos, and Maria de Natividade Pires. *História Crítica da Literatura Portuguesa, vol. V-o Romantismo.* Lisbon: Verbo, 1993.

Rodrigues, António Gonçalves. *A Tradução em Portugal.* 4 vols. Lisbon: INCM, 1992-94.

Santos, Maria de Lourdes Lima dos. *Intelectuais Portugueses na Primeira Metade de Oitocentos.* Lisbon: Presença, 1988.

_____. *Para uma Sociologia da Cultura Burguesa em Portugal no Século XIX.* Lisbon: Presença, 1983.

Saraiva, António José. *Herculano e o Liberalismo em Portugal.* Lisbon: Bertrand, 1977.

_____. *Para a História da Cultura em Portugal.* Vol. 2. Lisbon: Publicações Europa-América, 1961.

Saraiva, António José, and Óscar Lopes. *História da Literatura Portuguesa.* 17th ed. Oporto: Porto Editora, 1996.

Serrão, Joel. *Antero e a Ruína do seu Programa (1871-1875).* Lisbon: Livros Horizonte, 1988.

_____. *Temas Oitocentistas.* Lisbon: Livros Horizonte, 1978.

Simões, João Gaspar. *História da Poesia Portuguesa: das Origens aos Nossos Dias.* 3 vols. Lisbon: ENP, 1953-55.

_____. *História do Romance Português.* 3 vols. Lisbon: Côr, 1967-72.

Tengarrinha, José Manuel. *História da Imprensa Periódica Portuguesa.* Lisbon: Caminho, 1989.

Works Cited

Bourdieu, Pierre. *La distinction. Critique sociale du jugement.* Paris: Minuit, 1979.

Castelo Branco, Camilo. *Obras completas.* Porto: Lello, 1983.

Dinis, Júlio. *Obras completas.* Porto: Lello, 1985.

Garrett, J. B. de Almeida. *Obras completas.* Porto: Lello, 1985.

Herculano, Alexandre. "Various titles." Lisboa: Bertrand, various dates.

Mendonça, Antonio Pedro Lopes de. *Memorias de um Doido.* Lisboa: INCM, 1982.

Quental, Antero de. *Odes modernas.* Lisboa: Sa da Costa, 1952.

_____. *Sonetos completos.* Lisboa: Lello, 1983.

◆ Chapter 7

Decadence and Fin-de-siècle Literature in Portugal

J. C. Seabra Pereira

Critical consideration of Decadence in Portugal was for a long time limited to occasional references marked, nearly always, by an annoying curiosity about dreamy, "decadent" attitudes and figures belonging to an eccentric trend that dissipated at the turn of the century, after giving rise to a renewed, more pretentious symbolism. Symbolism proper, on the other hand, did garner scholarly and critical attention, particularly in retrospect, when the canon was revised and updated by new generations of writers (Pessoa, Régio, etc.). Even after fin-de-siècle literature, including the work of the Decadents, began to be studied in greater depth (Ramos, *Eugénio de Castro e a Poesia Nova*; Silveira, various works listed in Works Cited; Ferro, both works listed), to the point of figuring promiJ.ortuguese literary history (Ramos, *História da Literatura Portuguesa*), the genesis, character and range of Decadent literature continued to be suppressed, due to a generalized tendency to see it as an epiphenomenon subsumable under Symbolism and due, as well, to the misconceived view of it as a watered-down version of that same Symbolism (Simões, *Itinerário histórico da poesia portuguesa*).

The critical misfortune of Decadence in Portugal was owed in part to the reluctance of foreign literary history and criticism (particularly French, all too readily followed by others) to recognize analytically the movement's interactive autonomy and its importance for the construction of a coherent and intelligible picture of the post-Naturalist and pre-Modernist literary dynamic.

In Portugal, as elsewhere, the critical fate of the Decadent movement changed (Pereira, *Decadentismo e Simbolismo na Poesia Portuguesa*) when it began to be studied as a period style whose origins may be firmly fixed in the late nineteenth century (the eighties), without forgetting the intricate and overlapping circumstances of its emergence and development. Decadence preceded Symbolism only slightly and continued as a parallel and somewhat subordinate phenomenon, sometimes participating in resurgent, neo-romantic manifestations, while at other times (particularly in magazines, then much in vogue) getting diluted in the intrigues of arts and letters that rode the ornamentalist tide of the first years of this century. On the other hand, as an antirational and spiritualist reaction against Positivism and Scientism, and in the wider context of an anti-Naturalist and anti-Parnassian aesthetic renewal, Decadence embodied an artificial revival of romantic tendencies, in symbiosis with an agonizing pessimism and a morbid aestheticism, making for a kind of "verbo-musical" poetics of perceptual nuances, opposed to the architectural tradition of literary discourse subject to the principle of thematic and formal decomposition.

Students of Decadence in Portugal are only just beginning to appreciate that the evolutionary paths traced for twentieth-century vanguard movements by scholars such as Poggioli, Calinescu, Kenner and Sontag confirm Decadence as a link in the post-Baudelairian chain of aesthetic modernity, in conflict with the socio-scientific modernity descended from the Enlightenment. Decadence is also now seen, in accord with what the surrealists intuited, to have opened new artistic paths for liberating and for probing the imagination, the neurotic and the subliminal, desire and taboo.

Decadence, then, prevailed at the end of the nineteenth century not only as an artistic expression of Western man's crisis of confidence in urban industrial society but also as a skeptical reaction to the injunctions that modern scientific and pragmatic rationality wished to place on Transcendence and Nature, whether in our symbolic systems or in the social sphere.

Decadence gave expression to this twofold concern—intellectual and existential—through a set of thematic and formal characteristics that were polarized by the coexistence of an inward *horror vacui*, an obsession with the new, the cult of the artificial, and an individualism founded on a fragmentary or unstable identity.

To be sure, the reactive motivations of Decadence were nearly always shared by Symbolism, which likewise adopted the cosmopolitan, individualist, elitist, antimimetic, ultra-aesthetic and *"novista"* credo that gave rise to the Decadent movement's thematic and formal characteristics, and some of those same characteristics also showed up in certain phases or facets of authors who came out of the Naturalist school or evolved into Symbolists. But none of this invalidates the appropriateness of studying Decadence as an autonomous literary and aesthetic system.[1]

The potentially pejorative association of the Decadent movement with various psychosocial phenomena also denominated by the words *decadent* and *decadence* made for a slippery terrain where criticism only slowly found its footing and unraveled the reasons why the true Decadent writers—far from accepting any deprecatory connotations in the designation—considered, on the contrary, that their sophisticated artistic nonconformity was an irrevocable manifestation (extreme or paradoxical) of cultured modernity and a personal transcendence of the decadence that surrounded them (an attitude exemplified in Portugal by Eugénio de Castro, whose literary trajectory was informed by an "ethics of aestheticism" set forth in his article "João de Deus," in *Arte*, 1896).

By now a thorough reanalysis has been made of the complex boundaries and basic distinction between decadence and Decadence as expressions of ideological disenchantment and self-disillusionment that contributed to the evolution of modernity (Pereira, *Decadentismo e Simbolismo na Poesia Portuguesa*, "No centenário de *Oaristos*," and Pimentel, *Literatura Portuguesa e Modernidade*). The Decadent writers adopted an attitude that was parallel but axiologically opposite to the correlation between social decadence and artistic excellence formulated contemporaneously by Karl Marx, and they articulated it with Spenglerian visions of civilizational decline or even with inverted millenary mythifications. In the substratum of Decadence, in fact, a blasé enjoyment of scientific and technical achievements in a degenerate culture of luxury freely cohabited with the Baudelairian reversal of art's relationship to the natural world and with the sense of entrapment, emptiness and alienation in the modern City. This explains the compensatory search for aesthesia in writers who either split themselves, like the *nefelibatas* ["cloud-walkers"] of Oporto, between anarchist attitudes (militant or merely rhetorical) and literary creations ruled by a highly critical, snobbish egotism and by a hazy aesthetic mysticism, or who dissociated anarchism from individual revolt and rejected the need for political and social commitment in their life and work. Taking to heart both the tenet that Art is superior to Nature and should serve as its model and the priority attributed to bookish culture and the "religion of literature," the Decadent writers (such as the young António Nobre and Eugénio de Castro) strove to make their life and work conform to the same egotistic and aesthetic parameters.

In the case of Portugal, it is important not to confound the Decadent period style with the problem of national decadence that obsessed the late nineteenth-century intelligentsia (Martocq, Lopes). The Decadent movement that flourished among us also flourished in countries such as Germany or Victorian England that were not afflicted by a feeling of languor and decline, success rather than decadence having apparently graced their bourgeois societies and ruling national powers, so that the existential and spiritual trouble they felt was only latently perceptible in their behaviors. But in Portugal, as in certain other countries (France, Spain, Italy), debate on the problem of national decadence had marked the whole of nineteenth-century culture, becoming even more acute with the "Geração de 70" [1870 Generation] (Serrão, Pires). The Decadents in Portugal merely took on the preexisting theme of national decadence as one of their various concerns, using it as an instrument for magnifying their pessimistic vision and for expressing their anguished state of mind, according to the reversible relationship of poet to generation to nation, illustrated in A. Nobre's *Só* and in A. Lopes Vieira's *Naufrágio*. Indeed, they transferred the contingent and circumstantial fact of decadence to the final and necessary national decline instead. The fate of the national race emerged as a confirmation of their sense of universal crisis and their fatalistic world view, and it served— looking now from the other side—as a ready justification for the apathetic stance of the Poet and of the Decadent (anti-) hero, in accord with their affectation of a sophisticatedly skeptical modernity, and compensated by a D'Annunzian "aphrodisiacal aesthetic conceit." The self-representation of the artist was merely a metamorphosis of romanticism's predestined and *maudit* Poet, now subject to the fate of a demoniacal corruption, so that his or her creative gifts and aesthetic refinement are accompanied by a psychosomatic imbalance or cynical degeneration (cf. João Barreira, *Gouaches*, A. Nobre's *Só*, Eugénio de Castro's *Interlúnio*, António de Cardielos's *Agonia*, Gomes Leal's *A Mulher de Luto*, etc.).

The fin-de-siècle period was one of profound renewal for Portuguese literature, prompting a shift in the forces that ruled the aesthetic and ideological systems. Although Realism and Naturalism continued to reach a vast public through their presence in narrative fiction and plays, they lost prestige and the capacity to vie for hegemony. Realism was largely rejected as an ideology, being reduced to a loose set of procedural norms for structuring narrative, for formulating and describing characters and settings, and for using language with accuracy and restraint. Naturalism, always an ambiguous doctrine in Portugal (Jesus), now fell clearly out of favor in the literary programs, debates and critical appraisals that filled the pages of magazines and newspapers. The same was true for the tenuous Parnassian movement, but that did not prevent fin-de-siècle culture, in search of a new synthesis, from inheriting its artistic rigor, its post-Realist wariness of emotional and verbal effusiveness, and its cultivation of formal elegance—in short, its aestheticism and culturalist inspiration (music, however, came into prominence over and above the visual arts).

In the meantime Portuguese neo-romanticism emerged, initially participating—in a secondary and ideologically indefinite role—in the reaction against Scientism and Naturalism and becoming more firmly established when it went on to oppose the depressive and cosmopolitan aestheticism of the "novista" movement (as it was christened by Armando Navarro, the best of its critics), which spearheaded the renewal of fin-de-siècle literature in conformity with the tenets of Decadence and Symbolism.

If prior literary models and schools continued to operate into the late nineteenth century, they were overshadowed by a new literary dynamic that revitalized the traditions of bohemian art and literary circles, resurrected the ephemeral but important chapbooks and group reviews, revived the practice of manifestos and literary debates, dragging established figures from the preceding period into the fray, and invaded the cultural journals, the general interest magazines and the large-circulation newspapers. The "novista" artistic movement imposed its hegemony over this new literary dynamic, adopting an aesthetic of contraposition (in the Lotmanian sense) and a criticism that dismissed as outdated the norms and conventions that had prevailed until then, setting forth its own new poetics in a dense series of volumes (and scattered texts) remarkable for the originality of their content and mode of presentation.

The "aesthete" became an emblematic figure, inextricably linked to an audacious and laborious strategy of intervention in the institutional workings of literature according to the dictates of elitism and the paroxysms of originality. The first and best example of the "aesthete" figure—although his poetry does not attain the complexity and subtlety of Camilo Pessanha's symbolist verse (Lemos; Lopes; Pereira, "A condição do Simbolismo em Portugal . . ." and De Fim-de-Século ao Modernismo) nor the captivating singularity of António Nobre (Castilho; Morão; Pereira, "A dúplice exemplaridade de Só")—was Eugénio de Castro (Ramos, Eugénio de Castro e a Poesia Nova. Ensaio; Pimpão; Castro), beginning with his "Visões de haschisch" (1887), followed by the propitiatory sacrifice of Novas Poesias (c. 1888), by the prologues and texts proper of Oaristos (1890, 2nd ed. 1900), by Horas (1891) and the other works leading up to his Poesias Escolhidas (1902), and concluding with Interlúnio (1911) and Horas (1912). Exemplary in his ethics of aestheticism, Eugénio de Castro forged an uncommon and imposing literary career, following his own path toward maturity with discernment and determination. His poetic creations were accompanied by a cultural and literary activity that was versatile, well informed, stimulating and uncompromising, and he made of his work a living lesson of nonconformity (Pereira, "No centenário de Oaristos").

Animated and guided by this spirit, fin-de-siècle literary texts and activity stand out for their emphasis on the power of the new to rend and rupture, for their relish of the odd and extraordinary in discourse and sensibility, for their spiritual restlessness, for their militant aestheticism (art for art's sake, rejection of moral, didactic and political concerns, the substitution of art for life, the alleged dependence of nature on art, the recreation of existence according to artistic models), for their cosmopolitan development and orientation, and for their concomitant attitude of elitist differentiation, of withdrawal into closed groups or aristocratic isolation. For this reason, according to the lesson of Baudelaire, the "novistas" considered exhibitionism, a dandy or snob mode of behavior, and even the promotion of their books as precious objects to be subjective factors of demarcation and rupture necessary for the development of an artistic spirit and a truly innovative literary practice. Furthermore, they saw their attitude as an esoteric concentration (perhaps the only one possible) necessary for the only redemptive or exalting activity, which they felt should be the fruit of inspiration in conjunction with culture and technique.

The same may be said of the prominent attention that such matters as the musical and graphemic aspects of signifiants, details of rhythm and rhyme, and oddities in syntax, vocabulary and suffixes all received in the Decadents' theoretical texts and poetic productions, as well as in the literary debates on the relative ranking of each personality in terms of who best represented the new styles. Their occasional lapse into reductionist formulas and petty formalism and the provincial disputes over who was responsible for introducing one or another novelty from Paris do not annul the positive aspects of those literary phenomena. As certain Modernist metamorphoses will confirm, we are partly indebted to Decadence—though more so to Symbolism—for a new consciousness of literature as a textual artifact and of literary language as ineluctably *other* (Guimarães, *Linguagem e ideologia, Poética do Simbolismo em Portugal*, and *Simbolismo, Modernismo e Vanguardas*), for restoring dignity to poetry, which had been tending toward confessionalism and light verse uninformed by aesthetic concerns, for giving greater weight to the intellect and the will in poetic creation, and for defending the aesthetics of suggestion, via the symbols, allegories, metaphors and similes of the fin-de-siècle "novistas," with the theoretical potential in this area surpassing the actual achievements, some of which were nonetheless quite impressive. At the turn of the century Decadence and Symbolism clearly ebbed before the vitalist, "saudosista" ["nostalgic" but with specific reference to Portugal's past], nationalist neo-romantic upsurge, and the movement that introduced them into Portugal dissipated, but the styles they embodied were only temporarily eclipsed, for they would be metamorphosed and embraced by the Modernisms of *Orpheu* and of *Presença*, as well as by the revival movements surrounding them (Pereira, "A condição do Simbolismo em Portugal e o litígio das modernidades.")

In the overall panorama of Portuguese fin-de-siècle literature, Decadence prevailed in quantitative terms, but Symbolism[2] produced the texts of highest quality, by writers such as Pessanha, Roberto de Mesquita, Alberto Osório de Castro, João Lúcio, Eugénio de Castro and Carlos de Mesquita. This is explained by the Decadent movement's propensity to thrive in the limited cultural conditions and depressed socioeconomic and political situation of late nineteenth-century Portugal. The Decadents were less demanding in terms of underlying aesthetics and subtlety of creative gifts, falling more easily into a rehashed version of sentimental sub-romantic poetry or into an ambiguous appropriation of Naturalist aspirations with an aesthetic perspective of superior degeneracy.

On the other hand, and given the fundamentally polygenetic indoctrination of the movement's practitioners, neo-romantic elements were relegated to the secondary plane of a given work or appeared sporadically in the career of a given author or group—occupying, in whatever the case, a minor place (e.g., the prophetic moralism of Jaime de Magalhães Lima, the literary nationalism of Trindade Coelho or Luís Osório, the neo-Garrett style of Alberto de Oliveira, the "novolusismo" of Manuel da Silva Gaio, the Anteroesque mode of Carlos de Lemos and his promotion of the work of the "Portuguese Musset," Fausto Guedes Teixeira).

The 1880s correspond to the gestation period of Portuguese Decadence, which became firmly established between 1889 and 1891, had its heyday from 1892 till the end of the decade, and then receded until it was metamorphosed and incorporated into the Modernisms of *Orpheu* and *Presença* and invoked by the revivals that flourished on the fringe of these movements. Portuguese Decadence, then, was important above all as a dominating force in the fin-de-siècle literary renewal, which was polemically launched by a group of "nefelibatas" from Oporto (Raul Brandão, João Barreira,

Dom João de Castro, Justino de Montalvão and others) and by the groups formed around the Coimbra reviews *Boémia Nova* and *Os Insubmissos* (António Nobre, Alberto Osório de Castro, Alberto de Oliveira, Eugénio de Castro, etc.), seconded by isolated figures such as António de Oliveira-Soares and by disseminators of literary novelties from Paris such as Xavier de Carvalho, and soon afterwards joined by established authors (in particular Gomes Leal and Fialho de Almeida) and by certain "novos" or "novistas" from Lisbon and the rest of the country (Carlos de Mesquita, Henrique de Vasconcelos, Roberto de Mesquita, João Lúcio, João da Rocha, António de Cardielos, Júlio Dantas, Martinho de Brederode, José Lacerda, José Duro, and so on), followed in our own century by Alfredo Pimenta, Judite Teixeira, Luís de Montalvor and others.

The Decadent style is most evident in the poetry of these authors. It found little expression in dramatic literature but had a significant presence in fiction and in the prose poem, thanks to Fialho de Almeida and Raul Brandão (in his "nefelibata" phase), João Barreira and the partisans of his *Gouaches* (brief texts with symbolic-poetical ambitions, but limited by their affected impressionism: *Tristia e Além*, by Antero de Figueiredo; *Alva*, by Alberto Pinheiro Torres; *Aguadas*, by V. Ortigão Sampaio; and so on), and short story writers that could be occultist and anguished (e.g., João da Rocha, *Angústias*), ostentatiously morbid (e.g., Júlio Dantas and Manuel Penteado, *Doentes*), or inspired by a worldly culturalism (e.g., Henrique de Vasconcelos, *A Mentira Vital*, *Flirts*, and so on)—tendencies which carried into the twentieth century through authors such as Vila Moura or Albino Forjaz de Sampaio and, in a different way, through the fictions of Mário de Sá-Carneiro.

But it was indisputably lyric poetry that gave fullest expression to Decadent themes and formal devices. These include an agonizing pessimism and the flaunting of psychological imbalances, eccentric religiosity and occultism, a dandyish image overlaying a morbid hedonism of beauty and passion, satanism and sacro-sensualism, sadomasochistic perversion, extravagant obfuscation, ritually lascivious and illicit love, initiation into aberrant eroticism, exoticism of declined empires (Alexandrian, Roman, Byzantine) and Far Eastern preciosities, transgressive voluptuousness of vice, blood, pain and (anti-heroic) death, escapist pursuit of the mythic and legendary, musicality and a disconcerting prosodic liberation (sometimes already exploring subjectified mystery in accord with Bergson's *durée*), the primacy of suggestion through reliance on sensualist images instead of direct allusions or symbolic transpositions, a creative imagination that is both sordid and luminous, pathological and liturgical, necrophiliac (with the emblematic motif of the "dead city") and ambivalently monstrous (centaur, hermaphrodite, Sphinx, Chimera . . .), a *recherché* syntax and lexicon (rare words, unusual suffixes, and so on), an "écriture artiste" marked by affected, "incoherent" or anaphoric digression, and the atomization of textual units (Pereira, *Decadentismo e Simbolismo na Poesia Portuguesa*).

Portuguese Decadence was receptive to the Spencerian doctrine of the Unknowable and to the pessimistic philosophies of Schopenhauer and Hartmann (*Belkiss* and other works by Eugénio de Castro, Gomes Leal's *A Mulher de Luto*, etc.), and until Veiga Simões it embraced Wagnerism and its fusion of religious syncretism with intellectual eroticism. From out of the devastating individual or generational loss of faith (cf. A. Nobre's *Despedidas* or Henrique de Vasconcelos's *Flores Cinzentas*) and the bitter experience of appealing to a *Deus absconditus* (Roberto de Mesquita's sonnet "Eli! Eli!") there emerged the metaphysical anxiety of *Só* (A. Nobre), of *Jesus* and *Via Dolorosa* (Dom João de Castro), of *Almas cativas* (Roberto de Mesquita), and of poems such as "Madame Bovary" (Carlos de Mesquita). The subsequent religious compensation dissipated into a deism à la Guerra Junqueiro (*Jesus*, Júlio Brandão's *O Jardim da Morte*), sacralized panpsychism and metempsychosis (Eugénio de Castro's *Sagramor*), took on a fantastical or spiritist tinge (*Só, Almas cativas*), assumed Swedenborgian or ritual magic airs (*Sagramor*, Henrique de Vasconcelos's *A harpa de vanadio*), steeped itself in the "spirituality of lust" and in the dreadful illumination of black magic (*A Mulher de Luto, Flores cinzentas*), mixed ecstasy and hysteria (particularly in the psychopathological disfigurement of Saint Theresa: Dom João de Castro's *Alma Póstuma*, João Barreira's *Gouaches*, Júlio Brandão's *O livro de Anglaïs*), and combined spirituality with sensualism (cf. Eugénio de Castro's "O anjo e a ninfa"), delighting in the dazzling beauty of liturgical implements, in the splendor of acts of worship, and in the inebriation produced by incense and hymns.

The defeatist attitude of the Portuguese Decadents led to fatalism and a shocking defense of infertility, directly or metaphorically expressed in works such as *Só, Despedidas,* Castro's *Interlúnio*, José Duro's *Fel*, Júlio Dantas's *Nada*, Oliveira-Soares's *Paraíso Perdido*, and João da Rocha's *Nossa Senhora do Lar.*

Their skepticism (cf. *Despedidas*), on the other hand, conduced to apathetic withdrawal (cf. "Fins de Outono" in *Depois da ceifa*, or "Nirvanâncias" in *Flores cinzentas*), to "ineffable lethargy" (Carlos de Mesquita), and to sheer fatigue or *abulia*, setting the stage for their aspiration to lethal insensibility: all of which reinforced the themes of tedium, Baudelaire's spleen (*Só, Flores cinzentas*), "mortal boredom" (*Nada*), and a "loathing of life" accompanied by physical and psychological insularity (Roberto de Mesquita).

The stigma of the man who has come "sur le tard d'une race" (Bourget) translated—for the Portuguese Decadents— into physical enfeeblement, effeminate fragility, and premature decrepitude. Coherently enough, they hyperbolized their fondness for the swooning hour of the sunset, for the Autumn of the sweet and lifeless decline of things, for lulling or mournful sounds, for fading reflections of light, for misty airs and for shadowy places, insofar as these correlated with reverie, with weeping, with narcissistic consolation, and with fanciful retreats into the lost paradise of childhood or elsewhere in the "archeology of nostalgia" (as Nemésio defined Roberto de Mesquita's project).

Vis-à-vis the elusiveness of all that is real, Portuguese Decadence evinced subjective duplicity (cf. *Alma Póstuma, Sagramor* and "Hermafrodite," by Eugénio de Castro, and *Poesia humana*, by Xavier de Carvalho) as well as feverish agitation, the vertigo of mental derangement, an ominous foreboding, and neurosis allied to "the pain of thinking" (cf. *Só, Interlúnio, Fel*, and Henrique de Vasconcelos's *Os Esotéricos, Exiladas, Agonias*). It therefore sought, on the path forged by Baudelaire and Huysmans, "artificial paradises" and intoxication through rare and composite perfumes. It drowned the tormenting *horror vacui* of the modern soul in extraordinary flowers and gems, in the deceitful world of glitter and show, but it accompanied this obfuscating and hallucinatory lavishness with the spectacle of perverse deformation, with the horrifying and macabre, with rottenness and disease, and from *Só* to the already late *Nova Safo*, by Vila Moura, it wallowed in sadistic and necrophiliac practices and fantasies, in sexual neuroses and erotic deviations (cf. the work of Eugénio de Castro, Xavier de Carvalho, José Duro, Júlio Dantas, Oliveira-Soares and Henrique de Vasconcelos).

As in all of Euro-American Decadence, whose exotic and ghostly world of fantasy was inhabited by idolatrous or Medusan *femme fatale* figures in alternation with delicate but no less fateful *femme fragile* figures, so too in Portuguese Decadence love became an incoherent and impossible attraction, a burning but unrealizable desire, inspired by the same female types: Salome first and foremost (e.g., in Eugénio de Castro, whose *Belkiss* should also be remembered here), followed by Ophelia and Saint Iria (A. Nobre, J. Brandão), Mesquita's "Tanit" and Herodias, the "fatal virgin" that aroused an impossible, cathartic love in Oliveira-Soares, the sensuously and coldly fascinating woman found in Henrique de Vasconcelos, and so on.

Linking its formal and stylistic renewal to its altered world view (e.g., Armando Navarro, 1893), the Portuguese Decadents—from the time of Eugénio de Castro's *Oaristos*—prized prosodic and imagistic novelty and "rare words" as a quasi-aristocratic training for achieving a literary language and as a stimulus to artistic evolution. These purposes help us understand the excruciating detail employed in certain literary debates (particularly the one between *Boémia Nova* and *Os Insubmissos* over the issue of Alexandrine trimeters, in 1889).

Rejecting realist and Parnassian objectivity and descriptiveness, the Portuguese Decadents followed Verlaine's poetics of the hazy and indefinite, reflected in their conspicuous search for unusual adjectival and suffixal forms. Though occasionally harking back to the emotional/rhetorical mode (from Dom João de Castro to João Lúcio) and to narrative verse (achieved in Eugénio de Castro, mediocre in other authors), Portuguese Decadent poetry—beginning with Oliveira-Soares's *Azul*—sought to follow Verlaine's example of eschewing eloquence in favor of musicality. This, in turn, required a freer verse line and stanza and conduced to promotion of the poem and of poetic prose, as well as to the lyrical refashioning of drama and narrative prose.

I have made the point on more than one occasion that the incessant nourishment of nineteenth and twentieth-century Portuguese literature on the motives and proposals of romanticism—and we may even speak of the incessant proliferation of metamorphic "romanticisms" within this literature, since in Portugal, as Joaquim Manuel Magalhães has written, "the aesthetic category commonly known as Romantic became a kind of endemic echo without roots"— encompasses as a less positive aspect, or presents as an unfortunate byproduct, a misguided "sincerity" or aesthetic of moral-psychological authenticity. It suffers the ill effects, in other words, of the expressionist poetics that emerged very appropriately in the pre-romantic phase of literary history and persisted throughout romanticism as a concept of the creative process that ran parallel to the doctrine of the creative imagination, but at a level that was both more accessible and less seminal. It was a poetics that betrayed the derogation of the (neo-) classical aesthetic of representation, for it merely shifted mimesis to the plane of subjective description of experience, as a (preferably spontaneous) confessional expression of the writer's personality and intimate life.

Exacerbated egotism, emotional and verbal incontinence, and a slackening of critical awareness and of creative craftsmanship were some of the harmful consequences of the sub-romantic expressionist tradition. But it is also true that this tradition sometimes enabled the limited national literary-aesthetic experience to gain access, even if only secondhand, to the most varied stylistic programs and trends. And it occasionally found ways to redeem itself—if not through high-level integration into new aesthetic creeds, then at least by assimilation into more worthwhile discursive practices (with their different creative imagination and their own diction).

The Decadent movement played a role in this process, and—I will argue—at two critical junctures:

1. first of all, at the close of the nineteenth century, when Decadence, unlike Symbolism, continued to reelaborate a sentimental, sub-romantic poetry. At the same time it participated tenuously or intermittently in the aesthetic of suggestion and in the antecedents of the doctrine of poetic dissimulation that Symbolism fully assumed (and passed on to the Modernism of *Orpheu*), thereby acquiring antibodies—not always sufficient, to be sure—against the vices of an overly confident and prolix egotism.

2. secondly, at the turning of the century and in the several decades that followed, when derivative extensions of Decadence redeemed themselves as bulwarks (inappropriately decked out in finery, to be sure) against the torrential wave of emotional rhetoric produced still and always by sub-romantic expressionism, which had found fertile territory in the lower strata of the then predominant neo-romanticism. Then too, at least a bit of credit must go to the Decadent movement for the fin-de-siècle legacy that enabled the Modernism of *Orpheu* to reject "sincere" egotism and the inertia it bred.

But what has not been seen or stressed is that the most relevant path of literary "salvation" for that precocious, sub-romantic form of expressionism was formed by the intermittent, partial manifestations of Expressionism proper in Portuguese literature—from Raul Brandão to José Régio. Probably in all of European Expressionism, and most certainly in its Portuguese version, the Decadence movement made a crucial contribution.

The tenacious sub-romantic tradition of expressionist poetry and the crisis aesthetic of Decadence crossed paths in this artistic trajectory of "effusion and violence" (Ferriot) and were transformed in the chaotic clamor of Expressionism, which eventually gave rise to the psychological moralism of José Régio and some of the literature of *Presença*, though it was present already at the end of the last century in the extraordinary and uneven work of Raul Brandão.

So it was with the first jolting awareness of crisis: still in the wake of romanticism, the entire oeuvre of Raul Brandão was an attempt to come to grips with this anxiety and bitterness, succinctly expressed in the preface to Volume 1 of his *Memórias*: "Our age is dreadful because we stopped believing—and we still don't have new beliefs . . . . And here we are with no roof over our heads, amid ruins, waiting . . . ." So it was with one of the most spectacular anti-Naturalist manifestations, unrealism, particularly in the form of the grotesque, since all ostensible reality appeared as a mere, conventional deformation of the truly real. So it was with the radical pessimism, the nihilistic attitude and the sense of existential guilt, which were hardly offset by the ontic or collective nostalgia that at times was paradoxically invoked. So it was with the exacerbated, visionary and problematic exploration of lofty, canonical themes belonging to the Western humanist tradition (God, Love, Brotherhood . . .) and with the metaphysical and prophetic view taken of various sectors in the surrounding world. So it was with the indiscernible link between radical subversion and redemptive utopia that gave rise to an apocalyptic climate, apocalyptic myths, and the discourse of apocalyptic circularity (to underscore the contradictions of bourgeois morality, to evoke the bad conscience of the prophetic speaker, and to update the literary imagination of propitiatory catastrophe that would prelude the millenarian emancipation). So it was in the dialectic of the pathetic with the grotesque, ideal beauty with the repugnant, the sublime with physical and moral horror. So it was with the ambiguous character of pathos, at once psychological and metaphysical, ethical and revolutionary, and with the ramification of the comic into irony, black humor and nonsense. So it was with the appropriation of the nocturnal imagination of anarchic discourse, with the taste for obsessive and "strange" metaphors (Harald Weinrich), and with the simultaneous disjunction of antitheses and integration of oxymorons. So it was with the obsessive and tumultuous energy applied even to the formal deconstruction of the narrative (in favor of an unconventional, fragmentary and recurrent structural format) and to the play of repetition and variations of themes and motifs, characters, stylistic devices and lexemes: *dor* "pain," *ternura* "tenderness," *bolor* "mold," *absurdo* "absurdity," *espanto* "awe" and—above all—*grito* "shout or cry."

Notes

1. With respect to the vast bibliography on Decadence, see the studies indicated in Pereira, *Decadentismo e Simbolismo na Poesia Portuguesa* (particularly the classic work by Mario Praz, *La carne, la morte e il diavolo nella letteratura romantica*) and the following, more recent studies: L. Hönnighausen, *Präraphaeliten und Fin de Siècle* (Munich: 1971); A. Thomalla, *Die "femme fragile"* (Dusseldorf:, 1972); E. Koppen, *Dekadenter Wagnerismus* (Berlin: 1973); Roger Brauer (ed.), *Fin de Siècle* (Frankfurt: 1977); Jean Pierrot, *L'imaginaire décadent* (Paris: 1977); Linda C. Dowling *Aestheticism and Decadence* (New York: 1977); Enrico Ghidetti (ed.), *Il Decadentismo* (Rome: 1977); H. Hinterhäuser, *Fin de Siècle* (Munich: 1977); J. M. Fischer, *Fin de Siècle* (Munich: 1978); Ian Flechter (ed.), *Decadence and the 1890s* (London: 1979); (various authors) *L'Esprit de décadence*, 2 vols. (Paris: 1980, 1984); U. Horstmann, *Ästhetizismus und Dekadenz* (Munich: 1983); B. K. Timmons, *Decadent Style* (Ann Arbor

Mich.: 1984); Eugene Webwe, *France, Fin de siècle* (Cambridge: 1986); Józef Heistein, *Décadentisme, Symbolisme, Avant-Garde dans les Littératures Européennes* (Wroclaw/Paris: 1987); C. de Deugd, "Towards a Comparatist's Definition of Decadence," in D. W. Fokkema (ed.), *Comparative Poetics* (Amsterdam: undated), 33-50.

2. With historical fortune on its side, Symbolism, much earlier than Decadence, was clearly delimited as a term with a specific semantic and pragmatic scope for the style and period to which it corresponded. But that has not prevented Portuguese historical literary criticism, in slavish dependence on its French counterpart, from alternating between this specialized usage of the word symbolism and its much wider sense. Given the current state of scholarship on Symbolism and its presence in Portuguese literature (Pereira, "A condição do Simbolismo . . ." and *Decadentismo*; Guimarães, *Poética do Simbolismo em Portugal* and *Simbolismo, Modernismo e Vanguardas*), there is no more excuse for imprecise labeling with only a hazy notion of the period's chronological demarcations (e.g., Gomes, *O Poético: Magia e Iluminação* and *Poesia Simbolista—Literatura*) or for corruptions that would make Symbolism correspond to a highly vague anti-Positivism and anti-Naturalism (e.g., Simões, the three works listed in Works Cited). On the other hand, as shown by Guy Michaud's monumental and paradigmatic *Message Poétique du Symbolisme* (1947, 1969), an alternating usage for the term may have its place: (1) Symbolism in the stricter sense to refer to its genealogy, its canon and its embodiment as a system concerned with transcendental initiation—via musically recreated language—into a world view founded on analogy, and (2) a wider application that would allow us to speak of the *symbolist corpus*, which derived from a looser definition of the thematic and formal Symbolist system and whose makeup was gradually identified (Cidade, Régio) and finally delineated with rigor by Jacinto do Prado Coelho, having served ever since as a general framework for much of the Portuguese and Brazilian criticism on the matter.

Symbolism, in short, should be understood as an aesthetic-literary system and textual strategy that surpasses Decadence (while sharing its aristocratic, cosmopolitan and aesthetic attitude as well as its antimimetic, "novista" stance) in a dynamic that moves to a plane of original calm or esoteric optimism, attributes a supreme and transrational gnomic function to poetry, and presupposes an analogically constituted reality that derives from a primordial unity and survives in a hidden harmony, translatable only in the symbolically and musically structured text, in reforged language and, occasionally, in free verse (Pereira, *Decadentismo e Simbolismo* . . .).

It is important to understand that this hub imparted a specifically symbolist dimension to a whole range of more diffuse characteristics that surrounded it (and that were sometimes also explored, in different ways, by Decadent literature and by neo-romantic literature):

> revival of the Romantic fondness for the vague, hazy and impalpable;
> love of shadowy and melancholy, autumnal and crepuscular

landscapes; a pessimistic view of existence and painful awareness of its fleetingness; themes relating to tedium and disillusion; withdrawal from Reality, aristocratic egotism, and subtle analysis of sensorial and emotional nuances; rejection of confessional lyricism in the expansive and rhetorical Romantic style, and a preference for the indecisive suggestion of mental and emotional states taken out of the biographical context, impersonalized; thanks to an alert and sensitive aesthetic intelligence . . . , a highly effective combination of "inspiration" (surrender to spontaneous associations and appeals from the unconscious) and "lucidity" (control and exploitation of these irrational elements), with entirely new results in poetry; wide usage not only of the entirely symbolist, free-floating and untranslatable symbol, but of allegory, of images clearly and deliberately endowed with symbolic value, of express or implicit comparisons, of synesthesia . . . , and of merely decorative images; concrete or even impressionistic language, insofar as the mental or emotional state expresses itself through fragmentary images from the outside, from Nature, or imbues with psychic elements the landscape it describes (pantheism and panpsychism are relevant here); the dynamic, fleeting character of the image, ready to dissolve in the emotional tonality and musical flow of the poems, and this musicality is not limited to the play of sonorities in the verses but . . . is felt through inner resonances even beyond the reading of the text; liberation of rhythms and a rich vocabulary of highly evocative words, thanks to their own phonetic expressiveness or to a subtle playing off of words against each other . . . . (Coelho, "Simbolismo . . . ," 1026-27)

Works Cited

Castilho, Guilherme de. *António Nobre—a Obra e o Homem*. 3rd ed. Lisbon: Editorial Presença, 1988.

Castro, Aníbal Pinto de. "Tradição e renovação na poesia de Eugénio de Castro." *Arquivo Coimbrão*, 24 (1969): 154-81.

Cidade, Hernâni. *O conceito de poesia como expressão da cultura*. 2nd ed. Coimbra: A. Amado, 1957.

_____. *Tendências do lirismo contemporâneo*. 2nd ed. Lisbon: Portugália Editora, 1939.

Coelho, Jacinto do Prado. *Ao Contrário de Penélope*. Lisbon: Bertrand, 1976.

_____. "Simbolismo." *Dicionário de Literatura*. 1026-30. Oporto: Livraria Figueirinhas, 1969.

Ferriot, H. R. "L'effusion et la violence. Symbolisme et Expressionnisme." *Revue de Littérature Comparée*, 54 (1980): 71-79.

Ferro, Túlio Ramires. "Breves notas sobre as tendências da literatura portuguesa no final do século XIX." *Vértice* 10. 84, 87, 88 (1950): 71-84, 277-95, 366-77.

122 ◆ J. C. SEABRA PEREIRA

_____. "Raul Brandão et le Symbolisme portugais." *Bulletin des Ètudes Portugaises et de l'Institut Français au Portugal* 13 (1949): 210-28.

Gomes, Álvaro Cardoso. *O Poético: Magia e Iluminação.* São Paulo: Ed. Perspectiva, 1989.

_____. *Poesia Simbolista—Literatura Portuguesa.* São Paulo: Global, 1986.

Guimarães, Fernando. *Ficção e Narrativa no Simbolismo.* Lisbon: Guimarães Ed., 1988.

_____. *Linguagem e ideologia.* Oporto: Editorial Inova, 1971.

_____. *Poética do Simbolismo em Portugal.* Lisbon: INCM, 1990.

_____. *Simbolismo, Modernismo e Vanguardas.* 2nd ed. Oporto: Lello, 1992.

Jesus, Maria Saraiva de. "Erotismo decadentista e moralismo romântico n'*O Livro de Alda* de Abel Botelho." *Diacrítica* 6 (1991): 141-62.

Lemos, Esther de. *A "Clepsidra" de Camilo Pessanha.* 2nd ed. Lisbon: Verbo, 1981.

Lopes, Óscar. *Entre Fialho e Nemésio* Vol. 1. Lisbon: INCM, 1987.

Lourenço, Eduardo. "Salomé icône du Symbolisme." *Nova Renascença* 35-38 (1989-90): 515-21.

Lourenço, M. S. *Os Degraus do Parnaso.* Lisbon: Ed. O Independente, 1991.

Magalhães, Joaquim Manuel. "Coisas Gerais." *Os dois crepúsculos.* Lisbon: A Regra do Jogo, 1981.

Martocq, Bernard. "Le pessimisme au Portugal (1890-1910)." *Arquivos do Centro Cultural Português.* Vol. 5, 420-58. Paris: 1971.

Morão, Paula. *O "Só" de António Nobre. Uma leitura do nome.* Lisbon: Caminho, 1991.

Pereira, José Carlos Seabra. "A condição do Simbolismo em Portugal e o litígio das modernidades." *Nova Renascença* 35-38 (1989-90): 143-56.

_____. "A dúplice exemplaridade do *Só.*" *Colóquio/Letras* 127-28 (1993): 27-44.

_____. *Decadentismo e Simbolismo na Poesia Portuguesa.* Coimbra: Centro de Estudos Românticos, 1975.

_____. *De Fim-de-Século ao Modernismo*, vol. VII of *História Crítica da Literatura Portuguesa.* Ed. Carlos Reis. Lisbon: Author edition, 1995.

_____. *Do fim-de-século ao tempo de Orfeu.* Coimbra: Almedina, 1979.

_____. "No centenário de *Oaristos*: Em Prol de Eugénio de Castro-A ética do esteticismo." *Colóquio/Letras* 113-14 (1990): 68-88.

Pimentel, F. J. Vieira. *Literatura Portuguesa e Modernidade.* Ponta Delgada: Published by the author, 1991.

Pimpão, Álvaro J. da Costa. "Eugénio de Castro" and "Eugénio de Castro em Coimbra." *Gente grada*, 163-84, 185-96. Coimbra: Atlântida Editora, 1953.

Pires, António M. B. Machado. *A ideia de decadência na Geração de 70.* 2nd ed. Lisbon: Vega, 1992.

Ramos, Feliciano. *Eugénio de Castro e a Poesia Nova. Ensaio.* Lisbon: Edição Ocidente, 1943.

_____. *História da Literatura Portuguesa.* 6th ed. Braga: Livraria Cruz, 1963 (1st ed. 1950).

Régio, José. *Pequena história da moderna poesia portuguesa.* 2nd ed. Lisbon: Editorial Inquérito, undated [1941].

Serrão, Joel. *Temas da cultura portuguesa—II.* Lisbon: Livros Horizonte, 1983.

Silveira, Pedro da. "Alberto Osório de Castro." *Seara Nova* 1470 (1968): 122.

_____. "António Bandeira" and "Os Bárbaros." *Grande dicionário da Literatura Portuguesa e de teoria literária,* 587, 591-92. Lisbon: Iniciativas Editoriais.

_____. "A propósito duma homenagem e dum projecto." *Diário Ilustrado,* 25 Feb. 1958: 53.

_____. "Carlos e Roberto de Mesquita." *Estrada Larga.* Vol. 1, 140-43. Oporto: Porto Editora, undated [1959].

_____. "João Barreira, prosador-poeta simbolista." *Seara Nova* 1456 (1967): 52-53.

_____. "Uns simples apontamentos-I." *Vértice* 22. 228 (1962): 442-48.

Simões, João Gaspar. *História da poesia portuguesa.* Lisbon: Empresa Nacional de Publicidade. Vols. 2 (1956) and 3 (1959).

_____. *Itinerário histórico da poesia portuguesa.* Lisbon: Editorial Arcádia, 1964.

_____. *Perspectiva Histórica da Poesia Portuguesa (dos Simbolistas aos Novíssimos).* Oporto: Ed. Brasília, 1976.

Viana, António Manuel Couto. *As (e)vocações literárias.* Lisbon: Author edition, 1980.

_____. *Coração Arquivista.* Lisbon: Verbo, 1977.

◆ **Chapter 8**

Before the Barbarians

M. S. Lourenço

> *Wir sind zivilisierte Menschen, nicht Menschen der Gotik und des Rokoko; wir haben mit den harten und kalten Tatsachen eines SPÄTEN Lebens zu rechnen, dessen Parallele nicht in perikleischen Athen, sondern im cäsarischen Rom liegt.*
>
> O. Spengler

> *Wir—wieihr—zeigten glücklichen barbaren daß höchster stolz ein schönes sterben sei.*
>
> S. George

I.

The Winter exists, after all, or rather still exists, if one considers the visible traces left in the last few days by the rain, the wind, the weak and ambiguous morning light. The small crystals on the window glass, the hexa- and octogonal frozen particles sparkle against the dusky light, like messengers from a more brilliant world, more open to the definition of ever more complex and thus more perfect forms. Even if it is uncertain for how much longer one is going to have this Winter, or any form of Winter, due to the greenhouse effect, we should nevertheless demand a minimum of poetic justice in favor of the season that teaches us, even in the gloom of morning, the principle that all perception is composite, the musical law to be discovered through the window glass: that these icicles can only be perceived as a dramatic shape if there is a background surface to secure harmony. It is only relative to this space, like a *cantus firmus*, that it becomes possible to perceive in their shape the complexity of a stalactite.

But it is an illusion, after all, that the Winter still exists, even if it is not the last one, because the sense of doom is now too deeply rooted, in view of the certainty that in a near future the greenhouse effect will reach irreversible values, so that we are living now the certainty of its agony. The death of Winter will also entail the end of a sense of form, or rather of the perception of form as this is ruled by the musical law already mentioned, *cantus firmus* against discant, without which the perception of the external world will show us only a cloud, bigger than Moses's own cloud, the representation of which will bring about the Mallarmean *Crise de Vers*. From the asthetical point of view the ominous agony of Winter casts some light on the *vexata quaestio* of the relation between the work of art, even literary art, and the objects found in Nature. We want this relation to stay very far from being that of an attempted imitation, or even that of a resemblance between the work of art and the perceived natural object.

But if the polyhedric particles on the window glass can be interpreted as a symbol of the form of the work of art, including the literary work of art, it is revealing to separate the form from the physical object. We will then have a clear ontology of the physical objects of Winter, like crystals and light rays reflected by puddles of water, on one side, and the also no-less-clear ontology of the abstract object form, on the other, which is not perceived by the senses but whose meaning is then secured by the perceived relations between the physical objects. This is the sense of the word "form" which W. Pater calls "mind in style," a sense according to which a work of art has form when it has structure, when it consists of a complex unity built up from simpler elements. Without structure the work of art will be the unfastened sequence of its parts and for that reason unable to address the intellect, since only consistent relations can be understood and therefore, without these, there is no form. From our knowledge of the external world we also gain the vivid insight that we can only understand what is bound by specifiable parameters, since there is no actual perception of an indefinite extense object.

And so the question which is the form of a work of art, we could call it the test of form, can only be answered by analysis. This is the *basilikos odos* to arrive at a perception of the whole as a function of the perception of the component parts. The most expressive way to capture W. Pater's conception of form is to bring to mind his latent logical metaphor of the work of art as a functional structure, and thus we shall talk about a logical conception of form and of Logicism as its aesthetic theory. The crucial point of this view is that the ultimate value of the whole depends upon the integrating values of the the component parts, which we find by analysis, and these like the motif, the theme, or the period make then possible the perception of the more complex structures.

A very vivid expression of a similar view of Nature and of the work of art, in this case the literary work of art, is provided by the well-known poem by Cesario Verde on the crystals of a Winter morning, the title of which is "Cristalizações." But again typical of Cesário is not the static contemplation of the polyhedric particles on the glass window of his room but his active merging, on the street, with the Winter landscape, the physical and the human, as it was to be expected from a fin-de-siècle "flâneur." Once on the street his visual sensations are more intense due to the sharp clarity of the morning light. A number of rain showers in the last few days have made the air colder, and the small water puddles have now an iridescent texture, with a play of glittering and changing colors. To him the tree in the Winter landscape no longer seems to be three-dimensional but has now a linear outline with only half-suggested colors. The contrast between foreground and background, or rather the relation between one and the other, is exemplified by an acoustic sensation, where the sound of a hammer against a piece of stone is first heard and then fragmented in its reverberations through the air.

The world of form, which Cesário senses in the sharp Winter morning, is contrasted or negated by the amorphous world of the street workers, dirty and busy, setting cobblestones on the pavement around which he is taking his walk. Some are described as rough and shabby and the description is an accumulation of images calculated to represent the dissonance of their appearance with the sensations caused by the refined and sparkling form of the Winter landscape. This first part of Cesário's poem can be considered as being the object side of the cognitive relation; the second part is dedicated to the perceiving subject, not only in isolation but also in relation to the representatives of the workers' world. This part is introduced by the statement of his thoughts or rather the paradoxes produced by them, an example of which is his feeling himself somewhere in the north of Europe when he sees himself somewhere in the south, in a dismal and suburban part of the city.

As he walks on, he feels that the Winter light glitters in the water puddles and that these have the brilliancy of diamonds of the finest cut. But the diamond sharpness of the morning light acts upon all his other senses, with such intensity that the new sensations range over all four elements, water, air, earth and fire. The fullness of his diamond vision can hardly be shared by the workers around him: they are weak and inhibited, the body is deformed by heavy physical labor, they have no access to the poet's joy of seeing a world which has the clarity and precision of a precious stone. He looks at the workers also as they are, with no bias or comment on their condition; he just notices that some spit on their hands, some look fat and lazy, others seem mindless, bent by a burden like an animal.

Once arrived at this point Cesário has to resolve the dissonance created by the conjunction of the two contrasting themes, the elegance of the Winter morning and the pathetic triviality of the workers' world. He succeeds with the resolution of dissonance by introducing a new entity in his walk: an actress, warm and cosy in her fur coat, on her way to a rehearsal in the theater. He shifts to her all the properties that up to now he ascribed to the Winter morning: the elegance, the refinement and the air of distinction, that one can only find in Northern European faces. The paradox that in a dismal and suburban place in the south one finds, in the crystal clear December morning, someone of that Northern distinction, enhances the still greater tension of the change of images just mentioned. The initial contradiction between the mindless workers setting the cobblestone pavement and the diamond light is now the tension between these and the actress in her fur coat on her way to a rehearsal. The poem closes with the gradual resolution of the conflict, or with the transition from dissonance to consonance. The workers look at the actress in such a way that she has the impression of a latent sexual threat. She has a moment of doubt and hesitates, undecided as to what the outcome is going to be. But then taking her destiny in her own hands she is able to run the risk, she overcomes the fear of sexual abuse and crosses over, toward her theater.

And so the denouement of our little drama in the winter morning represents the victory of the artist over the brute force of nature, of the artifice of thought over the sheer organic drive. Prima facie it would be also the triumph of the conscious over the unconscious mind, symbolized in the poem by the heaps of rubble, dirt and mud that our artist has to step over. But this very symbol shows that the reduction of art to the reasoning mind is merely provisional, in spite of the sparkling icicles and the diamond light. And although we cannot doubt that Cesário wrote a work of art which reflects itself the perfection of the crystal, we should not be misled by the beautiful natural image. The work of art does not arise from Nature but from an artifice of the Mind, and from that region of it which the heaps of rubble, dirt and mud are a revealing symbol. By removing the work of art from Nature and inserting it in the artificial allegories of the unconscious, we also create the possibility of the experience of Nature as a representation of the Unconscious. Nature is a reflection of the Unconscious, and thus subordinated to art, even literary art, a good example of which is the poem by Álvaro de Campos, a follower of Cesário, "O dia deu em chuvoso." But whereas Cesário's poem is the miniature of a drama, with crisis and peripeteia, and its hundred verses have a crystal clear symmetry, the poem by Álvaro de Campos suggests rather a cyclical form with an alliterative refrain. One has the impression that the poem never ends, and works rather like a perpetuum mobile.

Cesário's lyrical subject is the Flaubertian and impartial mediator between his characters, the natural and mindless workers on the one side, and the elegant and studied actress on her way to rehearsal, on the other. We see him only as a recipient of all the stimuli that reach him from the external world; we participate in his sense of joy as he becomes conscious of his new sensations. Campos's lyrical subject is the disturbed protagonist of the minimally narrated plot. There has been a change of weather, he is going to have to face a rainy day and he is gripped by a resilient anxiety over this relentless fact. But the rain which is there to spoil his day is actually the depression that he can no longer deny. The sky may have been blue once, but with this change of weather he is being reminded that blue skies belong now to his buried past. He knows that there are sudden changes like this one, as we infer from the poem "Súbito, uma angustia," but knowledge alone is no relief of depression.

Cesário ends his walk on a much higher note. He seems to be convinced that the "paradise within" comes from the expansion of consciousness by the simultaneous stimulation of the senses. But this stimulation instead of binding him to Nature releases him from it, because it is the source of the synaesthesias he uses in his poems. Like the fragile actress he meets on the winter morning he will also cross over from sense perception to Imagination, and thus from Nature to Art.

II.

Aristocracy, luxury and sexual perversion are the Three Fallen Graces, the literary value of which can only be gradually revealed by the character who at a given time is its embodiment. Proust used the power of this law to frame the harmonic progression that begins with Swann, who represents luxury without aristocracy or sexual perversion, and from Swann one can go to the Duchess of Guermantes, who represents aristocracy and luxury without sexual perversion, the last chord of the progression being the Baron de Charlus, who embodies the Three Graces at the same time.

In 1874 Cesário Verde created a duchess with enough luxury and sexual perversion to be able to throw a neurotic poet into a cataleptic fit, on the *trottoir* between Chiado and Rua do Alecrim. The then realist and republican Establishment received Cesário's poem with contempt, unable to hear the musical virtuosity of a 19-year-old who wrote alexandrinian lines with a precise stacatto punctuation, only and where it was absolutely needed.

The sky is mild for a Portuguese winter day, a sweet wind rises in the Rua do Alecrim, where the horses of a landau shorten their trot and begin to change to a slow walk on the way to Chiado. The landau belongs to a duchess whose lifestyle belongs to the outer circles beyond Good and Evil, and for that reason, around her body, Cesário senses the morbid call of her diamond aura. She is pale and thinks, her eyes are closed and her body leans against the dark blue satin of her seat. The young Cesário is unable to guess the content of her thoughts. He is only drawn by the magnetic pull that comes from that body. He is seized by the thrill created between the tension of her black silk dress against the golden greens of the tiger skin with which she warms her fingers. He is no more than a bundle of nerves, hopelessly aroused by the exuberant and voluptuous tranquility inside the landau. But this is in the end what he wants, to be bound, unfree, to give up his own identity, to be punished rather than to receive from her the gifts of love.

This profession of faith in the Keatsian form of love of "La Belle Dame sans Merci" is the content of the poem "Esplêndida," from 1874, which was the target of a biting reception on the part of the Naturalist Establishment represented by Ramalho Ortigão, the main tenor of which revolved around the degrading influence of Baudelaire's work on young Portuguese poets. But having to concede that the poem "Esplêndida" still lacks the perfection of Cesário's future work, it nevertheless represents a last extension of the scope of the love poem in the Portuguese language. As far as Ramalho's philistine reception is concerned, it is instructive to remark that we are now in a position to see that Cesário gave to the Portuguese lyric poets what Eça de Queiroz offered to the prose artists: they both proved that the anxiety of influence was to be overcome, that the Oedipus complex was to be resolved and "Sentimento de um Ocidental" or "Os Maias" could escape the depressing power of Baudelaire or Flaubert. Cesário and Eça have both understood that the resulting depression could only be lifted by finding a new equivalent of the body of experience articulated by their awesome literary fathers. It is perplexing to realize that Cesário's heritage was to bear fruit, whereas, contrary to appearances, that of Eça remained unclaimed.

But of course in our poem "Esplêndida" Cesário is not yet fully successful in resolving his Oedipus complex. Although the poem is by no means a translation, literary or otherwise, it is still what one might call an *imitatio*, the main models of which are "Tableaux Parisiens," "À Une Passante," "Danse Macabre" and "L'Amour du Mensonge," each of which contains a reworking of the theme "femme fatale." Nevertheless, the rigorous choice of material, the sensitive metrical and rhythmical work, and above all the studied discontinuity of composition are already integral features of the poem and, in fact, they will form the uniqueness of Cesário's future work.

Thus one cannot accept A. J. Saraiva's judgement, according to which Cesario's poetry, by being such a "unicum," remained without following. As it was already said the immediate influence of Cesário was experienced by Pessoa and in fact this influence, or rather this "Wirkung," is twofold: the spiritual posture of Álvaro de Campos presupposes that of Cesário in poems like "Nevroses," a fact easy to trace in Campos's poems "Tabacaria" and "Poema em linha recta"; secondly, the turn to pastoral in Cesário's last phase of production (1881-86) was to be followed and reformulated by the pastoral poet of Modernism, Alberto Caeiro.

In the Portuguese language Cesário is actually the first poet to articulate the theme of consciousness. Pessoa's contribution to this theme is an expansion of Cesário's work, and common to both is the (simplified) conception that consciousness is essentially the experience of the so-called sense-data, as it is stated in his poem on the crystals of a winter morning:

> Lavo, refresco, limpo os meus sentidos.
> E tangem-me excitados, sacudidos,
> O tacto, a vista, o ouvido, o gosto, o olfacto!

The prime function of consciousness is here the correct perception of the objects of the external world, and for that reason for both, Cesário and later on Caeiro, abstract insights are no more than a redundant exuberance of language, to be replaced by knowledge about particulars.

But what makes the incipient art of Cesário so attractive is his awareness of the existence of those domains which, according to Stefan George, were for the first time opened for us by Baudelaire. They refer to the area of experience that one can capture with the general formula "symbolist sensibility": the sense organs are simultaneously stimulated by the colors of silk, by the texture of the tiger skin or by the smell of incense. But whereas in "Sentimento de um Ocidental," in relation to which our poem is to be considered as a preliminary study, the sense-data lead to a higher reflection, here in the foreground stays the sexual perversion, the desire to surrender to the feline beauty of "La Belle Dame sans Merci."

We know that such a sensibility takes time to be schooled, as it can be inferred from Huysmans's novel "À Rebours," and for that reason in our poem Cesário does not quite yet master it, in spite of the fact that his images "velozes como a peste," or "atrai como a voragem" do convey a symbolist perceptual modus. But they still lack the surprise of translating one sensation type into another, the synaesthesias of his later work. However, he is already quite advanced in his musical representation of the Three Graces. The duchess warms her very long fingers under a tiger skin, about which we come to know that it is a present from a lover who is devoted to Eastern religion and who has just returned from India. But his mentioning this fact does not lead to a formulation of its meaning and within the poem's own logic nothing follows from it. The tenor of his statement is rather to be found in the previous stanza, where the sexual perversion is the source of the magnetic aura that radiates from the Medusean beauty of her tainted body. The poem glows with lust and luxury ever since its first stanza, and this glow is actually intensified in the last stanzas, where the image of the neurotic and shabby poet on the *trottoir* emphasises the brilliance of the duchess and her *equipage*. But the world of the landau and that of the neurotic poet on the *trottoir* are going to remain forever separated: inside the landau the duchess is already on the way toward achieving the sensuality in tranquility which was announced by Baudelaire in "Invitation au Voyage," whereas on the *trottoir* the Keatsian poet is only seized by the gloomy desire to become the powerless victim of a rage of the beautiful aristocrat. But being forever excluded from her world, without even being seen by her, without ever being invited to ride along with her, his only nemesis is to become the Angel of Evil and announce the uncanny discovery of a nerve that reconciles pain with ecstasy.

III.

Sometimes one hears the ticking of the moments of one's life, and the perception one has of oneself is then that of a prisoner, solitarily confined to a hermetically sealed capsule of anxiety and delusion from which no escape is possible, and which one calls one's "ego" or one's deluded "identity." In an exceptional moment, under the influence of tobacco, hashish or opium one can have a glimpse of a crack in the wall of one's prison and come to realize, during that short moment, what it is to be free, to unbind the fetters in the caves of existence. But as Baudelaire has shown in his "Paradis Artificiels" and Álvaro de Campos in his poem "Tabacaria," this intimation of freedom is soon followed by a return to the previous state, a return so ruthless and bitter that the ticking of time in the mind becomes louder and each moment appears now even more meaningless than before.

Campos describes this experience in his poem "Tabacaria," from 1928, a poem which follows the introspective kind of statement of Cesário's "Nevroses," in spite of the fact that Campos's diction does not aim at the elevated regions of the mind but rather to what one can feel as a manic-depressive melancholy. Thus typical of Campos's poem is the inexistence of a cycle which takes the mind from an initial state of depression to a redeeming insight in the end. Instead one finds in the poem a circle, where the closing lines "sem ideal nem esperança" reassert again the sense of delusion at the beginning. One can also describe "Tabacaria" as a musical and philosophical drama in which the mental and physical motions of the only protagonist are framed within a ternary form of rising tension where a climax is reached, and from here the action then drops to a number of circular substatements. The philosophical claim of the poem is already present in the narrative texture, with a direct allusion to Kant and an indirect one to Descartes's "Cogito ergo sum." Its "Hauptsatz" is then reached in the already referred to moment of the intimation of freedom, when he comes to realize the Nietzschean truth that metaphysics is only the by-product of an illness, an undesirable consequence of ill health, and thus liberation is actually the victory of being over knowledge.

But he also has a musical claim for his poem since he ascribes to it a "musical essence," which is basically founded in the construction and arrangement of the narrative material in a ternary form, very much like that of the first movement of a sonata, with an Introduction, a "Durchführung" and a "Reprise." From the aesthetical point of view his sonata form ranges over two separate goals: a late romantic diction, as a global assertion on the higher value of self-awareness, and an avant-garde tone, to be heard in the formal treatment of the poem, in its prosody and in the predominant role of his rhythmic imagination, documented by the well-known patterns of repetition, variation and parallelism.

The minimal plot has a Beckett-like simplicity: in a room with a view over a dismal street with a tobacco shop, in a state of mind fragmented by the contradiction between insight and delusion, Campos's thoughts circle around three sets of problems, without ever finding a satisfactory solution to any of them. The formulation of the problems and the search for solutions are described together with the physical unrest of the protagonist. In spite of the fact that the poem begins and ends at the window with the view over the street, he walks from his chair to the window and from this back to his chair, unsettled, changing his position five times.

He begins with a review of his past failures, coming to the sober conclusion that he was a failure in everything he undertook. To this feeling of failure he adds the burden of self-consciousness, his inability to reach that form of innocence which is represented by the dirty little girl eating chocolate. Thirdly he lacks the talent to unravel the meaning of reality using the tools of reason. But whereas the existential failure, that is, the relentless fact of having been a failure in everything, can be ascribed to his lack of genius, the ontological failure, that is, the burden of self-consciousness and the compulsive use of thought, seem to him to be more a feature of how the world is, or how the human mind works, against which nothing can be done. In a short moment, reclined in his chair, smoking, he can experience the relief from thought, the bliss of no self-consciousness, but then the internal objects of the mind reassert themselves again and with them the reality of an external world, which moves without a goal and does not strive for ideals.

The first part, the Exposition, takes us to the first walk from the window, where he finds himself at the beginning of the poem, to the chair, and it includes the first soliloquy in which the poem's subject matter is introduced to us. The Exposition begins with an Introduction, where a smaller version of both themes is formulated, and one finds this introduction between the first quatrain and the image of Fate leading the cart of Being through the path of Nothing. Both themes, the theme of the subject and the theme of the object, are represented—the first by the motif of the finite existence and the second by the motif of the street, where the ontological mystery is buried under the pavement and Death writes on the walls. They are then fully stated and thus the basic contradiction of the whole poem, the contradiction between Idealism and Realism, between what is real outside and what is real inside, remains unsolved during the Exposition. Also in the Exposition two subsidiary themes are also stated, the first to the effect that the ontological mystery is not conceptually accessible and the second about the personal failure in everything he attempted, captured in the formula "Falhei em tudo."

The second part, the "Durchführung," begins when he walks from the window to the chair (he asks himself, On what shall he think, and thereby starts a first working-through of the first theme) and ends again at the window, when the owner of the tobacco shop appears for the first time at the door. This is the longer section of the poem in which both themes are reworked twice, following the scheme A-B-A-B. The first reworking of the A-theme begins with the already mentioned allusion to Descartes's "Cogito" and the motif of the ontological failure is reworked in a crescendo which ends precisely beyond the limits of the solar system, what he calls the Indefinite. Thus the contrast with the parenthetical episode of the dirty little girl, whom he sees from his chair eating a piece of chocolate, supports the juxtaposition of the contradictory images, the cosmic space on one side and the trivial space of a Lisbon street on the other. But on the whole, the dirty little girl eating a piece of chocolate is a symbol of non-self-consciousness, that state which would allow him, the observer in his chair, to be released from the bonds of thought, to reach unmediated experience. And thus, still in his chair, and realizing his inability of ever reaching that kind of experience, he returns to the self-recriminations of the first theme. And as he is hurt by the contempt beyond tears or self-pity with which he reviews his life, he gets up, walks to the window and considers one by one the objects on the street, the people crossing over to the sidewalk, and concludes that his own life adds up to no more than a sinister and undeserved exile.

And we reach the last section of the poem, the Recapitulation of both themes with a Coda. Two formal features separate this section from the previous ones very clearly: the length of the narrated action (or the introduction of new characters) and the use of the technique known as "Trugschluss," or false conclusion, in which the underlying contradiction is provisionally resolved while he smokes, but then is once more restated. Once again sitting in his chair he turns his attention yet another time to the world outside. The tobacco-shop owner stands at the door, motionless. It is not possible to understand reality: and following the uncanny sensation aroused by his insight he conceives the idea of writing a poem. He smokes and, for a moment, he reaches the unmediated freedom he has been looking for: all questions have found their answers.

It is now that we enter the Coda, as such, which begins exactly with his perception of Esteves's coming out of the tobacco shop. Esteves is also a symbol of another form of innocence, different from that of the dirty little girl eating a piece of chocolate. The innocence of this new character is that of a simpleton, of a mind not before but without experience, the unstudied simplicity of natural mind. From the street he greets the poet, now again at his window. The poet returns Esteves's greeting, shouting his words, and we hear in his shouting the pain of separation and the longing for unity. But this sense of unity he will never reach: Esteves walks away, the owner of the tobacco shop remains at the door, with a smile forming itself around the corners of his lips: it becomes the point where the despair that comes from the world above meets the sinister emptiness of the world below.

IV.

It is not difficult to picture to oneself the walk that Cesário takes in the misty twilight of the day described in his mature poem "Sentimento de um Ocidental." He begins along the river, on the way to the Santa Apolónia train station, and from here he goes up the hill to Alfama, and then down the hill to the Lisbon Cathedral, from where he reaches the Baixa, the downtown center of the capital, only to go up the hill again to Chiado, and finally once more down the hill to Baixa. In what we might call his *via dolorosa* he opens himself up to the music of the city, to the wave of sound that expresses the ennui endured by its captives who, like those in Hell, will forever know that redemption is no longer going to be possible. As the sun is setting, his external journey becomes the frame inside which something in his mind begins to fall, from mourning into depression, slowly, by stages, like the approaching night.

On the 10th of June 1880 the newspaper "Jornal de Viagens" came out with a special edition under the motto "Portugal and Camões," in which Cesário Verde, then no more than 25, published the most refined Portuguese poem of the nineteenth century, the poem with the numinous title "Sentimento de um Ocidental." But in his poem Cesário hardly mentions the celebrated object, and in Part II of the poem Camões is only the statue of an epic poet of the past, in bronze, on a pedestal. He is presented to us in the typically Portuguese schizoid mixture of the sublime with the ridiculous, rising in the middle of a rather vulgar square, where young working-class lovers have come to sit and chat. In the remaining parts of "Sentimento de um Ocidental" one finds, in Part I, a rather vague allusion to Camões. After that the epic poet and the epic subject cease to be mentioned, and the sfumato evocation of the glorious past is replaced by the ghastly experience of the depressing present, as both mist and darkness become thicker. Thus no resurrection for Camões or for the epic genre in general, as this cannot escape the Spenglerian laws of its own obsolescence.

Milton distinguished two kinds of epic poetry, to which he gave the names of brief and long epic. The long kind of epic poem is set in the well-known canon of twelve cantos, where the journey of a nation and its leader is narrated. In general they travel from their place of birth to a new country, where a new political and religious order will be created and a new era begins. One finds this kind of Milton's long epic in Homer, Virgil, Tasso and of course Camões. The brief epic is, as the name already suggests, shorter in size but above all the theme of the journey, the subject matter common to both kinds, is to be now understood in a purely spiritual sense: the two points, the point of departure and the point of arrival, both lie in the soul of the temporal and spiritual leader. Actually in the brief kind of epic the leader mainly leads himself. He no longer founds a new religious and political order, he founds or rather finds a new kind of knowledge, the journey being now one from an initial state of ignorance to a higher cognitive order. The example adduced by Milton for the brief kind of epic is in the Old Testament, the Book of Job.

It is only the long kind of epic that cannot be saved from the obsolescence of the underlying concept of State or Nation. On the contrary, the brief kind is independent from such assumptions and therefore able to survive, as Cesário has proved. "Sentimento de um Ocidental" is a brief epic poem in which the heroic action is the inner change experienced by the poet as he wanders, in ups and downs, in the misty twilight, all over the sad city.

In the representation of twilight in poetry, which goes back to classical antiquity, the associated context is always Nature, in most cases the setting being pastoral. The twilight hour plays a symbolic role in the semantic definition of the emotions to be described. Baudelaire was the first to eliminate the pastoral or even natural context of the dying day, indeed at a time in which also pastoral poetry, just like epic poetry, had fallen victim of the laws of its own obsolescence. Baudelaire shifted the twilight from Nature to anti-Nature, from shepherds leading their flock home after sunset to the prostitutes which emerge at the same hour on the streets of the overpopulated metropolis. Indeed in the second half of the nineteenth century Nature, as Eça de Queiroz puts it, no longer exists, having been replaced by neo-pharaohnic buildings and meaningless industries with their dismal factories. Thus the early pantheistic lyric poem of romanticism is also no longer possible: the romantic poet could merge with the sublime, with God as Nature, but not with the trivial artifacts of man. And so it is at this crepuscular moment that Baudelaire is lead to meditate upon the chaos which unfolds itself before his eyes, as he listens to the sinister music with which the metropolis represents the dereliction of man. In his poem "Crepuscule du Soir" prostitutes swarm the streets of the city, man has emptied himself of his original nature, and the music of the night falling upon the city ranges from the simple melodies of the orchestras to inarticulate sounds coming from hotel kitchens.

The influence of Baudelaire's poem is known to be present in Eliot's "Prufrock" and "Waste Land." But in the Portuguese language the nineteenth-century fictive poet Fradique Mendes is the author of two poems both under the manifest influence of "Crepuscule du Soir." The poems are "Serenata de Satã as Estrelas" and "Noites de Primavera no Boulevard." But both poems, apparently written by Eça de Queiroz, are far from having reached the refinement of Cesário's "Sentimento de um Ocidental": firstly because the musical content of the city is rather poorly represented in Fradique's poems, and this is again due to the fact that there is no original and transforming perception shaping the represented objects; secondly, because the poems are too near to their model, and that prevents Fradique from reaching some form of anagnorisis, the change of perception by means of which the initial chaos, in the end, creates the possibility of insight.

Cesário shares with Baudelaire the ambition to treat poetically the theme of the "Musikalität des Leidens," the new decadent image of the implicit music of mourning, when mist and night cover the city and intensify the sense of loss. In one of his letters Baudelaire explicitly mentions the musical potential of the city, when he talks about the "prodigieuse musique qui roule sur les sommets." In Cesário's poem this potential is realized in two different but converging ways. As far as form is concerned, the poem uses a set of principles to define its musical structure. The choice of the Alexandrinian meter makes it possible to formulate the line as a composite of two smaller units, the antecedent and the consequent, separated by a caesura, each of which is carried by a flowing legato articulation. But Cesário goes a step further and undoes this too smooth running of the legato with a surprising turn to stacatto, with an almost onomatopoeic effect, an example of which are the well-known lines:

> E sujos, sem ladrar, osseos, febris, errantes,
> Amareladamente, os cães parecem lobos.

The most obvious way in which the musical potential of the city is realized takes place in the poet's own consciousness, in its shift from the visual to the acoustic perception, in a permanent effort to "sonos insinuare oculis," to integrate the visual in the acoustic image, indeed to subordinate one to the other. When he looks at the double row of houses along the street he sees the lines of a musical score.

Cesário differs essentially from Baudelaire by the scope and depth of his perception. In the city Baudelaire hears the expression of pain articulated by the human voice, the formless kitchen sounds, but also the orchestras whose music offer or rather suggest the new pleasures of the night ahead. Cesário in his longer poem hears not only with more discrimination but he is also aware of more possibilities. His ear is so accurate that he not only hears the obvious grinding of keys in their locks but also, and above all, the unique sound of a screw falling on the stone pavement or, in another range, in the nearby hotel, the harmonic tones reverberated by two crystal glasses as one touches the other. In the human voice he includes the monochordic repetition of a cough, the shrill dynamics of a scream of pain and the easy structure of a melody being sung. In his wanderings through the dismal city streets he also integrates the musical instruments that come to the attention of his ear, the different sounds of bells, from church and prison, and the distant notes of a flute, which remind one of the lost world of the pastoral. Of course the city is no *locus amoenus* and in it the despondency of man is expressed through the piano music that reaches him from a nearby window. For Cesário, as for Crashaw, everything that exists is musical and one can be sure that he hears it.

Baudelaire stops to hear in order to think, to contemplate a procession of beings who remain forever unborn, whose form of existence is poisoned by the paradox of a death for which no previous life has to be assumed, and their abortive existences simply crowd the depressing city. In Baudelaire there is no hope of a rebirth, in whatever form; he sounds unaffected and factual, he just notices that most people die without ever being born first, he neither proposes nor articulates a comforting facit: the metropolis is just Hell; it depends on its death for its survival. At the end of his poem Lisbon is for Cesário also a Dantesque Hell, a dark valley surrounded by misty walls from which there is no escape. The images of Gustave Doré express the ruined churches of the city, the mindless masses that crawl like ants through the streets are now Hell itself, not an imaginative representation of it. And Cesário walks on, listening to the music of the city, up to the end of his *via dolorosa*. And while he walks on in the dead hours of the night, something is falling inside himself; his mind turns from mourning to depression. This is a reversal of the topological concept of the *ascensio mentis*, which in its substance comes from Plato, where Socrates is described as embarking on a second cognitive journey, rising from the perception of the objects of the external world to the higher knowledge of their Forms. This Socratic second journey becomes in turn a Christian topos, refering to the ascending movement of the soul from the world of the senses to the contemplation of God.

But by the time Cesário wanders up and down the city, platonic forms and, for that matter, God himself, belong already to the ruins of Western culture. The only motion left is that described in Parts I and II of the poem, from chaos and dream to, in the poem's latter parts, reflection and analysis. And thus he is now led to give to the topos of the *ascensio mentis* a darker kind of meaning, with an ironical twist to the Pauline *eauton ekenose*, by means of which he offers the ruined soul in the West the somber prospect of its impending destruction. He actually comes to reflect upon a new state, an intimation of infinity, in which the soul finally journeys beyond the horizon, its own horizon, to search out for a perfection without end. But now he sees that he is doomed to fail.

Chapter 9

Fernando Pessoa's Odd Epic

António M. Feijó

Aside from a few poems in English published in Lisbon in 1918 (*Antinous* and *35 Sonnets*) and 1921 (*English Poems I and II* and *English Poems III*), *Mensagem* is the only book of poetry published by Fernando Pessoa in his lifetime. The ostensible reason for its publication was a literary contest sponsored by Salazar's National Office for Propaganda in 1934 with a prize to be awarded to a work of "high nationalistic exaltation." Pessoa was awarded a special prize on a technicality pertaining to the required number of pages, the first prize going to *Romaria*, a poem by Father Vasco Reis which has been utterly forgotten (Blanco 251).

Four days after the prize was awarded, Pessoa published in an evening paper an article on Father Reis's poem. He was originally invited by the paper's editor to write a piece on literary contests in general but, he claims at the onset of the article, since he had recently been involved in one, whatever he might write thereon may be misunderstood. Instead, he would make a brief critical reference to the poem which the first prize of the *National Office of Propaganda* made public. He then proceeds to detail what makes *Romaria* a remarkable, thoroughly Portuguese poem: its eminently Christian paganism, its human supernaturalism. The paradoxes in such a description of *Romaria* as a poem which is "Christian, in the particular sense of Catholic, and, in that exact measure, pagan" are only apparent. Pessoa explains how the Church of Rome, although Catholic, is a large aggregate of particulars, "like a régime of moral municipalities centralized in an imponderable empire." In the case of Portuguese Catholicism, and in accordance with the native trait of indulging emotion over passion, its central feature makes it a form of Franciscanism. Of the paganism latent in Catholicism we find in Portugal not its aesthetic aspect as, in different forms, it manifests itself in Italy or in Spain, nor its imperial intent, which may be found in Spain or France, but rather the "dispersive and fluid" aspect which characterizes the sway of emotion. Catholicism is in Portugal "without contour, a religious tenderness lazily unsure of what it believes in." This explains why the manifest God is neither One nor any of the persons of the Trinity, but a "Catholic Cupid" who is Jesus in the manger, or why our saints are either John the Baptist as a child, much before he became the Baptist, or infantile adolescents such as Saint Anthony miraculously repairing broken water pitchers. "As to the Devil no Portuguese has ever believed in it. Emotion would never allow it." This circumstantial background leads to a final evaluative paragraph: "Father Vasco Reis, whom God has made a Franciscan for symbolic ends, belongs in true Portuguese fashion to this brand of loving Catholicism." His book shows, like no other, "in so Christian a fashion, in so pagan a fashion, the religious soul of Portugal." And, albeit barely perceptible, there is something emblematic in it which touches "not exactly our emotion, but our intelligence . . . . This, however, is not Portugal anymore: it is talent." (*Prosa*, 357-58).[1]

There is a guarded irony in this apparently graceful bow. Its true import can be appreciated in the brief introductory note which Pessoa inserted eleven months later, in November of 1935, in a special number of the review *Sudoeste*. This number of *Sudoeste* was to include pieces by those who had participated twenty years earlier in *Orpheu*, the ephemeral and scandalous 1915 literary review, as a late commemoration of a poetic and public disturbance which Pessoa had led with gusto. In his editorial note Pessoa names the *Orpheu* participants who have been included and explains the reasons for two absences. One of them, Ângelo de Lima, has been abducted by madness; the other, Côrtes-Rodrigues, to whom

Pessoa had been so close in the heroic years of *Orpheu*, has moved to the Azorean islands and is therefore not easily reached. Pessoa salutes him and expresses a telling wish: that Côrtes-Rodrigues not lapse excessively into the "rustic Catholicism which he has been pursuing for some time," a form of piety which has led to a sharp rise in the "number of literary victims of the blunted and Asiatic whimpering of St. Francis of Assisi, one of the most poisonous and treacherous enemies of the western mind." (*Prosa* 407).

This harsh indictment is not a mark of resentment which the incident of the *National Office of Propaganda* award might conceivably have led to. In an unpublished note of 1917, for instance, one of Pessoa's heteronyms, the classically minded Ricardo Reis, criticizes his master, Alberto Caeiro, because he detects in Caeiro's unpublished book "a naturalist Romanticism similar to that which was taught to the European mind by the dulcet canticles of the abominable founder of the Franciscan order" (Pessoa, *Caeiro* 33—see also pp. 133, 160, 183, 256*n*.)

This note is not a stray occurrence and could, in fact, be instantiated further. Pessoa's positions on Christianity are consistently antithetical, countering what he sees as its nefarious influence either through a rival teosophic inquiry, through Shelleyan claims for a most eminent status for poetry, or, more importantly, through a lengthy theorization of a resurrected "paganism" to be systematically enacted by his several heteronyms, that set of poets, markedly distinguished by diction, stance and biography, whom, as he puts it, he "mothered" within himself (*Prosa* 96—see also 82, 413, 433). *Mensagem* has had an uneasy posterity: praised by some as Pessoa's masterpiece and loudly decried by others as ideologically deleterious in its high nationalism, it nevertheless became an inescapably canonic monument. The régime's suspicions seem to have been caused by the gnostic nature of the poem's overt nationalism, by its peculiar choice of representative historical figures, by its general layout as a heraldic field, by the anti-Romanism of its occultist tenor, and by its abstract intellectualism. The pragmatic usages of the text as propaganda were justifiedly recognized as negligible. The intractability of Pessoa's text seemed to be compounded shortly thereafter by an article he published in a national newspaper defending the existence of the Masonic lodges which the régime intended to outlaw under a blanket proscription of all "secret societies" (*Prosa* 568-76). The canonic ambivalence which ensued remains. Intended as an epic, the poem seems designed as the counter-*Lusiads*, not only in the obvious sense of an *agon* with Camões as precursor apparent, but in the severely internalized nature of its nationalism. After a brief analysis of the topics and tensions I have described, I focus my attention here on a hitherto neglected, and most pertinent, trait of Pessoa's text: its dependence, as stated in a brief note kept in Pessoa's voluminous mass of unpublished materials, on Keats's "Hyperion."[2] This transnational crossing is, of course, highly disruptive of a text intended as a gallery of prosopopoeias set to intone a "high nationalistic exaltation."[3]

Written between 1913 and 1934, the terse poems which make up the volume are carefully divided in three major sections: the first part is made up of nineteen poems which cumulatively detail the Portuguese coat of arms. This mythic *ekphrasis* first describes the coat's two underlying "fields": the first bears seven "castles," the second five "shields." Above the "fields" is set a "crown" topped by a three-parted "crest." Every number in this description stands for a separate poem. Except for the initial two, setting up the fields which partition the body of the blazon, these poems are, for the most part, either epitaphs of, or apostrophes to, particular historical figures deemed emblematic. (The five "shields" are dramatic monologues of two kings and three princes martyred to duty.) This hieratic structure is intended as a description of the origins and of the apotheotic high curve of the history of the country. The chronology is therefore precise: from Ulysses, the mythical founder of Portugal, who, as an instance of mythical pregnancy, "without existing, sufficed us," to the central figure in the poem, King Sebastian, dead on a Moroccan beach in 1580 in a foolhardy imperialist incursion. The battle of Alcacer-Kibir in which he died led to a temporary loss of Portuguese independence, fallen under Spanish rule. A millenial reverie ensued, grounded upon the disappearance of the king's body on the battlefield and upon the messianic expectation of his return on a misty, redemptive morning. (The two main, and early, advocates of this Fifth-Monarchy millenium, a visionary cobbler and inchoate poet Gonçalo Mendes Trancoso, o Bandarra, and a seventeenth-century Jesuit orator who is the author of, arguably, the greatest prose in the language, Father António Vieira, are the object of two of the poems in a three-poem sequence entitled "The Warnings" included in the final third of Pessoa's book. The final poem of this sequence is the speech of an unnamed Jeremiah usually, and justifiably, identified as Pessoa himself, who, yet once more, in the wake of his two prophetic predecessors, ruefully calls for the return of the lost king.)

Following the initial lengthy heraldic description, the second part of the book is made up of a set of 12 poems detailing the Portuguese discoveries and their final collapse in the defeat of King Sebastian, which a most grievous form of contemporary decline underwrites. (A melancholy tone affects here, as it does all other such references anywhere else in the book, what Pessoa perceives, at the time of writing, as a stagnant and decayed present.) This whole section had already been published in 1922; it is the most coherent segment of the poem. In fact, its overt nationalism is only made problematic if the contextual pull of the two parts which frame it is ignored. The cultural branch of the régime was aware of the need for editorial discretion: the whole central section was excerpted from the book and published independently in 1936 under the aegis of the Cultural Propaganda Editions to commemorate the tenth anniversary of the régime.

The third and final part of the book is divided in three sections: the first is a set of five poems which a brief note in English in Pessoa's papers sums up as: "1) King Sebastian, the man, 2) King Sebastian, the hope, 3) King Sebastian, the symbol, 4) King Sebastian, the master, 5) King Sebastian, the Christ" (*Mensagem* 366). As to the fifth heading ("Sebastian, the Christ"), its Christian allusion is, in its conflation of the two figures, that of Christ and that of the king, an instance of what Pessoa elsewhere describes as the thoroughly "heretic" (*Páginas íntimas* 434) anti-Romanist tone of the poem. From a normative point of view, such a conflation of roles makes for a profane declension of Christ. After the brief middle section celebrating the three authors of prophetic warnings, Bandarra, Vieira, and Pessoa himself, comes the final section entitled "The Times," in which five poems chart the dark night of the country's soul ("Night," "Storm," "Calm," "Dawn," and "Mist"). The last poem is a messianic appeal from the nadir of the country's history: kingless, lawless, neither at peace nor at war, Portugal is, "as it saddens," a "dim lustre of the earth." The final line of the poem is therefore hushedly hortatory: "It is the Hour!" followed by a

Latin inscription which is a hermetic greeting of good health: "Valete, Fratres." And even the colophon itself is to be read as an integral part of the book, as, after indicating the place of printing, it lists the date, "the month of October of the year 1934, of the era of the Christ of Nazareth." This extended formula is not a periphrasis for *Anno Domini*, but a final intimation of how Christianity is to be sublated by a national millenium. In turn, this national messianic myth only reiterates Pessoa's most consistent position: the resurgence of paganism from the long eclipse which has dimmed it since antiquity and which a few flares but for a brief, malformed moment were able to lighten, the Renaissance and Romanticism. (This paganism is theorized at length and haltingly embodied in the poetry and prose of Pessoa's heteronyms. See, for instance, António Mora's "The Foundations of Paganism (a counter-thesis to Kant's *Critique of Pure Reason*)" or *The Keeper of Sheep*, the astonishing book of poems of Alberto Caeiro, the acknowledged master of all the heteronymic poets for whom Pessoa claimed to be but the dutiful scrivener [*Prosa* 82].)

Let me briefly sum up a few important positions: the historical cycle to be detailed in this brief epic starts with the earliest mythic precursors, retroactively construed by the poet as foretellers of a nation's history, and, as it advances through historical time, it restricts itself to a few select figures of the country's first two ruling dynasties which the national collapse of 1580 brings to a close. The tone of this celebration is melancholy because of the contemporary conditions of utterance for Pessoa himself, fallen as he is on hard times. Also, the depicted figures are consistently addressed or portrayed as objects uplifted from time, as mythic *eidólons*, in Whitman's terms.[4] History is thereby eroded. There is no time here but that of a perpetual fall. The same freezing of time, albeit in a more exuberant, less melancholy vein, is found in one of Pessoa's more often quoted descriptions of his several heteronyms which has consistently, and too hastily, been read as the preferred self-description of an essentially dramatic poet. In the passage I have in mind, Pessoa himself seems to support this view: his, he says, is a dramatic nature, but, instead of a drama unfolding in acts ("um drama em actos"), his drama unfolds in people, in individuals ("um drama em gente"). Thus the heteronyms: Alberto Caeiro, the blue-eyed, blond-haired, self-taught bucolic recluse; Ricardo Reis, the monarchist in his Peruvian exile, a reactionary and a classicist by training; Álvaro de Campos, a naval engineer with a degree from Glasgow, hysterical and futurist; and so on. But the burden of the passage lies less in the dramatic aspect proper than in the constitutive sequential nature of the drama, in the timely succession of the discrete individuals which embody it. What must be underlined here is how individual figures stand for acts of a drama, how the heteronyms are said to equate the formal units of a play. The several stations in the unfolding of the diachronic arc of the play, not its dramatic nature as such, is the ground of comparison. This is, in fact, Pessoa's own intention—he claims elsewhere that an intelligent man has the duty of being an atheist at noon, "when the clarity and materiality of the sun pervade everything," and an ultramontane catholic at sunset when the shadows gradually invest the clear presence of things (*Prosa* 446—cf. also 543, 555). (A weary type of worldly wisdom would undoubtedly read this as the typical shape of biography.) It is therefore fitting that, as he does elsewhere, Caeiro be repeatedly equated with the morning, Reis with noon, and Campos with the evening twilight. In their allegorical inception, these names succeed each other as, in the economy of a drama, acts do. But the diachrony in the composite day drawn by the heteronyms is frozen; there is no dénouement here, only markers of particular timeless stances with variable families of traits (corroborating Pessoa's claim not to evolve or grow as a poet but, rather, to "travel" (*Prosa* 101). Or, if diachrony there were, we would have to see it as decay: Caeiro, the source and concertmaster, is the first "act" which the others must follow. In short, time is as much absent from the genesis and function of the heteronyms as it is from the "transcendental cosmopolitics" of *Mensagem*.

"Transcendental cosmopolitics" is Leigh Hunt's description of what goes on in Keats's "Hyperion" (Bate 402). In a brief, cryptic plan for *Mensagem*, probably drafted in 1920 (*Obra poética* 727-28), Pessoa invokes Keats's poem on the destruction of the Titans by the Olympian gods, in the final mopping-up operations of which only Hyperion remains to be dethroned by Apollo, as the model of his poem. His epic will detail the Portuguese discoveries as an episode of the war between the old and the new gods. A nationalistic construal of this mythological parallel would predictably make the discoverers the new, olympian gods who claimed for themselves the old, listless realm of Saturn, as, in fact, several poems in *Mensagem* do. The poem on Magellan, for instance, tells of the titans's furor at the eponymous hero's rape of their mother, the Earth, graphically displayed in his circumnavigation of the globe, while that on Vasco da Gama's ascension to heaven describes the stunned gaze of both the olympians and the titans as they momentarily stop their battle to watch the induction into heaven of a national hero. Pessoa's 1920 plan is more complex than this, however. Its main section reads:

PORTUGAL
1. The idea of an epic poem representing the navigation and discoveries of the Portuguese as resulting from the war between the old and the new gods—Hyperion, Apollo, and so on (how does Christianity fit in here? How does it work? As an *attrait* used by the old gods to deflect men from the faith in the race of Jove?).
In the same way that in the *Iliad* war is a reflection of the war among the gods, the navigations are here the war between the old gods and the new ones, who lay obstacles in their path: Neptune his storms; Jove his lightning; Venus corruption; Mars, seduced by Venus, the conquests which followed the *Discoveries*.
The victory belongs to the new gods (what of Christianity, then?), and
It is Mars who achieves it in Alcacer-Kibir.
Taking up, in a fashion, Keat's life of Hyperion.

It will be noticed that, in this cryptic note, the Portuguese are equated *with the old gods, the Titans*,[5] while the innumerable obstacles which they face are seen as canny battle moves of the new gods, the Olympians. A listing of the latter's deployed weapons, which is but an epitome of *The Lusiads*, makes this identity clear: "Neptune with his storms, Jove with his rays, Venus with corruption, Mars . . . with the conquests which followed the discoveries." (Mars's role here is crucial: the imperialist consequences of the discoveries are denounced as a ruse and an instance of loss. The crucial link of Pessoa's inquiry on the causes of Portuguese decadence lies in its affinity with the Romantic historiography of Oliveira Martins.[6]) And, in fact, the note goes on to say that victory belonged to the new gods, the Olympians, who sealed it through Mars in Alcácer-Kibir. What, in fine, this means is that the high point of the country's history, the discoveries, is in itself a massive defeat—a defeat with momentous consequences: in his note Pessoa tries to grapple with the role of Christianity in the struggle related in this peculiarly inverted epic, wondering whether it might have been used as an expendable tactical unit, as bait ("attrait"), by the old gods to entice men away from any "faith in the race of Jove." The old gods' tactical usage of Christianity as an exoteric lure gives rise to a tremendous historical irony: the implication seems to be that upon their defeat by Mars Christianity was kept by men, unaware of its oblique origin, and is now the dim refraction of a vanished deeper faith which Pessoa calls "paganism." To the notion of empire as loss must then be added the perverted role of Christianity. "Perverted" is, in this case, very much to the point: the genesis of Christianity is agonistic but virtuous, deriving in syncretic fashion from the old gods' efforts at persuasion. Made rootless by the defeat of its creators, it has become an overpowering mistake.

Rootlessness is of the essence here. A difficult excerpt from a planned "Theory of Paganism" (*Textos filosóficos* 2: 96-101) defines Christ as sheer crossing: "Christ is a humanized, symbolic representation of the process which paganism does not, or cannot, tell, whereby Reality passed from Chaos and Night (Fate) to the Gods." The "causal abyss" bridging the Formless and the Formed is deliberately silenced by paganism because it is part of a "truth which precedes the gods." The Christ is but an imprudent, intransitive symbol of this bridging, which merely symbolises itself. Or, better, the Christ is not even *a* symbol, but the symbol *qua* symbol, the "Absolute intermediary," a paradoxical loss of function "which is absurd" and denotes nothing. It is a sacrilegious attempt, "nocturnal" and "left-handed," to reveal that which is not revealable. In a silent rewriting of a celebrated passage of Gray's "Elegy" which topples its latent political content into a gnostic insight, Pessoa adds: "It is as if there were a jewel or a flower whose magnificent colour could only exist in the night, vanishing on the spot were light to be shed."[7] (This passage is also a theory of subjectivity, of "sentiment," gnostically translated here into that which the Christ inhumanly signifies, as, later in this same text, Pessoa adds that "to feel is to exist irreparably alone," whereas "to think is to exist with the gods and with the harmonic and visible substance of the world.") In turn, the pagan gods are real and "fleshy in their flesh" (99); they are but magnified human possibilities. Only Fate, the Ananke, rules above them. (Christ is a fumbled schema, forged "at the height of the abyss," attempting to connect Fate and the gods.) Pessoa consistently reiterates this position which he sees as a fundamental axiom nowhere more perfectly condensed than in a passage by Pindar which he often quotes: "the race of men and the gods is but one."[8]

In history, the "Nation" fulfills a role functionally homologous to that of Christ (*Prosa* 71). (The fourth armorial "castle," on D. Tareja, echoes the gnostic theory of subjectivity as Christ alluded to above: "All of the nations are mysteries. / Each one is the whole world alone.") It bridges "Humanity," "a zoological concept," an "animal species," and the "Individual," a "biological concept." Its nature as a functional crossing is explicit: "The Individual and Humanity are *places*, the Nation the *path* between them." In its use of history, *Mensagem* is an attempt to map out a particular path. To those who walk in it the nature of a path is prospective, always ahead. But, in the same way that Christ is insusceptible of being intuited, "intuition" conflating two different senses of a *negative* faculty ("coming from *intus*, 'inside,' and signifying 'an understanding coming from inside,' it may also mean *in-tuitio*, not to see, not to protect" [*Textos filosóficos* 98]), the Nation is in itself always already a broken path. Pessoa's poem chronicles this constitutive interruption, its messianic import lying less in its topic "sebastianism" than in its tonal pathos. It is therefore sacred history. The protracted debate which has characterized its reception, broadly opposing nationalist apologists and enlightened secularists, is, therefore, given the cheerless nature of the epic, wholly beside the point.

Notes

1. All translations of Pessoa's texts are my own.
2. See Santos, *"Hyperion."* "Sistema."
3. See Tamen.
4. Cf. Vendler 3: "The actions we call history, and their written chronicles which we also confusingly call history, need to be converted into what Whitman in 1876 Platonically called 'eidólons.'"

152 ANTÓNIO M. FEIJÓ

5. See the variant poem on Affonso de Albuquerque, published in 1934 in *O Mundo Português,* where the eponymous hero is a Titan (*Mensagem* 41*n.*).
6. See Lourenço.
7. The crucial text here is, of course, Empson 5-6.
8. On Pindar, see *Textos filosóficos* 2:97. Cf. also *Prosa* 148, 169, 175, 178, 181-82, 232, 245, 549.

Works Cited

Bate, Walter Jackson. *John Keats.* Cambridge: Harvard University Press, 1963.

Blanco, José. "Nota." Ed. Adolfo Casais Monteiro. *A Poesia de Fernando Pessoa,* 251-*ff.* Lisbon: Imprensa Nacional-Casa da Moeda, 1985.

Empson, William. *Some Versions of Pastoral.* New York: New Directions, 1974.

Lourenço, Eduardo. "Oliveira Martins e Pessoa." *Revista da Biblioteca Nacional* 1-2 (1995).

Pessoa, Fernando. *Mensagem. Poemas Esotéricos.* Ed. José Augusto Seabra. Madrid: Archivos, 1993.

_____. *Obra em Prosa.* Ed. Cleonice Berardinelli. Rio de Janeiro: Editora Nova Aguilar, 1985.

_____. *Obra Poética.* Ed. Maria Aliete Galhoz. Rio de Janeiro: Nova Aguilar, 1986.

_____. *Páginas Íntimas e de Auto-Interpretação.* Ed. Georg Rudolf Lind and Jacinto do Prado Coelho. Lisbon: Edições Ática, 1966.

_____. *Poemas Completos de Alberto Caeiro.* Ed. Teresa Sobral Cunha. Lisbon: Editorial Presença, 1994.

_____. *Textos Filosóficos.* Ed. António de Pina Coelho. Lisbon: Ática, 1994.

Santos, Maria Irene Ramalho de Sousa. "A hora do poeta: o *Hyperion* de Keats na *Mensagem* de Pessoa." *Revista da Universidade de Coimbra* (1992).

_____. "A poesia e o sistema mundial." *Portugal: um Retrato Singular* Oporto: Afrontamento, 1993.

Tamen, Miguel. "Podiam Explicar-me O Que Devo Fazer Com Esta Espada?" *As Escadas não têm Degraus* 4. Lisbon: Edições Cotovia, 1991.

Vendler, Helen. "Robert Lowell and History" in *The Given and the Made: Recent American Poets.* London: Faber and Faber, 1995.

◆ Chapter 10

Notes for a Cartography of Twentieth-Century Portuguese Poetry

Manuel Gusmão

Genealogical and Historical Questions

It is not my intention to propose a canon of twentieth-century Portuguese poetry: not merely because of prudence or incertitude, but because even though "in poetry [there's] always war" (Osip Mandelstam), I prefer to attempt a few syncopated gestures—flashes—that might serve as the outline of a tentative, incomplete cartography of Portuguese poetry in this century. On the horizon of the possible study that might be made, I will merely try to plot a few criteria for determining (never with exactitude) the changing lay of the land over the course of time.

I will accept and build on the oft-repeated hypothesis that twentieth-century Portuguese poetry reveals a complex and insistent relationship between romanticism and modernity—this notwithstanding Gastão Cruz's observation that "poetry, in Portugal, has always been the most modern of the arts. Which is to say, the most relentless in its search, the most restless in the organization of its discourse" (*A poesia portuguesa hoje* 209).

Nemésio, in his preface to the 1961 edition of *Poesia (1935-1940)*, wrote that "the poetry that fundamentally interests our mental and emotional universe—classical or otherwise—passed through the crucible of Romanticism, a

154 ◆ MANUEL GUSMÃO

movement that transformed a culture of essential forms into one of existential forms. And since it was not only a revolution of taste, valid within historical limits, Romanticism affected and revised the entire Western poetic heritage, from Homer to Dante as well as from Dante to Shelley and—even today, however far from the Romantics we may feel—from Shelley to Rilke" (705).

In 1985 Herberto Helder published *Edoi Lelia Doura, Antologia das vozes comunicantes da poesia moderna portuguesa*, which he characterized in an introductory note as "univocal in its vocal multiplicity, and fiercely biased." The bias, readily apparent but more complex than it may seem at first glance, is in favor of those poets who are committed "to a shared art of fire and night, to the same stellar aegis." This image corresponds to what, in other texts, Helder takes to be a (heterogeneous) romantic tradition that he tends to confound, in a certain way, with poetry itself.

Joaquim Manuel Magalhães has at various moments insisted on the importance of romanticism as "an ever present aesthetic category" in modern Portuguese poetry. He links that importance to the "fact of Portuguese poetry never having recognized Romanticism as a precise historical category" (*Os dois crepúsculos* 290) and to the relative weakness of Portuguese historical romanticism in the European panorama, resulting in a species of romanticism that lingers on as "an endemic echo" (291).

Despite their notable differences, there is a common thread running through all of these examples: romanticism as an active force is understood as a transhistoric rather than period-specific category, and it is seen as modulating if not actually modeling modernity in Portuguese poetry. But let us consider the differences in these examples. In Nemésio, romanticism prompts a reflection on the relationship between poetry, metaphysics and mysticism which is basically an expanded version of the relationship between poetry and philosophy and which recognizes the first discipline—poetry—as yet another form of understanding, one that need not suppress the "web" of its poetic and artistic modes. In Herberto Helder, romanticism can be read as the expression of one intellectual and aesthetic current in tense conflict with another, on the plane of a bipolar poetic confrontation: "voyants" and "artistes" (Marcel Raymond), "Terror" and "Rhetoric" (J. Paulhan), "inspired" and "craftsmen" (Mikel Dufrenne), "orphics" and "hermetics" (Gerald L. Bruns). Though their terms cannot be entirely superimposed over each other, both of these poetics call to mind Plato's and Aristotle's conceptions of the poet and of poetry, both are suggestive of the distinction between the two principles of the scientific imagination, the "flame" and the "crystal," and both evoke the duality between form and force.

In Magalhães, on the other hand, the romantic tradition contains within itself an oscillation between two aesthetic categories: that "of sentimentalized realism and that of the sentiment that requires expression" (291). This duality is reflected in the juxtaposition between "a Romantic disequilibrium of the sensibility, such that emotions and the dream state govern how reality is apprehended" and "a Romantic equilibrium whereby reality is the platform of resistance for organizing intuitions of extrasensory reality" (*Um pouco da morte* 147). This is a crucial observation for a romanticism seen not as "contrary to [the category of] classicism but contrary to that of Positivism" (147), which may help explain, for example, how elements of the romantic ethos are present in certain anti-romantic reactions such as those of Ducasse in his *Poésies*, or—in Portuguese poetry— those of Fernando Pessoa. Furthermore, Magalhães's attention to matters of poetic *techne* and prosody urge us to consider the historical experience of form as meaning.

I would like however to continue exploring our subject on a horizon of reading which, while keeping in mind these dualities and their distinguishing characteristics, postulates a genealogical network allowing for the informal crisscrossing of different traditions, namely: (a) discursive exuberance, which may be reflected in the diversity of verbal registers and poetic forms as well as in the visionary ethos, and whose most fertile terrain may or may not be the long poem; (b) severe restraint or purification; (c) colloquialness, or the reinvention of an oral or quasi-oral speech, tending toward irony or self-irony; (d) scorn and satire, which has accompanied the history of Portuguese poetry ever since the *cantigas de escarnho e maldizer* of the medieval *cancioneiros*; (e) the discourse of citation or allusion, in explicit as well as veiled forms. It is important to remember that in the work of certain poets several of these traditions are combined. For the proposed cartography to arrive as close as possible at the uniqueness of each author, we would also need to analyze in their writing (our reading) the various figures of the narrator and the forms of autobiography, the depictions of reality and schemes of reference, the nature of the populations or characters that inhabit their poems, and the time-space dimensions of the worlds their poems invent. Then we would still need to see how their verbal worlds cohere or transform, and ditto for their specifically poetic gestures and figurations.

Border Questions: When Does Twentieth-Century Portuguese Poetry Begin?

Nuno Júdice proposes a literary turning of the century that precedes its chronological or historical turning. "Around 1900, four names stand out in Portuguese poetry: Antero de Quental, António Nobre, Cesário Verde and Guerra Junqueiro" (*Campos* 47). Gomes Leal (1848-1921) should be added to this list. It is with Leal that Oscar Lopes ends the "Sixth Period—Romanticism" of *Historia da Literatura Portuguesa* (Saraiva and Lopes), and it is Leal that opens Helder's aforementioned anthology. Oscar Lopes, furthermore, taking advantage of the fact that *O Livro de Cesário Verde* was not widely circulated until 1901, and giving great importance to this main nucleus of the poet's work, significantly places Verde at the beginning of the twentieth century and even on the threshold of Modernism (Lopes, both titles in Works Cited).

Antero de Quental (1842-91), whose work was a poetic dramatization of philosophy, may be considered a romantic still strongly influenced by classical procedures. Gomes Leal produced a vast and uneven body of work, with certain poems, stanzas and verses that resonate with a peculiar strangeness. Junqueiro (1850-1923) stands out for his long verse line and his pamphletary, moody truculence. António Nobre (1867-1900) left us his transparently fashioned bitterness, fruit of his "voluntary" (?) exile in Paris. Cesário Verde (1855-86) is an odd figure in the Portuguese poetic panorama. He *saw* nineteenth-century, urban Lisbon, and also *saw*, from the country, "'as maçãs de espelho' / Que Herbert Spencer talvez tenha comido" ['the mirror apples' / That Herbert Spencer may have eaten]. He assimilated Baudelaire, in certain of his poems, as well as the major stereotypes of his day, and he also delighted in lexically, syntactically and rhythmically configured realistic detail. Yet he was also the poet who transfigured reality, employed surprising images, and fostered an ironic, incisive first-person narrator that could be colloquial and talk poetics, with a vision both emotive and transgressive. For these reasons, some of the greatest and most disparate poets of this century have time and again gone back to Verde. And even when they have not, it is good to know that this hybrid of the Enlightenment, romanticism and modernism, exists in Portuguese literary history.

Already in the twentieth century, from out of the mists of Symbolism, Decadence and "saudosismo" there emerged the prominent figures of Camilo Pessanha (1867-1926), Teixeira de Pascoaes (1887-1952), Mário de Sá-Carneiro (1890-1915), Fernando Pessoa (1888-1935) and Almada Negreiros (1893-1970). Pessanha is the music that was missing from the rest of Portuguese Symbolism (Eugénio de Andrade would hear it later on); his work is like the prosodic trail of a missing subject, for whom poetry is invention and the crisis of feeling set to words. Pascoaes is the long poem, the dream of a new religion, syncretic (or synthetic?), the air of expanding heights, the image that suddenly flashes. The others fall between Symbolism and modernism. All of these poets are cited, invoked or playfully "used" in the praxis of subsequent poets and the rival movements of genealogical demarcation, but those that will be most genuinely and dynamically appropriated are Gomes Leal, António Nobre, Cesário Verde, Pessanha, Mário de Sá-Carneiro and, of course, Pessoa. Pascoaes will be used more as a foil against Pessoa. Or perhaps this is an illusion deriving from personal taste.

The World of Pessoa: "An Entire Literature" or an "Over-intelligent Fear"?

Perhaps today it is no longer necessary (if ever it really was) to forget Pessoa's contemporaries in order to appreciate the power and fascination of the poet of many masks, whose long-lasting impact is due in part to the stretched-out publication of his oeuvre. Perhaps today it is easier to *see* these others without having to *reduce* Pessoa. On the one hand, we may observe that, besides drawing on English poets, French poets, Poe and Whitman for his poetic development, Pessoa inherited some of Antero's philosophical poetic vocabulary, prolonged something of Gomes Leal in his "paulismo," appropriated Cesário Verde, albeit through a "misreading" of Alberto Caeiro, and evoked—in world-weary Campos—the weariness of Sá-Carneiro's last poems, in an attempt to exorcise Teixeira de Pascoaes. On the other hand, we may observe how a number of great poets who came after Pessoa have felt close affinity not with him but with one or another of his contemporaries or with poets from the turn of the century.

In one of his drafts (1930?) for a preface to his works, Pessoa announced that he had made himself into "at least a lunatic with lofty dreams, at most not only a writer but an entire literature" (*Páginas Íntimas*, 98). Beyond the bravado employed to cast out fear, this passage expresses his tremendous ambition, evident in the way "Pessoa's oeuvre evokes a reasonably complete image of literature (primary and secondary texts, poetics and poiesis) corresponding to a space circumscribed by the *grammar* of the canon" (Diogo and Monteiro, 84). This is probably *one* of the reasons why the literary establishment has for so long been interested in Pessoa's work. Heteronymy is also this constellation and representation of "an entire literature," and we may read it on various levels:

1. As a theory of authorship within a poetics of simulation. A poetics of the "artistic lie" (relatable to Oscar Wilde) or of the poetic fiction (in Nietzsche). A poetics that oscillates between a theory of impersonality—à la Mallarmé, Proust, Eliot, Valéry—and a theory of "othering," most akin to Keats's "poet-chameleon" and Browning's or Rimbaud's use of dramatic monologues.

2. As a *fiction* that yields a highly diversified and disorganized *novel* composed of letters, biographical passages, prefaces, commentaries and horoscopes; an autobiography told through author-characters; a fragmentary, incomplete and incompletable story emblematized in the *Livro do Desassossego*. Or a *drama* whose dialogues would be all the poems, in a theater where the dramatic poem *Fausto* —likewise incomplete and incompletable—would be the ruins. In any case, "all fragments, fragments, fragments," as Pessoa said of the *Livro* in a letter to Armando Cortes Rodrigues dated November 19, 1914.

3. Independent of the poetics inscribed therein, heteronymy is Pessoa's radical way of making poetry, his poetic praxis. And

it is also a bending and stretching of the Portuguese language, placed at the disposal of its poets.

The word *heteronym* emerged only after he had spoken of *pseudonyms* and when it no longer made sense to use pseudonyms for hiding one's identity or for evoking an aura of disquieting strangeness. The heteronyms, as Jorge de Sena first pointed out, expanding on what Pessoa himself had indicated, include the so-called orthonym, which divides heteronymically into the Pessoa of *Mensagem*, the Pessoa of the *English Poems*, and the Pessoa who wrote esoteric poems. "Heteronym," in this wider sense, means estrangement, an "othering" of the self. And the poetry of each of the main heteronyms undergoes further subdivision, in a contra-diction that subverts the transparency of its fictive project, role, excess, or "erro próprio" (the expression is the title of a text by the surrealist António Maria Lisboa). This subdivision can also serve as a means for understanding heteronymy. In Alberto Caeiro, the fictive project shows, in the way it is expressed, its impossibility in reality, and the "shepherd," when "in love" or "sick" is already another. Ricardo Reis so completely simulates transcendence over death that his mental gymnastics to achieve that simulation are obviously rooted in a horrible fear of death. Álvaro de Campos is divided between modernist exuberance and an ironic, blasé colloquialness, now effusive now contained. The *Livro do Desassossego* disseminates the differences between them all, while *Fausto* presents the stage that imprisons them all, the impossibilities and fears they all repeat and variously attempt to respond to. The *English Poems* variously express, in another language, and *only in another language*, the ways of Eros, which in the other voices we meet as the tragic impossibility of accepting the flesh, as the obliteration of sexuality, or in the form of Campos's sadomasochism, and very occasionally as a homoerotic suggestion.

Heteronymy as a mode of poetic creation is a desire for and struggle of language, a verbal proliferation, a series of "language games" that conceive "forms of life" for responding to the unbearably hard task of living. It involves grandiloquence and restraint, vehemence and irony, syntactical inventiveness, the aristocratic and colloquial versions of modernity and modernism, compulsion and premeditation. And so various currents are assumed by Pessoa and pass through him to subsequent poets. Pessoa is at his most fascinating when he upsets the dichotomy between form and force, "classicism" and "Romanticism," and that perhaps explains why even today he is most resisted by certain "Neoromantic" versions of poetry.

The Post-Pessoa World:
Modernity after Modernism

Pessoa is not an absolute meteor and obviously not the sum of all poetry. There were, as already indicated, echoes of other poets who preceded him or were contemporaries.

Four families—internally heterogeneous and, on the other hand, more interconnected than they may seem—knew Pessoa's influence, even if they minimized or resisted him: (1) those associated with *Presença* (1927-40), such as José Régio or Adolfo Casais Monteiro (or writers from that time, such as Miguel Torga), who had the undeniable merit of having published, studied and promoted Pessoa; (2) the neo-realists of the poetry series *Novo Cancioneiro* (1941-44), which published Álvaro Feijó and Políbio Gomes dos Santos posthumously, and others such as Mário Dionísio, J. J. Cochofel, Joaquim Namorado, Manuel da Fonseca, and Carlos de Oliveira, with Armindo Rodrigues and José Gomes Ferreira joining the group somewhat later; (3) a group of "isolated" voices to which we will return; (4) the self-denominated surrealists.

Many of the great poets who came after Pessoa—who knew that they could only come "after" him—read him, paid him homage, and answered him, each in their own way.

The year 1942—when the *Obras Completas de Fernando Pessoa* began to be published—is a good point in time for directing our focus on what others were doing. In that year a number of key poets from mid-century either began to publish, had already published, or were about to publish. Their strategies for answering to and for distinguishing and freeing themselves from Pessoa vary, but they coincide at certain points. What follow are a few possible readings.

The heteronymic explosion of the "I" is answered by Vitorino Nemésio (1901-78) with "the harmonious animal," the "poetic double" of the author, the envisioning of the "I" as a fantastic creature of poetry and of life, a unicorn or phoenix reborn out of the discursive metamorphoses and eroding action of time; by Ruy Cinatti (1915-86) with the author's nomadic lifestyle and the anthropological construction of one's personal destiny; by Jorge de Sena (1919-78) with the spreading out of the author across various genres and registers; by Carlos de Oliveira (1921-81) with the reserve or withdrawal of the immediate authorial presence; and by José Gomes Ferreira (1901-85) with his long and ironic autobiographical project, the creation of a role as witness of our century (evident in the parenthetical notes that accompany many of his poems, as if they were his acting roles), and the ironic personalization of the pamphletary mode.

Pessoa's discursive originality is answered by Nemésio and Sena with their verbal, discursive and formal/technical multiplicity and exuberance, while other poets—Oliveira, Eugénio de Andrade (b. 1923) and Sophia de Mello Breyner Andresen (b. 1919)—respond with forms of restraint and a voice or writing style marked by cohesive intensity.

The poetics of simulation is answered by Sena with a *sui generis* poetics of "testimony" (of himself and of his world) and of historical circumstantiality; by Oliveira with the impassioned craftsmanship that impelled him to rewrite continuously; and by Sophia de Mello Breyner and Eugénio de Andrade with various forms of lyric fusion.

The invention and deconstruction of dualisms in the incurably skeptical "poet animated by philosophy" (Pessoa, *Páginas Íntimas*, 13) is countered by a love of the concrete and a religious preoccupation (in Nemésio and Cinatti); by a voracious vitality, an exacerbated surrender to the finite and to the heartbeat of the world's and mankind's (trans)historical construction and transformation (in Sena); by imagining a materialist ontology of the world and the poem that would make for an altered "cartography" in which the poem and the world self-reflect, without any need for Platonic mediation, and an abstract writing that would retain—within poetry—the "surplus effulgence" of the real (in Oliveira); by an enchanted materialism (in Andrade); and by the "pursuit of reality" and a "rejoining" of the "I," poetry and the world, in a sunlit and mythic Mediterranean Sea, with the Greeks on one shore and the cradle of monotheistic religions on the other (in Sophia).

If Pessoa virtually expunges or at least evades the theme of physical sensuality, Sena celebrates it (and so, at times, does Nemésio, who never ceases to surprise) in many different forms, including poems made of invented, nonsignifying "words" (semantic but not semiotic) which, in his "Sonetos a Afrodite Anadiómena," suggest the meeting of slippery bodies, and also more overtly explicit poems, which are nonetheless (in the first section of *Exorcismos*, for example, or in *Sobre esta praia*, 1977) figurally and syntactically almost conceptualist. And there is Andrade, in whom the experience of the world is concentrated in the song of the body; "Um novo corpo nasce" with the memory of that other "nouveau corps amoureux," from the poem "Being Beauteous," in Rimbaud's *Illuminations*. Oscar Lopes and others speak of the music that can be heard in this poetry that incorporates silence as its own vibration. In yet another poet, David Mourão-Ferreira (1927-96), who began writing toward the end of the 1940s, a spirit marked by "classical" attentiveness and virtuosity obsessively invokes the experience of Eros as a concentration of pleasure and a contradiction of time.

To present these authors in this fashion is a hazardous expedient, for it might seem that they merely reacted to the ghost of Pessoa. The point, on the contrary, is that they have succeeded in being different. All are conscious of Pessoa's importance, but their relationship with him plays very different roles in their poetic formation. Sena takes him on hands first, as a critical reader (being one of the first to understand Pessoa in the complexity of his *fingimento*, or "feigning"), as a co-translator of the *English Poems*, for which he also wrote the preface, and as editor of some previously unpublished texts. At the other extreme is Carlos de Oliveira, who knows and can cite Pessoa but whose poetic world, in its substance and fabric, has only a tenuous relationship with him. Eugénio de Andrade recounts the fascination he felt on discovering Pessoa, whose work he has anthologized, but it is other poets who have inspired him, providing the motifs from which he makes the music of his verse. Sophia de Mello Breyner borrows a formula from Pessoa to tell how her poems *happen*, uses him as a character in her poetry, and writes odes in the manner of Ricardo Reis, but her keenly felt awareness of the separation that devastates the contemporary world and the religious promise she finds in the words of poems call for an adherence to language and the world that Pessoa could never consent to (not even in Caeiro).

All of these poets, in greater or lesser measure, went beyond Pessoa to find some of their emblems, and there does not seem to be any attempt here to exorcise an "anxiety of influence." For example, one of Cinatti's most beautiful poems, besides citing Shelley and Keats (his favorite), and Byron in another register, is dedicated "to the memory of António Nobre and Cesário Verde." Carlos de Oliveira composed a "Portrait of the Author with Verses of Camilo Pessanha (collage)" and paid homage, in verse, to what he learned from Gomes Leal and Cesário Verde. And one of his "poetic arts" is called "Collage/ with verses of Desnos, Mayakovski and Rilke"— verses that he lifts and significantly deforms. Thus this poet, who seemed to come out of a tradition of poetry as craft, embraces, in his own way, the ethos of poetry as inspiration.

Resistance to Pessoa, which these highly individual poetic voices successfully achieved for their time, can also be identified in the Portuguese surrealists. As a formally established movement surrealism was most active in the late forties and early fifties, but it has had long-lasting repercussions. Even before this time we can find various anticipatory signs, echoes and expressions from poets who had learned and appropriated certain surrealist procedures. One such example are the poems written by Edmundo de Bettencourt (1899-1973) between 1934 and 1940, only published in 1963, and subsequently issued autonomously under the title *Poemas Surdos*. Nemésio, always artistically open-minded, freely incorporated what he learned from surrealism about the verbal imagination, and Sena confessed he was "freed from myself by surrealism."

While it is true that surrealism flourished rather late in Portugal, coinciding with attempts to revive the movement in postwar France, we should note that Portuguese surrealism was very much integrated into the genealogical network of Portuguese poetry and the historical circumstances of its time, as is especially evident in Mário Cesariny de Vasconcelos (b. 1923). It was marked as well by a certain dimming of its potential luminosity and a downplaying of Éluard's and Breton's otherworldliness (one of the authors whose proclamations were most appreciated was Artaud, significantly enough). These aspects of Portuguese surrealism may well be inseparable. Appropriating Pessoa, particularly in his guise as Campos, the surrealists played against him, and also against Gomes Leal, Pascoaes, Mário de Sá-Carneiro and Pessanha. In Cesariny there are also signs of an appropriation (and not just mere homage) of Cesário Verde, whose prosaism and eschewal of easy sentimentality are directly relevant to the surrealist poet's strategy, in which lyricism and the epic mode combine formal aspects of modernism (namely, the confounding of images, sudden shifts in tone, phonetic and graphic games) with those of earlier traditions and with an admirable reinvention of everyday and popular speech. On the other hand, the violence that characterizes some of his poetry comes not only from the use of satire but from his bitter impatience with the "pouco de realidade" permitted by the Salazar regime and with the feeling of confinement created by the political, ideological and cultural repression of lifestyles and physical desires. In Cesariny the echoes of the "sexual sublime" are surpassed by a more fundamental and radical sexualization, in the gestures by which he protests and sings, in a discursive and symbolic mode that contrasts sharply with what we find in Eugénio de Andrade, a Rimbaldian "nouveau corps amoureux," the repressed and rebellious homoerotic body.

The scant body of work left by António Maria Lisboa (1928-53) is informed by a somewhat different surrealism, one that aims to go beyond itself, toward a kind of magic and occult utopia in which the "enriched body" would be one with the cosmos, and in which language would cease being an "add-on" and become fully integrated into the body, or else integrate into itself the "very movement of reality."

Traces of this specifically Portuguese brand of surrealism can also be found in the work of Alexandre O'Neill (1924-86), a "neo-realist surrealist" (to use Oscar Lopes's provocative but perceptive epithet) in whom we encounter Cesário Verde, the satirical tradition, humor and bitterness at play with the modernists' bag of tricks, and inventions based on popular speech. Still in the 1950s, surrealism left its mark on poets who were not strict partisans of the movement, such as Raul de Carvalho (1920-84) and Natália Correia (1923-93).

The Urgency of the New: Modernity between 1956 and 1969

This kind of "period," consisting of various poetic moments pivoting around the year 1961, is marked by an obsessive preoccupation with the new and innovative. This concern becomes particularly evident with the arrival of the sixties but is already discernible in poets who published their first books in 1956—Fernando Guimarães (b. 1928), Fernando Echevarria (b. 1929), Pedro Tamen (b. 1934)—or in 1958—António Ramos Rosa (b. 1924) and Herberto Helder (b. 1930). The first three authors opened important ground for poets who would pursue a course of discursive rarefaction. We will come back to the latter two. In 1960, M. S. Lourenço (b. 1936) published a strange, composite book, *O desequilibrista*, which included poems, prose texts and dramatic poems.

This urgent insistence on the new was linked to the problem of how to inscribe the (then) present moment into the historical continuum and of how to individuate each poetic voice within that moment. In crude and simplistic terms (since they seem to imply a cold premeditation that would exclude the undeniable role of unconscious or blind forces), we may state the problem as one of "how to come after." Or, in an expanded form: "Who am I coming after? How should I come after? With whom and against whom should I come? How should I represent, in the imminence of my own time, the present moment in which I have come?" What seems to be at stake, then, is the question of the possible paths toward discursive renewal and re-representation of the world and of life. A related question is that of appropriation and/or confrontation vis-à-vis the most influential poetic movements of the time, neo-realism and surrealism, and vis-à-vis the great—or at least widely read—poetic voices from the 1940s. Also related is the question of family resemblances identifiable in the poetry of other languages.

The new generation of poets seemed to find their answers in processes of discursive purification and restraint, which could be pursued by way of ellipse, hyperbation and, in general, a trenchant manipulation and transformation of syntax (Melo e Castro and *Poesia 61*), or by a more radical isolation of the word, eliminating nearly all syntactical links until arriving—in the most extreme version—at visual poetry (Melo e Castro and *Poesia Experimental*). But this period also saw the reinvention of the long free verse, which liberated itself from what was considered an excessive "informalism" (Cruz), from insistent and schematic repetition, and from what seemed to be random enumeration.

Answers were found in procedures of syntactical fragmentation within the verse or in syntactical linking between verses, in the blending of different discursive registers, in the playing off of words or playing within the word (e.g., segmentation), and even in recurrences of words, verbal motifs and images, which sometimes seem like re-elaborations of Mannerist and baroque techniques.

Significantly, the kind of procedures chosen is not in itself a sufficient criterion to distinguish between those poets whose work is founded on the transformation of realist tendencies and those who take surrealism as their starting point. Tied to the procedural questions are the ways that poets carried on—and transformed—the traditions of ideological commitment, "Romantic" visionariness, religious poetry, colloquialness, and scorn and satire.

António Ramos Rosa, whose *O grito claro* came out in 1958, published three books in 1960-61. Originally founded on a blend of neo-realism and surrealism under the aegis of Éluard, Ramos Rosa's poetry has undergone a dramatic evolution to become an admirable poetry of vehement restraint, a kind of verbal respiration of the world's silence, words concentrated on themselves to the point where all is transfigured and they are the *Incêndio dos aspectos* [Fire of Aspects] (1980) of the world's essential surface. Though generationally older, it was in the mid-sixties that he began to fashion his poetic time and space.

Herberto Helder (b. 1930), who had already published a chapbook, *O Amor em visita*, published his first volume of poetry, *A Colher na boca*, in 1961. It was a resplendent beginning, to be sustained over and over in his future work. With a definite surrealist streak and occasional points of contact with "experimental" poetry, Helder is the poet of the intense, cosmically constellated body and, at the same time, of the smattering of this cosmos and this body into streams of luminous verbal energy. He is the poet of obscure and evident symbology, that in which poetry comes closest to being "the genuine absolute real" (Novalis).

Furthermore, 1961 was also the year when Ruy Belo (1933-78) published *Aquele grande rio Eufrates*. Belo was likewise a poet whose discourse may be called exuberant, and in two distinct senses. On the one hand he used a wide variety of verbal and poetic registers, from the short poem and the poetic gloss (e.g., "Variações sobre 'o jogador de pião'") to long poems and a long verse line, which he came to prefer. On the other hand, his voice was marked by an expansive cadence, and he was able—through shifts in verbal tones and registers, an emphatic colloquialness, and taut modulation of his verses—to sustain the verbal tension that long forms require. His was not the long discourse of visionaries, however; it was a realism charged with hope and distress, solitude, questioning and listening. He struggled with how to find or make a "terra de alegria" in a country that embittered him. A poet whose culture is neither ornament nor submission and for whom the concrete corresponds to the verbal amalgamation of imaginative observation and human destiny, his poetry is of the sort that moves us without demagoguery.

Poesia 61 was the name of a set of five chapbooks, by Maria Teresa Horta (b. 1937), Casimiro de Brito (b. 1938), Fiama Hasse Pais Brandão (b. 1938), Luiza Neto Jorge (1939-89) and Gastão Cruz (b. 1941), poets who would evolve in very different ways. Attempts to renew a historically and politically committed realism now moved, significantly, toward verbal restraint, producing at least three poets who developed highly distinctive voices: Fernando Assis Pacheco (1937-95) published his first book in 1963, with Manuel Alegre (b. 1937) and Armando da Silva Carvalho (b. 1938) following suit two years later. While the last two names have gained recognition, Armando da Silva Carvalho is still waiting for the country of *brandos costumes* "mild manners" to read the angry but verbally rigorous violence of his best poetry, which resonates with the sound and fury of life in the world and of repressed desires. Again in 1961, Ernesto M. de Melo e Castro (b. 1932) published a book that included a text issued in chapbook form the previous year, and he subsequently collaborated (along with António Ramos Rosa, Herberto Helder and others) in *Poesia experimental*, nos. 1 and 2 (1964, 1966). Vasco Graça Moura (b. 1942) began publishing in 1963 and developed a poetry marked by technical prowess, ironic colloquialness and myriad cultural citations.

Of all the poets whose paths cross in 1961, Herberto Helder and Ruy Belo seem at this point in time to be the two who stand out as canonical figures. Without reducing their stature, we may also recognize the originality and value of other poets, most especially Luiza Neto Jorge and Gastão Cruz, while others, such as Fiama Hasse Pais Brandão, need to be reassessed.

To do this we must recognize that *Poesia 61* was not a very consistent or homogeneous "family." The subsequent evolution of its members shows their fundamental differences.

The development of Gastão Cruz, as Magalhães has indicated, was partly due to his confrontation with neo-realism and followed, in many respects, the evolution of Carlos de Oliveira, while Luiza Neto Jorge's work was initially grounded in a transposed surrealism. It is in Cruz that we can most readily discern a guiding strategy of stylistic purification, but his "realist" vocation is precisely the means by which he reinvents a rigorously constructed romanticism as an experience of form equal to force. If initially this romanticism, already citing Baudelaire, relies on contorted syntax and a strained syllabic percussion, as in a Mannerist recitation, it later becomes more fluid, stating more clearly its English references, to which may be added Valéry, whose incorporation adds strangeness and power. Cruz's work is, in these times, one of the most disturbing and crystalline protests against the death we must live, the death of beloved friends, and the violence that assails our body and time. It is the ambivalent song of the "ignoble art of verses" and of the scar that scorches the skin and memory.

For Luiza Neto Jorge, on the other hand, poetry is the song of sheer freedom, the sound and feelings of the "rebellious body." Her *Dezanove recantos* (1969), whose elaborate architecture ironically parodies the structure of the epic poem, is a book that rigorously exacerbates the internal fragmentation of the long verse, its verbal, prosodic and figurative inventiveness, weaving an elliptic mythography (full of ironic fury, humor and joy) of the female body and of the lover, of the family and of the history of her time, all of which will resurface in *O ciclópico acto* (1972). But Jorge also reveals, in a form diametrically inverse to what we find in Gastão Cruz, the capacity for distillation or intense concentration, giving rise to some exquisite poems, such as "A Magnólia" and "O poema ensina a cair."

If, added to what we have seen, we look at what was published in the 1960s by poets whose careers began in the 1940s, then we see a period truly bursting with creative energy. Many of these older poets now publish compilations of their early titles, but they also publish new books of tremendous significance for their personal oeuvre and for the decade. Taking just a few examples, we may begin with Jorge de Sena, whose *Metamorfoses* (1963), *Arte de Música* (1968) and *Peregrinatio ad loca infecta* (1969) were powerful books that affirmed his expansiveness, his anthropological perspective on the arts, his polyphony of voices capable of creative assimilation, and his practical humanism that transcends the limits of disembodied idealism and is not afraid of political statement. Sophia de Mello Breyner, in *Livro Sexto* (1962) and *Geografia* (1967), pursues her "just relationship" with things, which turns out to be inextricably linked to her pursuit of "a just relationship with man." And so the word "just," in the moral vision that informs her poetry, is used to mean "fitting, right" but also "fair, righteous." Carlos de Oliveira, in turn, pursues with ever greater insistence the admirable metamorphosis of his realism, giving his work an affinity with the distilled poetry of Eugénio de Andrade and Sophia de Mello Breyner but also with the poetry of the new generation. In 1960 he published *Cantata*, a transitional work of intense concentration. This was followed in 1962 by *Poesias*, which collected all of his earlier titles except the first (which would only reappear, considerably revised, in the complete edition of his poetry, *Trabalho poético*, 1976), and also included rewrites of poems by others. In 1968 he published two books in which his new mode of writing was honed and expanded. He is the great and impassioned craftsman whom Herberto Helder would include, significantly, in his "fiercely biased" anthology mentioned above. This inclusion can perhaps help us to understand that Oliveira and Helder, in their radical difference, produce a strange node of fire in Portuguese poetry.

Finally, in 1969, first books were published by Mário Cláudio (b. 1941) and by António Franco Alexandre (b. 1942), one of the leading poets of the generation to emerge in the first half of the next decade.

The End of What? New Mutations, New Forms of Newness

"Neo-romanticism," "micro-realism," "end of modernity" and "postmodernism" are some of the terms that have been used to try to characterize the constellation of poets that began to appear in the 1970s. It has also been proposed that we see melancholy not so much as a generalized theme but as the "atmosphere" in which the various poetic "programs" and "objects"—at least the more recent ones—have emerged. Another common observation is that recent poetry consists of free-floating, individualized manifestations that can no longer be grouped together in "movements" or trends.

The poets from this still evolving constellation insistently confront us with mutations of the various traditions enumerated at the beginning of this essay. In any event, the search is still for something new, even if this novelty is no longer conceived as "avant-garde." Of course, a number of the great innovators that came after Pessoa also did not talk about the avant-garde.

In order to characterize post-1970 poets, we may ask what relationships they have with the poets of the sixties. Do we find continuities, metamorphoses, transformations? Is there a clean break, a staggered break, an uneven break? Some of today's poets seem to have more in common with poets from previous generations than with their own contemporaries. This makes it easier to get a handle on the novelties their poetry presents, for we can see them as new modulations of some of the traditions and tendencies we have already come across. It may happen that there are links between modulations proceeding from different genealogies. What follows are some observations on just a few of the important voices.

Each new book by António Franco Alexandre is remarkably different. His latest, *Oásis* (1992), is one long poem almost always in tercets, through whose stream of invocation, declaration and conversation we can intermittently glean what seems to be a subjacent narrative, a narrative of someone roaming around the urban space of Lisbon, with echoes from other places. We are tempted to imagine a distant relationship between this work and poems like Apollinaire's "Zone" or Cesário Verde's "Sentimento de um ocidental," after more than a century of so much and such varied poetry has gone by. Franco Alexandre is the great "obscure" poet of this generation, a master of writing as palimpsest, whose subtext is only partially revealed.

António Osório, who was born in 1933 but did not publish his first book until 1972 (*A raíz afectuosa*), is a completely different poet. His poetry is a species of "return" (there are, of course, no true returns) to the wellspring of a lyricism understood as an equilibrium between *I, you and the natural world*, a verbal music of affections whose various parts include a gallery of "family" portraits, a sounding out of the "earth's movement" in the galaxy, the lesson of things, aphorisms or gnomic wisdom, and the convocation of animals, "from the inimical to the friendly," as if to gather them together in a new Noah's Ark. Poetry, in Osório, strikes us in various ways as a kind of ecology.

João Miguel Fernandes Jorge (b. 1943) seems to employ a strategy of depuration that reduces representation to a hazy sketch of the image, with references and a narrative thread that—though elliptical—demand to be read. He is a poet of the most ordinary and unsensational, of the faint music of daily life and its meetings and nonmeetings of affections, but also a poet who turns history into a myth that can be lived and allegorized by the characters of that ordinary daily life. He may perhaps be legitimately seen as the poet of a wise and discreet joy.

Joaquim Manuel Magalhães (b. 1945) is not only one of the most notable poets to emerge in this period; he is also the most informed and incisive poetry critic of his generation. In 1987 he published *Alguns livros reunidos*, which brings together, with countless alterations, the poetry volumes published since 1974 until *Alguns antecedentes mitológicos* (1985), with the exception of *Os dias, pequenos charcos* (1981), whose opening poem is an important *ars poetica*. Magalhães's alterations run deep. He eliminated or violently slashed numerous poems and stanzas, "corrected" and rewrote verses, and tampered with the order of the poems. Such heavy rewriting finds a parallel only in Carlos de Oliveira, though even this parallel is relative, since the nature of the rewriting is different. Magalhães seems to have tossed out or corrected all that might even remotely suggest poetic uses and language that he prefers not to be identified with. He excluded various prose poems, phrasal and lexical amplifications, and images, while at the same time creating new images. At the risk of oversimplifying, we may perhaps say that his rewriting has on the whole aimed at increasing the verbal and poetic tension and at bringing his work closer to the poetics underlying the introductory poem of *Os dias, pequenos charcos*. His poetry, rich in allusions and with considerable "autobiographical" power, has taken up and transformed traditional metrical schemes, enlisting them in a verbal music that is sarcastic and lyrically violent, reflecting the violence we live in today's world.

The thematic concerns and discursive register shared by these two authors (to produce two clearly distinguishable poetries) are not the same as we find, for example, in Nuno

Júdice (b. 1949), José Agostinho Baptista (b. 1948) or Paulo Teixeira (b. 1962). What immediately sets these three apart is the discursive and visionary exuberance found likewise in Herberto Helder, though other motives and procedures are at work.

Nuno Júdice's poetry derives, rather conspicuously, from a crisscrossing of traditions. It is as if—after Hölderlin and the threshold of modernity in French poetry from the final decades of the nineteenth century (Rimbaud to Mallarmé), after Pessoa and under the initial impulse of Saint-John Perse—Nuno Júdice had ironically appropriated the fin-de-siècle imagination and vocabulary to elaborate his sumptuous poetry, under whose many masks we can no longer find the "face" of any one person. He is a poet who constructs scenes, nowadays increasingly contemporary, though older scenes can still appear on the stage. In any case, the poet's exaltation is becoming less theatrical and more reflexive, as if his verse had acquired a calmer wisdom. Paulo Teixeira, for his part, pursues a recapitulation of poetry through epitaphs and dramatic monologues, as if—after Auschwitz and in this time of apocalyptic ideologies—poetry had assumed the task of mourning, lending its voice to the sacred dead, and still watched over the land.

Something of post-surrealism can be found in the work of poets as diverse as Al Berto (b. 1948) and Paulo da Costa Domingos (b. 1953), who have few points of contact with the poets discussed above.

And we could go on.

This generation of poets—up to Fernando Pinto do Amaral, whose *Acédia* was published in 1990—is still so close in time that they perhaps seem to occupy one and the same beach, despite their tremendous diversity. But it is probably a good idea to resist identifying, in the network of these differences, melancholy as a link left over from the absence of links. Instead we could borrow the title of Manuel António Pina's first book, from 1974: *Ainda não é o fim nem o princípio do mundo é apenas um pouco tarde* [It's still not the end nor the beginning of the world it's just a little late]. Yes. Or might it, rather, be just a little early?

Works Cited

Alegre, Manuel. *30 Anos de poesia*. Lisbon: Dom Quixote, 1995.

Alexandre, António Franco. *Oasis*. Lisbon: Assírio & Alvim, 1992.

_____. *Poemas*. Lisbon: Assírio & Alvim, 1996.

Amaral, Fernando Pinto do. *Acédia*. Lisbon: Assírio & Alvim, 1990.

_____. *O mosaico fluido—modernidade e pósmodernidade na poesia portuguesa mais recente*. Lisbon: Assírio & Alvim, 1991.

Andrade, Eugénio de. *O Sal na Língua*. Oporto: Fundação Eugénio de Andrade, 1996.

_____. *Poesia e prosa*. 2 vols. Lisbon: O Jornal/Limiar, 1990.

Andresen, Sophia de Mello Breyner. *Musa*. Lisbon: Caminho, 1994.

_____. *Obra Poética*. 3 vols. Lisbon: Caminho, 1991.

Aragâo, A., and Hélder H., eds. *Poesia experimental*. Lisboa: Assírio & Alvim, 1974.

Baptista, José Agostino. *O último romântico*. Lisboa: Assírio & Alvim, 1980.

Barrento, João. "Palimpsestos do tempo. O paradigma da narrativa na poesia dos anos 80" and "O astro baço. A poesia portuguesa sob o signo de Saturno." *A palavra transversal. Literatura e Ideias no século 20*. Lisbon: Cotovia, 1996.

Belo, Ruy. *Obra poética*. 2 vols. Lisbon: Presença, 1981.

Berto, Al. *O Medo (Trabalho poético 1974-1990)*. Lisbon: Contexto/Círculo de Leitores, 1991.

Bettencourt, Edmundo de. *Poemas*. Lisbon: Portugália, 1963.

_____. *Poemas surdos (1934-1940)*. Lisbon: Assírio & Alvim, 1993.

Brandão, Fiama Hasse Pais. *Obra breve*. Lisbon: Teorema, 1991.

Carvalho, Armando da Silva. *Canis dei*. Lisbon: Relógio d'água, 1995.

_____. *Lírica consumível*. Lisbon: Ulisseia, 1965.

Cesariny de Vasconcelos, Mário. *Manual de prestidigitação*. Lisbon: Assírio & Alvim, 1980.

_____. *Nobilíssima visão*. Lisbon: Assírio & Alvim, 1991.

_____. *O Virgem negra*. Lisbon: Assírio & Alvim, 1989.

_____. *Titânia e Cidade queimada*. Lisbon: Dom Quixote, 1977.

Cinatti, Ruy. *Antologia Poética*. Lisbon: Presença, 1986.

_____. *Corpo—Alma*. Lisbon: Presença, 1994.

Coelho, Eduardo Prado. "A poesia portuguesa contemporânea." *A noite do mundo*. Lisbon: IN/CM, 1988, 123-32.

Cruz, Gastão. *A poesia portuguesa hoje*. Lisbon: Plátano Editora, 1973.

_____. *As Pedras Negras*. Lisbon: Relógio d'água, 1995.

_____. *Órgão de Luzes (poesia reunida)*. Lisbon: IN/CM, 1992.

Diogo, A. Lindeza, and Rosa Gil Monteiro. *Um Medo por demais inteligente. Autobiografias pessoanas*. Braga: Angelus Novus, 1994.

Echevarria, Fernando. *Poesia, 1956-1979* and *Poesia, 1980-1984*. Oporto: Afrontamento, 1989 and 1993.

Gomes Ferreira, José. *Poeta militante*. 3 vols. Lisbon: Moraes, 1977-83.

174 ◆ MANUEL GUSMÃO

Guimarães, Fernando. *A poesia contemporânea portuguesa e o fim da modernidade*. Lisbon: Caminho, 1989.

_____. *Poesias Completas*. Vol. 1 (1952-1988). Oporto: Afrontamento, 1994.

Helder, Herberto, ed. *Edoi Lelia Doura: Antologia das vozes comunicantes da poesia moderna portuguesa*. Lisbon: Assírio & Alvim, 1985.

_____. *Poesia Toda*. Lisbon: Assírio & Alvim, 1995.

Jorge, João Miguel Fernandes. *Obra Poética*. 4 vols. Lisbon: Presença, 1987 (I-II), 1988 (III), 1991 (IV).

Jorge, Luiza Neto. *Poesia (1960-1989)*. Lisbon: Assírio & Alvim, 1993.

Júdice, Nuno. "Campos e contracampo na poesia portuguesa do princípio do século." In *Um século de poesia (1888-1988)*, 47-50.

_____. *Obra poética (1972-1985)*. Lisbon: Quetzal, 1991.

_____. *O movimento do mundo*. Lisbon: Quetzal, 1996.

Lisboa, António Maria. *Poesia*. Lisbon: Assírio & Alvim, 1977.

Lopes, Oscar. "Alguns Nexos Diacrónicos na poesia novecentista portuguesa." In *Um século de poesia (1888-1988)*, 208-23.

_____. *Entre Fialho e Nemésio. Estudos de Literatura Portuguesa Contemporânea*, I-II. Lisbon: IN/CM, 1987.

Lourenço, Eduardo. "Entre o ser e o silêncio. Cem anos de poesia portuguesa." In *Um século de poesia (1888-1988)*, 202-07.

Magalhães, Joaquim Manuel. *Alguns Livros Reunidos*. Lisbon: Contexto, 1987.

_____. *A poeira levada pelo vento*. Lisbon: Presença, 1993.

_____. *Os dias, pequenos charcos*. Lisbon: Presença, 1981.

_____. *Os dois crepúsculos*. Lisbon: A Regra do Jogo, 1981.

_____. *Um pouco da morte*. Lisbon: Presença, 1989.

Martinho, Fernando J. B. "Modernismo, vanguarda e pós-modernismo na poesia portuguesa contemporânea." In *Panorama da Literatura Universal, II*. Lisbon: Círculo de Leitores, 1991.

Melo e Castro, Ernesto M. *Trans(a)parências*. Poesia-I (1950/1990). Sintra: Tertúlia, 1990.

Moura, Vasco Graça. *Poemas Escolhidos*. Lisbon: Bertrand, 1996.

Mourão-Ferreira, David. *Obra poética (1948-1988)*. Lisbon: Presença, 1988.

Nemésio, Vitorino. *Obras Completas. I e II—Poesia*. Lisbon: IN/CM, 1989.

Novo Cancioneiro. (Poetry published in 1941-44.) Ed. Alexandre Pinheiro Torres. Lisbon: Caminho, 1989.

Oliveira, Carlos de. *Obras*. Lisbon: Caminho, 1992.

O'Neill, Alexandre. *Poesias Completas 1951/1986*. 3rd ed. Lisbon: IN/CM, 1990.

Osório, António. *A Raiz Afectuosa*. Oporto: Gota de água, 1984.

_____. *Planetário e zoo dos homens*. Lisbon: Presença, 1990.

Pacheco, Fernando Assis. *A Musa irRegular*. Lisbon: Hiena, 1991.

Pascoaes, Teixeira de. *Marânus*. Lisbon: Assírio & Alvim, 1990.

_____. *Regresso ao Paraíso*. Lisbon: Assírio & Alvim, 1986.

_____. *Senhora da Noite*. Lisbon: Assírio & Alvim, 1986.

Pessanha, Camilo. *Clepsydra*. Lisbon: Relógio d'água, 1995.
Pessoa, Fernando. *Fausto. Tragédia subjectiva*. Ed. Teresa Sobral Cunha. Lisbon: Presença, 1988.
_____. *Livro do Desassossego*. Lisbon: Ática, 1982.
_____. *Obra poética*. Rio de Janeiro: Aguilar, 1965.
_____. *Páginas íntimas e de auto-interpretação*. Ed. Jacinto do Prado Coelho and Georg Rudolf Lind. Lisbon: Ática, 1966.
_____. *Poemas Completos de Alberto Caeiro*. Ed. Teresa Sobral Cunha. Lisbon: Presença, 1994.
_____. *Poemas de Álvaro de Campos*. Ed. Cleonice Berardinelli. Lisbon: IN/CM, 1992.
_____. *Poemas de Ricardo Reis*. Ed. Luiz Fagundes Duarte. Lisbon: IN/CM, 1994.
_____. *Poemas Ingleses*. Ed. Jorge de Sena. Lisbon: Ática, 1974.
Rosa, António Ramos. *Animal Olhar (Obra poética 2)*. Lisbon: Plátano, 1975.
_____. *Delta seguido de Pela primeira vez*. Lisbon: Quetzal, 1996.
_____. *Matéria de amor* (Anthology). Lisbon: Presença, 1983.
_____. *Não posso adiar o coração (Obra poética 1)*. Lisbon: Plátano, 1974.
_____. *Respirar a sombra viva (Obra poética 3)*. Lisbon: Plátano, 1975.
Sá-Carneiro, Mário de. *Poesias*. Lisbon: Ática, 1993.
Saraiva, A. J., and Oscar Lopes. *História da literatura portuguesa*. Oporto: Porto Editora, 1995.
Sena, Jorge de. *Poesia I, II e III*. Lisbon: Edições 70, 1988 (1st ed. 1961), 1988 (1978), 1989 (1978).
Tamen, Pedro. *Tábua das Matérias (Poesia 1956-1991)*. Lisbon: Círculo de Leitores, 1992.
Teixeira, Paulo. *A Região brilhante*. Lisbon: Caminho, 1988.
_____. *As Imaginações da verdade*. Lisbon: Caminho, 1985.
_____. *Patmos*. Lisbon: Caminho, 1994.
Um século de poesia (1888-1988) (various authors). Lisbon: Assírio & Alvim, 1988.
Verde, Cesário. *Obra completa de Cesário Verde*. Lisbon: Livros Horizonte, 1992.

◆   **Chapter 11**

Contemporary Portuguese Fiction—Cases and Problems

Paula Morão

It is not easy to present a picture of current Portuguese literature, not only because of the quantity and variety of works available but also because some of the criteria traditionally used in studies of literary history have become largely irrelevant. Today, in whatever generation we consider, from the oldest to the youngest, we will not find the kind of organized movements or schools that once existed. Instead we see certain interactions—not always obvious—between writers of very different ages and generations, with established writers such as Eugénio de Andrade or António Ramos Rosa having an important influence on beginning poets, who closely model their work after those they look to as their masters until they (or the more talented among them) find their own voice. As for the traditional literary schools, there is no modern counterpart nor any magazines that define a group-supported poetic or fictional program, nor is there any sign of other forms of collective orientation likely to arise out of the new technologies or the media.

We may venture to say that current literature is marked by some of the same characteristics as contemporary society: territorial disputes, competition, and the emphasis on speed, the immediate and the perishable in place of a slower, inner time necessary to conceive and realize diverse art forms. It is not my intention to judge (and much less to judge negatively) this state of affairs; I am merely trying to *describe* what seems to me a relevant aspect of the current situation. Individualism (in general and as it affects literature) at least has the advantage of generating considerable stylistic variety. This variety is also due to the many intercultural relationships that currently exist, with the French model (that predominated for many decades) having ebbed. Today's taste and the range of interests of those who make literature are highly eclectic in origin, deriving from contact with Brazilian and other South American literatures, from Anglo-American literature, and from European literatures as diverse as those produced in the German, Italian and Spanish languages. Given this variety of intertextual relationships and models—without forgetting, of course, the presence of the national literary tradition (quite explicit in some authors)—it would not be very useful to attempt an exhaustive overview, an endeavor that in any case always proves to be impossible. Instead I will try to identify directions and trends that seem to me to be vibrant and dynamic among us today. This requires a broad definition of *contemporary*, for I will adopt a perspective that cuts across time, understanding as contemporary that which is currently "making waves," even if this might be Camões or Camilo Castelo Branco, Pessoa or the symbolists (thcse authors having all achieved a critical consensus); in some instances, it might even be a case of today's readers gaining access to works that were for a long time out of print or that can now be read as part of a complete oeuvre,[1] thereby acquiring an interrelationship with its formerly available parts.

Finally, as a methodological option justified by practical constraints, I will concentrate on works of fiction, though I will not hestitate, when the context demands, to mention other genres. This oscillation, prompted by the particular corpus under study, derives from a generalized characteristic of contemporary literature, true also for Portuguese literature: the traditional generic designations (novel, novella, short story and so forth) are inadequate for the narrative literature currently being published, for although some recent narrative works do tell a more or less typical story and portray a particular time period (the author's or one from the past or future), the fact is that most of our contemporary works are structured in terms that go beyond these terms. And so there has been an increasing reliance on the term *fiction*, which is more comprehensive and better able to accommodate the shifting boundaries of *impure* narrative subgenres, some of which are transgeneric, cutting across the different genres as traditionally conceived. We often find works with both rhematic and thematic indications[2] identifying them as "fiction," or that, without any explicit indications, are difficult to read if forced into the traditional designations.

In the case of Portugal, there is another reason for analyzing fiction from a historical perspective. For authors who began writing before April 25, 1974, it is often useful to consider the consequences of the Revolution on their creative output. Indeed a number of established and emerging authors, who had been writing under the constraints of censorship, passed through a period of adaptation (sometimes even a period of silence) to the new circumstances. Much had been said and written about all the works "on hold" that were waiting for Liberty, but it soon became apparent that the presumed works that would have been written had there been no censorship rested on mere hypothesis; the decades-long official censorship transformed into a self-censorship, and the years immediately following 1974 were an "empty place," according to Eduardo Lourenço,[3] who noted a relative "paralysis of our fiction during the first two years after the April Revolution." Certain writers who were already publishing before the Revolution, such as Agustina Bessa Luís and Vergílio Ferreira, continued their trajectories much as before, while others, such as José Gomes Ferreira, switched to a style that was more demonstrative and more tied to current events. Younger writers who began to publish in the 1980s or 1990s obviously did not face the same set of circumstances; the changes in Portuguese society, and specifically its approximation (at least in the more affluent social classes, with their easier access to culture and education) to the social models and lifestyles typical of the more developed Western countries, have created new conditions for life in general and for intellectual activities in particular. The arrival of Liberty, it may be said, ushered in the individualism I have already mentioned, and it is one of the defining traits of our contemporary society.

These and other historical, social and literary conditioning factors are especially relevant to three strands of the same general topic, which may be termed an inventory and analysis of the Portuguese imagination in the field of fiction. The first strand is concerned with the experience of the colonial wars

(1961-74), with texts that oscillate between the registers of "chronicle, fiction and history."[4] A significant portion of this literature recounts actual experiences, usually by officers, but if some texts border on quasi-direct testimony, others deal with the war's effects on the inner world of characters. Such is the case with António Lobo Antunes's early novels,[5] which used language in an innovative and at the time controversial way to portray characters who are inwardly falling apart (as we find in other war literatures). Works by two women, Wanda Ramos and Lídia Jorge,[6] focus on the "rear guard" occupied by wives and other women. Still other books, such as *Os alferes* (1984), a collection of novellas by Mário de Carvalho, depict daily life in a barracks during wartime with such realism that the reader is surprised to learn, in the case of Carvalho (who did not participate in the war, though he belongs to that generation), that the author did not actually witness the scenes he invents. An analogous case occurs with the first and so far only book of Rodrigo Guedes de Carvalho, *Daqui a nada* (1992). The author belongs to the generation that came after the colonial wars ended and therefore only knows about them secondhand, but he paints an intensely realistic portrait of a man overwhelmed by that past and struggling with a present that has been irrevocably changed by it.

A second strand in this inventory and analysis of the Portuguese literary imagination is formed by a vast and varied group of works that depict a family, a house (as the symbolic hub of collective identification and diffusion) or a generation. These works implicitly draw the portrait of an age, providing valuable material for literary studies and the social sciences, which implies no judgment on their artistic worth. (*Mutatis mutandis*, no one today would deny the literary importance of Balzac, whose novels are consulted by historians studying nineteenth-century French society.) Works in this area such as João de Melo's *Gente feliz com lágrimas* (1988), Maria Isabel Barreno's *Crónica do tempo* (1990), Helder Macedo's *Partes de África* (1991), Helena Marques's *O último cais* (1992), Fernando Assis Pacheco's *Trabalhos e paixões de Benito Prada* (1993) and Manuel Alegre's *Alma* (1995) form a jigsaw puzzle of contemporary Portugal and its roots, in which a realistic description of places, customs and social relationships is undertaken with ironic detachment. Other works constitute a kind of generational survey and chronicle.

Eduarda Dionísio,[7] for example, gathers the shattered pieces of the Sixties generation, while Paulo Castilho accounts for more recent years.[8] The same thematic material informs the highly wrought prose of Maria Velho da Costa, one of the writers who most successfully combines narrative and stylistic innovation with a renewed appreciation of the literary tradition, both in longer and shorter formats. In *Casas pardas* (1977), and continuing a process begun in *Maina Mendes* (1969), Velho da Costa painstakingly worked on the voice, which corresponds to different levels of language, composing the mosaic of a world through three female characters. This labor has been pursued with increasing intensity in subsequent volumes,[9] in which the rigor and versatility of the stylistic modes is combined with an intense exploration of the inner world and of human affections. Mention should be made here of Nuno Bragança, who in his short life was the author who dialogued most closely with Velho da Costa (with direct allusions from one work to another, as Manuel Gusmão has pointed out),[10] the two authors having occupied and defined the same lineage.

The third thematic strand of what I have denominated the Portuguese literary imagination is concerned with the fictional construction of historical figures from the past as well as from our own time. This tendency is probably due in part to the renewed interest, following the 1974 Revolution, in Portuguese history from the political and sociological perspectives, or from the point of view of mentalities, areas that the previous regime would not allow to develop to the extent they did in the rest of Europe. Fiction, it would seem, has in some cases assumed the role of historiography's co-helper. Examples of this genre include the fictionalized biographies of Agustina Bessa Luís,[11] the historical novels of Fernando Campos,[12] the record of the first decades of the twentieth century undertaken by Álvaro Guerra's works,[13] and the reconstruction of episodes or time periods in novels by José Saramago,[14] Jorge de Sena (*Sinais de fogo*, 1979), José Cardoso Pires,[15] and Mário de Carvalho (*A paixão do Conde de Fróis* , 1987).

The pursuit of an idea of Portugal sometimes has more radical consequences in terms of language, as in the works of Mário Cláudio, which as a rule take one of two basic approaches. The first consists of researching and appropriating the historical reality and the writing styles of a given time period so as to proceed by means of a quasi-pastiche technique. This method is used to evoke Camilo Castelo Branco in *A Quinta das Virtudes* (1990), to explore the language of the 1940s in *Tocata para dois clarins* (1992), and to recreate the figure and style of Eça de Queirós in *As batalhas do Caia* (1995). The second approach used by Cláudio was born out of commissions he received to write biographies of the modernist painter Amadeo de Sousa-Cardoso (*Amadeo*, 1984), the cellist Guilhermina Suggia (*Guilhermina*, 1986), and the traditional ceramist Rosa Ramalho (*Rosa*, 1988). In these works the writer conciliated the classical biography's aim to portray a life and an age with his own aim to write fiction, creating a narrator that interferes in the story as an organizer and supervisor, serving as a unifying element of the three volumes (thereby justifying their publication in a joint edition titled *A trilogia da mão*, 1993) while at the same time challenging the very concept of fiction, since the first-person narrative is combined with diaristic fragments or with biography. The text ultimately stands outside and apart from the various genres it evokes and crosses.

Other works and authors also follow this hybrid path between biography and pastiche in order to research language from markedly different periods. Teresa Veiga, for example, constructs episodes of the supposed biography of Florbela Espanca.[16] Nuno Júdice does something similar with the poet Manuel Laranjeira as his subject (*Roseira de Espinho*, 1994). Júdice alternates between essay, biography and the fictional autobiography of one who in examining the other is searching for his own self, testing and exploring himself through language. This will come as no surprise to readers who are familiar with Júdice's use of pastiche in his poetry or with his essays and critical work, concerned in particular with poets of the late nineteenth and early twentieth century, where Laranjeira fits in. Another incursion into prose by a poet interested in imitation is Luís Filipe Castro Mendes's *Correspondência secreta* (1995), which incorporates citations and a historical and intertextual memoir into a series of monologues alternately dating from 1762 and 1782 and pronounced by various figures of the Portuguese cultural world (e.g., the "Cavaleiro de Oliveira" and the poets Filinto Elísio and the Marchioness of Alorna). The narrative, in which directly quoted passages mix with the fictional monologue attributed to various voices, is framed by two opening

epigraphs—by Robert Browning and Agustina Bessa Luís—
and by a closing citation from Pessoa/Bernardo Soares's *Livro
do desassossego* that comments on the indefinite place of the
authorial figure, struggling between the voices he reads in the
tradition and the paradoxical uncertainty of his own position.
The author, in this book of Castro Mendes, is the one who
elaborates the apparatus of notes and who adds more text onto
the quoted speeches of each of his characters, which these
might very well have written. Such an author is quite literally a
paratextual figure.

Historical accuracy, in the realist perspective, has an
exemplary author in Mário de Carvalho, whose fictional
output is highly diverse but in all cases characterized by
eclectic and factually accurate references. This was already
true in several aforementioned books, *Os alferes* (1989) and *A
paixão do Conde de Fróis* (1986), a historical narrative
reminiscent of Camilo Castelo Branco (among others, for the
references underlying this author's fictions are always
plentiful and well researched). Two more recent and very
different works of fiction exemplify the author's consistently
high literary standards in whatever kind of narrative prose he
has written. *Um deus passeando pela brisa da tarde* (1994)—
a story conceived as the memoirs of Lucius Valerius, *duumvir*
of Tarcisis, in Iberia during the time of Marcus Aurelius—is
much more than a well-informed, accurate picture of an era; it
is an illustrious, lucid and cultured citizen's meditation on the
limits of power in a time of crisis. The serenity of the
protagonist comes from Marcus Aurelius, his contemporary,
and also has something of Yourcenar's Hadrian, but the voice
gives allegorical expression to our own day, in a utopian
dimension where time or what we may call—for lack of a
better term—the human condition endures without change. A
few months after this remarkable book was issued, Mário de
Carvalho published another, completely different book, *Era
bom que trocássemos umas ideias sobre o assunto* (1995), that
portrays and/or satirizes a certain side of contemporary
Portugal through a series of typical characters and vignettes
told in apparently banal and colloquial language, describing a
certain everyday Portuguese existence (the protagonist is a
man who, in order to feel part of a family, wants to join the
Communist Party, which the author happens to know quite
well, having been an active Communist for many years), with
all its twists and tricks for survival.

What I would now like to emphasize, in these very different works, is how much they also have in common. Both books are presented, in subtitles, as novels, prompting us to reflect on the present-day boundaries of this genre. However, is Mário de Carvalho using the term as a traditional designation, or does he employ it parodically (as he parodically employs various linguistic registers, in accord with the character and the time period represented)? Furthermore, the author's historical (or even historicist) program in these "novels" is joined by another aspect, irony, whose effect is to detach the writer. This rhetorical method for maintaining critical distance and a heightened awareness of the language and writing is always present—discreetly and without fanfare—in Mário de Carvalho's texts. Laughter combined with seriousness, erudition with the use of banal language, and his versatility of genres and styles make Carvalho one of the contemporary Portuguese writers whose work is most clearly stamped by an individual identity, autonomous from the voices of highly diverse origins that crisscross his books.

The passing reference to memorialistic writing in Carvalho brings to mind the increasing presence of intimist genres in current Portuguese literature. Miguel Torga regularly published volumes of his diary until the end of his life (1995), and Vergílio Ferreira published a two-series journal titled *Conta corrente*.[17] We also have *Na água do tempo-Diário (1948-1987)*, published in 1992 by Luísa Dacosta, whose entire oeuvre is centered on memory and the inner world, or Marcello Duarte Mathias's *Lembrar de raízes e outras coisas mais*, written in a fragmentary style resorting to aphorism, essayistic reflection and autobiography.[18] José Saramago, in turn, has already published three volumes of his diary, *Cadernos de Lanzarote* (1994, 1995, 1996). António Alçada Baptista, an author who since the 1970s has been publishing works that hover between memorialism and intimism, continues to forge fiction in which this source material is apparent, whether in *Uma vida melhor* (1984), with its childhood remembrances, or in books more akin to the traditional novel.[19]

In addition, we often meet up with works that are structured after intimist models: diaries, personal notes, and fragments of inner monologue. This occurs, for example, in Mário Claudio's aforementioned *Amadeo*, in Teolinda Gersão's *O Silêncio* (1981) and *Os guarda-chuvas cintilantes* (1984), in Yvette Centeno's *No jardim das nogueiras* (1983) and *Matriz* (1988), and in Maria Ondina Braga's *Passagem do Cabo* (1994). Refining procedures that the author had already experimented with, the most recent book by Rui Nunes, *Que sinos dobram por aqueles que morrem como gado?* (1995), is a good example of a cross between intimist and fragmentary writing, being elaborated on two textual levels, with the odd pages containing fragments of voices and discursive odds and ends, while the even pages are taken up by a diary that grows terser as the narrative progresses. This structure mirrors the deceptive universe that is the theme of the book, in which sickness deforms and infects everything, as in the realm of the grotesque (confirmed by a painting of Francis Bacon reproduced on the cover), here embodied by blindness, real for one of the characters and symbolically present at a more general level.

Some of these authors work in various genres, with their intimist writing affecting other sectors of their oeuvre. A case in point is the most recent novels of Vergílio Ferreira,[20] whose predominant technique—the inner monologue or reported dialogue—owes something to the cross between journal, memoirs and essay that the author simultaneously pursued, in full awareness of the fluid boundaries between these narrative subgenres, all of which were exclusively concerned to address certain central issues such as time, memory, the "I" in relationship to the other, and aging. All of these themes are summed up in the aphoristic title of one of his books, *Pensar* (1992), included in the author's list of diaries, a classification that—far from being obvious—calls attention once more to the whole problem of genres. For Vergílio Ferreira, as for Augusto Abelaira, literature is anything but innocent. These authors, well acquainted with the tradition, know that *essay* has been an ambiguous term since at least the time of Montaigne.

Critics have found rich source material for studying these matters in the singular oeuvre of Maria Gabriela Llansol, which in various ways cuts against the grain of canonical genres and the Portuguese cultural tradition. Forever treading a thin line between diary, fiction and essay, this author's writing is founded on the fragment and on a crisscrossing of cultural references that can make Fernando Pessoa and Camões coexist as characters in the same text with Thomas Muntzer, the Beguines of Flanders, Bach, Spinoza and others.

Standing apart from the fashions of the day and even, if possible, from time itself, Llansol conceives and elaborates a nonplace, a heterodox conception of the world in which writing coexists as a form of life with other forms of art and of being (with vegetable and animal entities being just as valid as human figures), to constitute one of the most intriguing, fascinating and challenging universes in contemporary Portuguese fiction. The author's list of works in her most recent book (*Lisboaleipzig 2-O ensaio de música*, 1994) keeps the reader uncertain. *Um falcâo no punho* (1985) and *Finita* (1987) are classified as "diaries," with the rest of her titles being designated as "fiction," but this category's further subdivision into "fiction" and "other works of fiction" shows how difficult it is to order or classify an oeuvre of this sort, even when nontraditional terminology is called in. The problem is that these texts form a system of inextricable parts that constantly play off one another, so that what we have, in the fullest sense of the term, is a single Work.

This brings us to another interesting aspect of the genre question in Portuguese letters, which has to do with the breakdown—thanks to various contemporary essayists—of the traditional distinction between fiction and essay.[21] I am referring not only to those authors who practice both kinds of writing, such as Vergílio Ferreira or David Mourão-Ferreira,[22] but to the fictional component that creeps into essays by Guilherme de Castilho,[23] Óscar Lopes,[24] António José Saraiva,[25] and Eduardo Lourenço.[26] The fictional "contamination" in these essayists is of immediate importance for appreciating the "poetic" system of titles they have been using (a point I will not pursue here). Fictional modes are also evoked, if not actually invoked, by the prefaces of the last books written by Jacinto do Prado Coelho[27] and by the long poem-essay of Vasco Graça Moura, "Regresso de Camões a Lisboa," a form that the author (also a poet and fiction writer) claims to have employed for lack of time to write the essay he would have liked to have written.[28]

An inverse contamination occurs with fictional works that mimic essayism. The very title of the novel *Ensaio sobre a cegueira* [Essay on Blindness] (1995), by José Saramago, is an explicit indication of how we are to read it, while in Luísa Costa Gomes's *Olhos verdes* (1994), which parodies the traditional "Life and Work" model, the fifth chapter surprises us with an essay on Berkeley's theory of sight. This essay reconsiders and implicitly proposes a rereading of the theme of looking as a means to know and to communicate (or not) that runs throughout the text, which had read as a mishmash but now gains coherency as an ensemble of fragments and speeches narrating the cruel everyday world we find in other texts by this author. If we add to these two books the aforementioned last work of Rui Nunes, whose theme is the progressive loss of vision and submergence into the state of blindness, then we have traced a thematic and symbolic line that merits our attention. In an age when our arts and techniques are investing heavily in the visual, it is significant that the metaphor of blindness, in these and in many other cases, is used to express the crisis of epistemology and of the contemporary world in general.

The poet and essayist Fernando Guimarães, long interested in literary and cultural self-reflection, has put these problems into sharp focus in his recent book, *As quatro idades* [The Four Ages] (1996), a title with classic resonance that the opening pages explore, transforming it into a program for the reader to develop. Composed of a stimulating and asymmetrical ensemble of radiating and disseminating fragments, this is a book of fiction but it is also essay, dialogue, poetry, literary theory and an analysis of literature's relationship to the visual arts, to philosophy, and to the classical tradition and its ways of abiding in the individual and collective memory.

The difficulty of using a definite taxonomy and the overlapping of genres in the same work (as I have tried to demonstrate) are only some of the characteristics that distinguish Portuguese fiction at the end of this century and millennium. The splintering of categories is conducive to their usage in complementary planes, in a movement of construction and deconstruction clearly linked to postmodernist thought. A paradox emerges from the picture that has been presented here: fiction writers do not seem to believe in the possibility of inventing something new, which is why they quote, resort to pastiche, or parody what others have done. But at the same time they continue to create, to pursue the not-yet-said, seeking through memory and fantasy to describe and understand the world, this world or another, and still another, always another. Perhaps literature is also, in each age and in each text, this impulse that prompts authors to invent by turning back to revise, repeat and vary, losing themselves and finding themselves in the varied and changing face of the Sphinx.[29]

Notes

1. Editions of the complete works of Teixeira Gomes, Irene Lisboa and Vitorino Nemésio are currently in progress, for example, while the complete works of Alexandre O'Neill, Carlos de Oliveira and Ruy Belo have been reissued. Considerable importance has also attached, in recent years, to the critical editions of works by Pessoa, by Eça de Queirós and, more recently, by Camilo Pessanha. The textual canon, when revised and debated by specialists, affects how these authors are read and interpreted by critics as well as by general readers, all of us feeling the practical effects of the scientific rigor applied to texts we thought were immutable.

2. To use the terminology of Genette.

3. "Literatura e revolução," in *Colóquio-Letras* 78 (March 1984). This article opens the special section "Dez anos de literatura portuguesa (1974-1984)," in which Maria Alzira Seixo surveyed fiction and Fernando J. B. Martinho examined poetry. Lourenço's essay was republished in *O canto do signo* . See Works Cited.

4. The phrase is taken from the subtitle of the most complete anthology of texts concerned with this theme (Melo).

5. *Memória de elefante*, 1979; *Os cús de Judas*, 1979; *Conhecimento do inferno*, 1980.

6. *Percursos—Do Luachimo ao Luena*, 1981, by Ramos, and *A costa dos murmúrios*, 1988, by Jorge.

7. See this author's titles from the 1980s (earlier works were published in the 1970s): *Histórias, memórias, imagens e mitos duma geração curiosa*, 1981; *Pouco tempo depois (As tentações)*, 1984; *Alguns lugares muito comuns (Diário de uns quantos dias que não abalaram o mundo)*, 1987.

8. *Fora de horas*, 1990; *Sinais exteriores*, 1993.

9. The main titles are *Lúcialima* (1983), *Missa in Albis* (1988) and *Dores* (1994).

10. See Bragança's *A noite e o riso* (1969), *Directa* (1977) and *Square Tolstoi* (1981). Gusmão's observations are made in his preface that accompanies the three reprintings of *A noite e o riso*.

11. *Florbela Espanca* (1979), *Fanny Owen* (1979), *Um bicho da terra* (1984), *A corte do Norte* (1987), *Eugénia e Silvina* (1989), and others.

12. *A Casa do Pó* (1986) and *A esmeralda partida* (1995).

13. *Café República* (1982), *Café Central* (1984), *Café 25 de Abril* (1987). In other works, such as Guerra's *Razões do coração—Romance de paixões acontecidas em Mafra ocupada pelos franceses no ano de 1808* (1991), the reader is forewarned that facts and fiction overlap.

188 ◆ PAULA MORÃO

14. The period of the dictatorship in *Levantado do Chão* (1980), the building of the Mafra monastery in the eighteenth century in *Memorial do convento* (1982), and the 1930s in *O ano da morte de Ricardo Reis* (1984).

15. *Balada da Praia dos Cães* (1982) and *Alexandra Alpha* (1988).

16. See "A minha vida com Bela," one of the novellas in *O último amante* (1990). Teresa Veiga has also published a book of short stories, *História da bela fria* (1992).

17. The five volumes of the first series were published between 1980 and 1987, the four volumes of the second in 1993-94.

18. Previous works by this author include *No devagar depressa dos tempos—Notas de um diário (1962-1969)* (1980) and *Mas é no rosto e no porte altivo do rosto* (1983).

19. *Os nós e os laços* (1985), *Catarina ou o sabor da maçã* (1988), *Tia Suzana, meu amor* (1989).

20. *Para sempre* (1983), *Até ao fim* (1987), *Em nome da terra* (1990), *Na tua face* (1993).

21. An idea doubly reinforced by the presentation, shortly before this text was written, of the Prémio Camões and the Prémio Vida Literária—two of the most prestigious prizes for Portuguese-language literature—to the essayists Eduardo Lourenço and Óscar Lopes.

22. His large output of short stories is joined by a single novel, *Um amor feliz* (1986), the portrait of a generation drawn with ironic detachment and writerly elegance, typical of David Mourão-Ferreira.

23. Apparent in some of the texts collected in *Presença do espírito* (1989).

24. See his recent essays, collected in *Cifras do tempo* (1990) and in *A busca de sentido* (1995).

25. Some of the essays in Saraiva's *A tertúlia Ocidental* (1990) are written in a fictional register.

26. I have in mind older essays, such as those that open the book *Tempo e poesia* (1974, republished in 1988), as well as essays from *Fernando, rei da nossa Baviera* (1986) or *O canto do signo—Existência e literatura (1957-1993)* (1994).

27. *Ao contrário de Penélope* (1976) and *Camões e Pessoa, poetas da utopia* (1983).

28. In *Oceanos* 23 (July-September 1995). This poem of 264 verses is an excellent example of the intermingling of genres that has continually informed this author's work. I am thinking particularly of the narrator of *Naufrágio de Sepúlveda* (1988), who prepares a biography of Luís de Montalvor, a modernist poet and publisher of some of his contemporaries.

29. Cf. Eduardo Lourenço's essay "Esfinge ou a poesia" in *Tempo e poesia* (1974, republished 1988).

Works Cited

Genette, Gérard. "Les titres." *Seuils*, 54-97. Paris: Seuil, 1987.

Lourenço, Eduardo. "Esfinge ou a poesia." *Tempo e poesia.* 1974. Lisbon: Relgio D'igua, 1987.

_____. "Literatura e Revolução." *O canto do signo—Existência e literatura (1957-1993).* Lisbon: Presença, 1994.

Melo, João de, ed. *Os anos da Guerra—1961-1975. Os portugueses em África—Crónica, ficção e história.* 2 vols. Lisbon: Dom Quixote, 1988.

◆ Chapter 12

Four Twentieth-Century Portuguese Critics

Victor Mendes

One of the explicitly or implicitly recurring themes of twentieth-century Portuguese criticism is the problem of its own birth and identity. Fernando Pessoa (1888-1935)—as well as João Gaspar Simões, whom I will discuss further on— belongs to the group of critics who deplore the absence of criticism in Portugal, themselves (implicitly or explicitly) excluded. Pessoa's writings on Portuguese literature—dating from the teens, the twenties, and the thirties—propose an inauguration of criticism and the need for a radical revision: "I call the attention of critically competent persons (whose existence among us is a hypothesis I admit out of courtesy) to the obvious fact that [Guerra] Junqueiro's *Pátria* is not only the greatest work of the last thirty years but the most outstanding work our literature has thus far produced. *Os Lusíadas* ranks an honorable second place" (*Obras em Prosa* 343). Pessoa's appreciation of Luís de Camões was never without reservation, but it was certainly greater than what he expressed for Eça de Queroz, as we will see.

Pessoa focused on two items in particular: (1) the failure, in poetry, for writers to remain true to their intention, and (2) the contradictions often apparent between a writer's work and the theories he or she propounds. In "A Poesia Nova em Portugal" (*Páginas de Estética e de Teoria e Crítica Literárias* 350-52), he offers us the examples of Milton and

Goethe. Milton, in *Paradise Lost*, intended to sing of the Fall in function of Man's redemption but ended up glorifying Satan and Adam and Eve, after the Fall. Goethe, on the other hand, "affirmed he was a classicist, and in his theory he surely was; his masterpiece, *Faust*, is the masterpiece of Romanticism" (*Páginas de Estética* . . . , 352). These observations suggest we would do well to look closely at the subsequent statements of intention, prefaces and commentaries made by Pessoa with respect to his own work, for this author remains one of the most forceful critics of his poetry, when his poetry is not itself a means of formulating critical problems (in the case of the poetry attributed to Alberto Caeiro, for example). Pessoa's creative writing has a strong critical component.[1]

By Pessoa's own terms, criticism is doomed to fail. Before looking any further, how does Pessoa's criticism fail in relation to his own work? The recent edition of *Poemas Completos de Alberto Caeiro*—which in spite of its shortcomings closely follows Pessoa's project, documented in a number of his papers—offers us a good subject of study. The accompanying prose texts written by Pessoa, "Prefácio do Dr. Ricardo Reis" and "Notas para a recordação do meu mestre Caeiro" [Notes to the memory of my master, Caeiro], were designed to furnish a definite interpretive program and a critical and ideological framework through the recognized instruments of a preface and an afterword. This strategy sought to show the future influences of Caeiro's work on his "disciples" Ricardo Reis and Álvaro de Campos, two other heteronyms of Pessoa. In this way Pessoa dodges another aspect of influence: to set up Caeiro as a master without masters and the great precursor in Pessoa's work is a way of saying that Pessoa is his own precursor.

Pessoa's attempt to establish himself critically as a beginning *ex nihilo*, evading the problem of a precursor, is patently evident in his texts. A case in point is the contradiction between the first and second paragraphs of the Preface written by Pessoa (in the name of Reis) to *Poemas Completos de Alberto Caeiro* (25-36). On the one hand he argues the impossibility of narrating Caeiro's life, since narration presumes a reality beyond or outside itself: "something to narrate." On the other hand, Caeiro's poems subsume his life; in them his life has no reality beyond. Therefore, and in this specific context, the work is the life, and vice versa: the life is the work. "His poems are what there was in him of life" (25). A kind of genealogical tension is established; the impossibility of "narrating" is juxtaposed to the possibility of poems.

We could say it is a matter of poetry *versus* narrative. But the poems, once incorporated into the life, also incorporate the narrative, since "apart from them there were no events and no history" (25). In other words; there is "life" in the poems; there are "events"; the poems contain the narrative content. A difficult problem arises at this point. How see *O Pastor Amoroso* ("The Shepherd in Love," a poetic sequence in *Poemas Completos de Alberto Caeiro*) as the result of a "brief, fruitless and absurd episode" (25) without giving this episode the status of an event? Since this poetic sequence is an anomaly in Caeiro's life (because an anomaly in his work) without history, this episode—according to Pessoa's own formulation—should be narratable. Therefore we can read in Pessoa's text the negation of his critical intention.

Pessoa's best critical writing is dedicated to poetry. With respect to Portuguese poetry he was especially concerned to defend three theses. The first was that Camões, though important, is inferior to the great poets Dante, Milton and Shakespeare. The second was that the Portuguese poets who preceded him, such as Guerra Junqueiro and Teixeira de Pascoaes, were among Europe's best and comparable to Wordsworth or Goethe. The third thesis was that the best of Portuguese literature was yet to come. In various contexts and at various points in his work, Pessoa clearly inferred that the future of Portuguese literature depended on the generation of *Orpheu*,[2] in which he played a leading role. Taken together, the second and third theses suggest that Pessoa's place in literature was very high indeed.

Let's look at these theses in more detail. With regard to the first one, it should be said that to minimize Camões's importance was part of Pessoa's overall strategy. This is evident in a number of texts and especially in his conception of a "Super-Camões." As for the second thesis, the poets who preceded Pessoa belonged to a movement described by Pessoa in a letter written in English to a British publisher (possibly in 1916):

Portuguese "transcendentalist pantheism" you do not know. It is a pity, because, though not a long-standing movement, yet it is an original one. Suppose English romanticism had, instead of retrograding to the Tennysonian-Rossetti-Browning level, progressed right onward from Shelley, spiritualising his already spiritualistic pantheism. You would arrive at the conception of Nature (our transcendentalist pantheists are essentially poets of Nature) in which flesh and spirit are entirely mingled in something which transcends both. If you can conceive a William Blake put into the soul of Shelley and writing through that, you will perhaps have a nearer idea of what I mean. This movement has produced two poems which I am bound to hold among the greatest of all time. Neither is a long one. One is the "Ode to Light" of Guerra Junqueiro, the greatest of all Portuguese Poets (he drove Camoens from the first place when he published "Pátria" in 1896—but "Pátria," which is a lyrical and satirical drama is not of his transcendental-pantheist phase). The "Prayer to Light" is probably the greatest metaphysico-poetical achievement since Wordsworth's great "Ode." The other poem, which certainly transcends Browning's "Last Ride Together" as a love-poem, and which belongs to the same metaphysical level of love-emotion, though more religiously pantheistic, is the "Elegy" of Teixeira de Pascoaes, who wrote it in 1905.—To this school of poets we, the "sensationists," owe the fact that in our poetry spirit and matter are interpenetrated and inter-transcended. And we have carried the process further than the originators, though I regret to say that we cannot as yet claim to have produced anything on the level of the two poems I have referred to. (*Páginas Íntimas e de Auto-interpretação*, 129-30)

The dash ("—To this school of poets we, the 'sensationists'") denotes direct discourse; Pessoa was the spokesman for his "school of poets." His hyperbolic praise of Guerra Junqueiro and Teixeira de Pascoaes was the critical groundwork for the glorification of the so-called "First Modernism," ushered in by the generation of *Orpheu* and Pessoa. This premeditated glorification would be confirmed by others in the second half of this century, with respect to his poetry more than his literary criticism. Pessoa's critical theses, therefore, do not adhere to the Kantian critical ideal, according to which the judge must be disinterested, and are significant in function of a critical program concerned with the fate of his own work.

To emphasize how an artist's work has little or nothing to do with his or her intentions, Pessoa offered various examples outside the domain of poetry. "Prince Henry the Navigator," he wrote, "though the most systematic of all the creators of civilization, had no idea of the wonder he was creating—the whole of modern transoceanic civilization" (*Obras em Prosa*, 337). In spite of Pessoa's frequently complex formulations, both in terms of syntax and ideas, his criticism was unable to achieve its objective in any rigorous way. Particularly in the case of Portuguese literature, one of the implicit functions of Pessoa's criticism was to *situate* his work in a history and above all in a hierarchy whose terms were his own, but this endeavor was compromised by the inevitable failure of art— and by extension, criticism—to remain true to intention.

João Gaspar Simões (1903-87) was the most prolific Portuguese critic of the twentieth century and one of the first to give critical attention to the work of Pessoa. Born at the beginning of the century and living almost to the end of its penultimate decade, he was in contact with writers from various generations. He wrote more than fifty works (including a few novels that no one reads anymore), the vast majority of which are taken up by essay and literary criticism covering virtually the whole gamut of Portuguese literature. He is decidedly out of fashion as a critic. The biographical thrust in some of his analyses has not helped him among younger scholars, most of whom were trained by disciples of French structuralism and poststructuralism. And yet from time to time in his books we find striking intuitions that merit being researched, particularly since some of them have not been at all developed.

The place Gaspar Simões reserved for himself in Portuguese criticism was that of founder, more or less as Pessoa had done. In his "Brief Introit" to *Crítica IV* (9-11), Gaspar Simões cites David Mourão-Ferreira's epithet for him: "the very *consciousness* of the literature being produced in Portugal in whatever form—from poetry to fiction, from theater to essay." By invoking this warranty, Gaspar Simões suggests that anyone interested in the workings of the *consciousness* of Portuguese literature should search among his numerous newspaper articles.[3] Gaspar Simões regarded his critical work to be the starting point of criticism in Portugal, and in parentheses he issued this challenge: "(and let anyone who doubts this boast prove the contrary)" (*Crítica IV*, 10).[4]

João Gaspar Simões wrote two large biographies, *Vida e Obra de Eça de Queiroz* (1945) and *Vida e Obra de Fernando Pessoa. História de uma Geração* (1951), this latter being the most celebrated Portuguese literary biography. Eça de Queiroz and Fernando Pessoa are the two figures that dominate Gaspar Simões's critical writings. He considered the first of these figures to be the greatest Portuguese novelist and even—in verses such as "Eu gosto pelas ruas da cidade / De ver uma velhinha corcovada" [On the streets of the city I like / To see an old hunchbacked woman]—a precursor of Cesário Verde (*Eça de Queiroz* 50).

I will examine three of Gaspar Simões's propositions concerning Eça de Queiroz's importance for the Portuguese novel. The first is that Eça, carrying out the project he announced in his Casino Conference (*Vida e Obra de Eça de Queiróz*, 293 ff.), introduced the art of the novel in Portugal. The realism/naturalism of Queiroz was to some extent original, making him the first Portuguese novelist to rise to the level of universal literature. His culminating work was *Os Maias*, an English-influenced novel. The second proposition is that before Eça there was no true novel in Portugal, mainly for philosophical reasons, since romanticism's idealism and aesthetic of feeling were incompatible with the art of the novel. Camilo Castelo Branco, according to this view, was not a novelist but a storyteller. If there were any precursor to Eça, it could only have been the Almeida Garrett of *Viagens na Minha Terra*. The third proposition is that in the thirty years after Eça's death, largely because his writing was clear and easy to imitate, his realist style dominated the Portuguese novel, with writers such as Aquilino Ribeiro (*Via Sinuosa*) and Fernanda Botelho being indebted to him.

Gaspar Simões passed critical judgment—positive or negative—on a number of Eça de Queiroz's works. Some of the so-called semiposthumous works, for example, earned the negative rating. *A Ilustre Casa de Ramires* "constituted a new kind of novel—the symbolic novel—and was only admissible as such: the story of Ramires, the greatest of all the puppets conceived by the novelist . . ." (*Eça de Queiroz* 191). "*A Cidade e as Serras* is, so to speak, the literary testament of a writer who stopped being true in his final days"[5] (*Eça* 191).

In the story of genius and decadence that Gaspar Simões tells about Eça, *A Correspondência de Fradique Mendes* occupies a special place, arousing a notorious ambiguity. The critic considers it a failed work, but successful in certain aspects.

A top rating, on the other hand, was attributed to the novel *Os Maias*, the "most perfect work of literary art that had been written in Portugal since *The Lusiads*" (182). This judgement has largely prevailed throughout the twentieth century, to the detriment of Pessoa as a literary critic. The pejorative link Pessoa had established between Eça and the French tradition was revised by Gaspar Simões: "*Os Maias*, his unquestionable masterpiece, shows that the writer's sensibility was influenced by long and close contact with specifically English fiction" (96).

One of Gaspar Simões's critical confrontations was with another self-styled founder of Portuguese criticism, namely, Fernando Pessoa. In *Vida e Obra de Fernando Pessoa*, Gaspar Simões—who made many friends and many enemies with his "life and work" approach—dedicated one of the book's "parts" to the critical texts published by Pessoa in *A Águia*, an Oporto-based review founded in 1910. The chapter is titled "The Error of *Saudosismo*,"[6] and its three subchapters ("The Poetic Error: from 'Gládio' to 'Ascensão,'" "The Critical Error: The 'Super-Camões,'" and "The Metaphysical Error: 'Pantheistic Transcendentalism'") invariably repeat the word error with respect to Pessoa the critic. A close reading of this part of the biography shows that Simões saw Pessoa, Eça de Queiroz and Antero de Quental as occupying essentially the same position vis-à-vis the complex problem of Portugal's renewal.

What Simões wants to show is that Pessoa the ingenious poet was preceded by Pessoa the failed critic, as evidenced by the several controversial articles he published in *A Águia*: "A Nova Poesia Portuguesa Sociologicamente Considerada" (April 1912) and "A Nova Poesia Portuguesa no seu Aspecto Psicológico" (November 1912). The conclusion, for Simões, is that Pessoa is not really a critic. This attitude is patent in a number of his assertions. Pessoa's notion of a Super-Camões, linked to a predicted Golden Age of Portuguese literature, is called an "astounding conclusion" (*Vida e Obra de Fernando Pessoa*, 161). The next page of the same biography affirms that "Pessoa offers a knowingly captious analysis of the conditions that will lead to a glorious social and literary life in Portugal." And on the page after that: "Unable to provide 'a corroborative reasoning' for the deductive reasoning he tirelessly pursued, Pessoa's thesis demonstrated nothing at all." Finally: "The overall architecture of his reasoning . . . is solid, but the weakness of its construction is readily apparent" (164). Gaspar Simões not only concurs with critics of Pessoa such as Hernâni Cidade; he also argues that Pessoa's elevation of "Pantheistic Transcendentalism" and poets such as Teixeira de Pascoaes and Guerra Junqueiro to superlative status was probably a sham. In support of this argument are Pessoa's letters to his friend and *Orpheu* colleague, Mario de Sá-Carneiro, in which he expresses only moderate admiration for Pascoaes and Junqueiro. The reason for the critical pieces in *A Águia*, according to Gaspar Simões, was to set the stage for the fulfillment of Pessoa's prophecy of a Super-Camões, who would be no other than Pessoa himself, writing as a poet.

Gaspar Simões finds fault with Pessoa as a critic on two grounds. The first was direct, insofar as the articles published in *A Águia* were seriously flawed and revealed a poor critic. The second implicit ground was Pessoa's failure to give sufficient attention to Portuguese fiction and especially to Portugal's greatest novelist, Eça de Queiroz.

Jorge de Sena (1919-78) was, in turn, a critic of Gaspar Simões. In "Ensaísmo crítico em Portugal" (*Estudos de Literatura Portuguesa—III*, 45-49), an article written in 1961, Sena challenged Simões's contention that Portuguese criticism was born at the end of the last century with the little-known Moniz Barreto. Taking a wider view of what constitutes a literary critic, Sena published a brief list of great Portuguese critics beginning with the medieval troubadours and continuing up to the present with names such as King Dom Duarte, Fernão Lopes, Sá de Miranda, Camões, Rodrigues Lobo, Francisco Manuel de Melo, Correia Garção, Garrett, Herculano, Camilo Castelo Branco, Eça de Queiroz, Fernando Pessoa, and Teixeira de Pascoaes. This list could also serve as a brief canon of Portuguese literature, and Sena surely did not want to reduce criticism to the trite observation that every author is a critic. His point was obviously polemical and aimed directly at Gaspar Simões. In fact, of the critics belonging to the so-called Second Modernism as represented by the magazine *Presença*, Sena emphasized José Régio, "with all his limitations," over Gaspar Simões.

In his article "A crítica portuguesa no séc. XX" (*Estudos* 95-106), written in 1969, Sena distinguished between "literary essay writing" and "book review criticism," giving greater importance to the former. The article stressed the relationship between literary and political criticism insofar as it gave considerable attention to the Salazar decades and to some of the political implications of criticism formulated by the anti-romantic *Geração de 70* [1870s Generation]. It also clarified why Sena considered António Sérgio the greatest Portuguese critic of the first half of the twentieth century. Sérgio, we are told, did not approach literature as an end in itelf but as a "pretext" for a vigorous defense of pedagogical, historical and political points of view. Sena, too, generally preferred not to reduce literature to the level of its linguistic factors.

In Sena's brief history of Portuguese criticism, Pessoa and Gaspar Simões emerge as the respective emblematic critics of the First and Second Modernisms, though they meet rather different fates. Pessoa's debut in the two pieces published in *A Águia*, in 1912, is characterized by Sena as a study lauding "the *saudosista* poets with demoniacal exaggeration" (Estudos 101). The use of the adjective "demoniacal" indicates that Pessoa, for Sena, was not ingenuous in the hyperbolic praise he lavished on Teixeira de Pascoaes and others. The split between "Saudosismo" and modernism occurred in 1915, with the appearance of the review *Orpheu*. Sena's assertion that from then on Pessoa and the vanguardist group of the First Modernism abandoned criticism and even their own critical promotion is hard to defend, particularly in the case of Pessoa. For one thing Sena, according to the wide view of criticism he took in his dispute with Gaspar Simões, considered Portugal's great poets and novelists to be also its best critics. For another thing, detailed analysis of Pessoa's oeuvre as we know it today[7] shows that the poet had a very definite critical strategy for situating his own work.

The demarcation that Sena tried to establish for his own poetry in relation to Pessoa's is best expressed in his preface to the first edition of *Poesia—I*, published in 1961. In contrast to Pessoa's poetics of dissimulation, Sena proposes a poetics of testimony, which is another path for avoiding the confessionalism associated with some of the poetry published by the magazine *Presença*. But Pessoa's solipsistic universe and Sena's *world that we live* (or *world that surrounds us*) intersect at various points, with the same or similar terms sometimes being used to characterize both. Both poetics presuppose virtual, potential worlds. For Sena, poetry expresses the revelation, in the "real" world, of other worlds invoked by human will. This "will," capable of transforming potential worlds into actual ones, is one of the elements that distinguishes Sena from Pessoa. Another differentiating factor apparent in Sena's preface has to do with time. The technique of dissimulation is synchronic, whereas the imperative worlds of Sena's "will" imply a diachronic movement.

With regard to Gaspar Simões's "impressionistic" criticism, initially inspired by the *Nouvelle Revue Française*, Sena, in "A crítica portuguesa no séc. XX," remarks on the practice of

> a critic using literature to justify for decades his own existence, as has been the case with Hernâni Cidade and Gaspar Simões, who are not only alive and well but highly respected, in spite of the regular heap of nonsense they serve to the Portuguese public and to the bibliographical ingenuousness of foreign scholars. (104)

Pessoa—with whom Sena had, so to speak, a poetic confrontation—is one of the poets occupying a major place in Sena's critical works; the other is Luís de Camões. Sena is in fact one of the great Camões scholars of this century. His extensive analytical work on the sixteenth-century poet can only be properly grasped from the theoretical perspective revealed in "Ensaio de uma tipologia literária," written in 1959 and now available in *Dialécticas Teóricas da Literatura.* This essay, participating in the campaign against impressionistic and biographical criticism, consists of twenty-two distinct, intersecting planes of aesthetic analysis ranging from linguistics to ideology. Their various combinations should make it possible to circumvent elementary forms of historicism and to gain access, in the manner of Hegel, to the whole of a literary work. It is the highest expression of Sena as *homo academicus*, notwithstanding the war he waged against a certain sterility in Portuguese academic criticism. This essay is interesting in how it is traversed by a creative dimension (an idealistic approach revived by a number of Marxists), though this is never made explicit. To put it another way, in Sena the aesthetics of reviewing a literary work depends on a poiesis. Literary criticism, therefore, occupies the same territory as literary creation. Sena's interpretation based on structural and typological methodologies is opposed to erudition pure and simple. Sena's brand of criticism, whose "cycle of critical research" required "a *mythographic* synthesis" (*Uma Canção de Camões* 39), consisted largely in integrating various critical methods—"statistical, topical, stylistic, semantic, etc." (40)—at various levels. Sena's reasoning seems to be that a coordinated synthesis of all available criteria of interpretation enable us to go beyond the arbitrariness of any one criterion.

The effectiveness of a method is measured by the interpretive results obtained. In the case of Sena, who left no disciples of his critical method, the best interpreter is himself. In *Uma Canção de Camões*, Sena's survey of the criticism on Camões showed that it had become thin in terms of internal analysis "because the exegetical traditions of the 18th century had been lost" (*Uma Cançao* 27). Examining the possible influence of Petrarch on Camões, he concluded there was none:

> The *canções* of Camões overflow with quintessentialized experiences, and in their poetic expression they sublimely surpass the criteria of external form that Petrarch explored. Reflecting their author's longing for an ideal, personal and austere model, they surpass the external in a way that majestically confirms a loftiness of spirit, a nobility of intentions and a dignity of man vis-à-vis his own destiny . . . . (186)

Relying on a rhetorical strategy of "objective" proof, Sena carries out an intense statistical labor (a mainstay of typological criticism) to produce page after page of meticulous charts showing the number of rhymes, rhyme groups, percentages, and so on in Petrarch and Camões, to conclude that the latter *surpassed* the former. This kind of comparison only makes sense if we take into account the dialectic of supersession inherent to this critical approach. Another presupposition is that *external form* necessarily implies an *internal form*. It was on this basis that Sena could attempt to go beyond critical impressionism through "concrete phenomenological research" (186).

The most trenchant criticism of Jorge de Sena's scholarly work on Camões is found in the article "Jorge de Sena camonista," by Vítor Manuel de Aguiar e Silva, himself a

distinguished specialist in Camões and Mannerism. Praising
the ingenious fragmentary approach of Sena's work on
Camões[8] but also noting the lacunae of one who kept his
distance from the academic community in Portugal, Aguiar e
Silva at one point reviews the negative results of Sena's
statistical objectivity:

a simple and fruitless catalogue of quantitative
observations; a gross reductionism of the "structural
models" proposed for describing the objects or *corpora*
under analysis, with highly flawed and unwarranted
conclusions being able to result from this statistically
"canonical" concept of the *corpora*; in short, a
manipulation *ad libitum* of the statistical operations
themselves, and not only of the conclusions they yield.
(48)

Aguiar e Silva seriously questions the results of Sena's
methodology, pointing out mistakes (some of which were
inevitable, due to the lack of bibliographical sources in Brazil,
where Sena lived for many years) in the application of his own
method. Aguiar e Silva also notes the seemingly unforgivable
lacuna of "escolaridade" [academic training]. In a defense
and apology titled "O ensaio e a crítica de Jorge de Sena,"
Luís de Sousa Rebelo affirms that Aguiar e Silva failed to see
that Sena was the precursor of an innovative critical program
that takes literary historicism to task, anticipates feminism[9]
(with respect to Florbela Espanca), and relies heavily on
comparative and multidisciplinary approaches (50).

Joaquim Manuel Magalhães (b. 1945), a great admirer of
Jorge de Sena, has established himself as the most interesting
poetry critic of the second half of this century. His two main
critical works are *Os Dois Crepúsculos* (1981) and *Um Pouco
da Morte* (1989). His venture consists chiefly in defining a
canon for post-World War II Portuguese poetry and in
redefining a genealogy for "Os dos anos 70" [Those from
the 70s], a group that includes himself as a poet. "Os dos anos
70" alludes to the nineteenth-century "Geração de 70,"
whose activity centered on fiction and argumentative prose
and whose writers, particularly Eça de Queiroz, brought the
nineteenth-century Portuguese novel to its highest level. "Os
dos anos 70" omits the word *geração*,[10] though the word
occasionally occurs in Magalhães's texts, always with a caveat

that a programmatic meaning is not intended. The new 1970s Generation is not one of narrative and expository prose but of poetry; the twentieth century in Portugal, contrary to the nineteenth, stands out for its poets.[11] But there is, as we shall see, a strong narrative component in this new generation, as suggested by the *historical* character of its very name.

Magalhães has developed a form of criticism that—contrary to most of New Criticism and French Structuralism—can and does resort to biography[12] as well as the daily world and external circumstances bearing on poetry. To defend his thesis that Portuguese literature, especially the poetry, is cosmopolitan, he points out that its internal evolution has yielded an overwhelming number of epigones. But his main critical task has been to formulate, for his own Seventies generation, a genealogy with alternatives to Fernando Pessoa. According to Magalhães, the 1960s marked a turning point at which Pessoa ceased to be an active influence on poets and moved, as it were, into the domain of critics. Ruy Belo, in this view, was the last poet to be influenced by Pessoa. The elaboration of alternative genealogies to Pessoa involves identifying precursors for twentieth-century movements and poets, with the nineteenth-century poets Cesário Verde, Camilo Pessanha and António Nobre constituting a crucial triad. Verde is considered a precursor for poets such as Teixeira de Pascoaes, but also for the neo-realists and for Mário Cesariny and Alexandre O'Neill. Pessanha's descendants include Sophia de Mello Breyner Andresen and Eugénio de Andrade. Nobre is seen as an important influence on poets of the Seventies generation such as Nuno Júdice and João Miguel Fernandes Jorge.[13]

In the blueprint of this genealogy for the Seventies generation, Jorge de Sena plays a preeminent role. Taking the somewhat Eliotic view that "literary historians and critics never count" for the essential core of poetic creation (*Um Pouco da Morte* 43), Magalhães regards Sena—a poet and critic (namely of Pessoa, for what interests us here) with a similar concern to condemn in no uncertain terms the Portuguese management of the State,[14] of Education and of Culture—as the first poet who understood, precisely because of his persistent heterodoxy, the importance of going beyond Pessoa. For Magalhães, Sena's poetry "achieved the great victory of freeing us from a certain hegemony of Pessoa" (*Os*

Dois Crepúsculos 53). Here the first person plural refers to the poets of the Seventies.

In exactly what way or ways did Sena surpass Pessoa? The word *surpass* [*ultrapassar*] is frankly infelicitous, and yet it recurs in Magalhães's critical texts, especially in those concerning Pessoa, Sena and the Seventies generation. This is explained by Magalhães's keen historical awareness and respect, causing him to accept a word passed down by tradition and employed by Sena himself, for whom Camões, as noted above, *surpassed* Petrarch. In the case of Magalhães, we meet with a relentless defense of poetry's influence on prose (*Dois Crepúsculos* 58), on criticism and on narrative fiction; the reverse also occurs, with the exception of criticism written by nonpoets. The Aristotelian concept of the poet is restored, even if some poets do not venture out of the lyric mode.

Magalhães uses the poetry of João Miguel Fernandes Jorge to insist on its narrative component[15] and to affirm the rebirth of the epic poem, now redefined to include the small incidents of daily life, thereby widening the prevailing concept that in Portugal derived from the paradigm of Camões's *The Lusiads*. The presence of narrative is identified by Magalhães in his reading of poems by Sena such as "Café cheio de militares em Luanda," which he analyzed from the narrative point of view (*Um Pouco da Morte* 55-56). A corollary of narrative's preeminence is the view that the best Portuguese novels are usually historical. Examples include Alexandre Herculano's *Eurico, o Presbítero*, Eça de Queiroz's *A Ilustre Casa de Ramires*, and two novels by Jorge de Sena: *O Físico Prodigioso* and *Sinais de Fogo*. Magalhães uses this last novel—whose action takes place in Figueira da Foz in 1936, at the time of the Spanish Civil War—to explore the theme of bodily exposure and repressed sexuality. Mário Cesariny, with *Titânia e A Cidade Queimada* (*Dois Crepúsculos*, 113-21), is another author in whom "the revolution reaches the body" (117).

For both of Magalhães's books, the table of contents is basically a list of Portuguese poets who are mostly from the second half of the twentieth century. The order is loosely chronological, according to the decades when the poets began publishing. A few names appearing in the contents of both books are those whom Magalhães canonizes: Ruy Cinatti, Jorge de Sena, Mário Cesariny, Herberto Hélder, Ruy Belo, Pedro Tamen, João Miguel Fernandes Jorge and António

Franco Alexandre. *Um Pouco da Morte* also proposes some new, post-1970s poets such as Gil de Carvalho, Fernando Luís, Paulo Teixeira and José António de Almeida.

In Magalhães's view, 1961 was the year when post-World War II Portuguese poetry came into its own, with the publication of Ruy Belo's *Aquele Grande Rio Eufrates* and Herberto Hélder's *A Colher na Boca*. These are seen as the two great poets of the 1960s, marking an end to the groups that had dominated Portuguese poetry. The affirmation of post-World War II poetry was accompanied by a change of paradigm. Instead of Pessoa's "tricks" with the subject or voice, inherited from nineteenth-century English poetry and depending largely on noncoincidence, on a failure to meet with the *consciousness of oneself* (this phraseology coming from another celebrated critic of Pessoa, Eduardo Lourenço), Sena proposes the subjective description of objects:

> The "dramatic monologue" of Browning, the heteronymic discourse of Pessoa and the "objective correlative" of Eliot were followed by Sena's "framed expression" [expressão enquadrada], which innovatively took its place in the anti-Romantic lyric tradition invoked by our age in an attempt to redefine itself vis-à-vis the imaginative incontinence that also, and no less tellingly, qualifies it. (*Dois Crepúsculos* 59)

The texts of Magalhães contain passages of intense admiration for Sena—"the greatest Portuguese intellectual" (*Dois Crepúsculos* 49), in whom "I admired the masters I was never able to have" (50)—and go so far as to justify his alleged megalomania: "greatness can only think of itself with greatness" (52). Various affinities between these two poet-critics could be explored, besides the implicit affirmation that *Pessoa is dead* (in the sense that it's time to move on) and their shared inclination toward Anglo-American literature and culture. But what about their differences? They exist, though they are not immediately obvious. For one thing there are no traces of Sena's methodological strategy in Magalhães's beautiful critical prose. Sena's Marxist criticism (even when this Marxism is concerned only with *transforming language*) is completely alien to the criticism of Magalhães, whose strategy of critical revision relies on omission. This explains why a critic such as João Gaspar Simões, who was not a poet, is never mentioned in Magalhães's two main books of literary criticism.

Notes

1. João Gaspar Simões wrote the following about the relationship of criticism to poetry in Pessoa: "The poet of *Mensagem*, when he could have still easily reclaimed his British 'naturalization' and become, perhaps, a great poet in English, preferred to remain in Portugal. There he laid the critical groundwork for the arrival of his own poetic personality. His future as a writer was always coupled with the future of Portuguese literature itself. For this reason Pessoa, hiding his ambitions as a poet, made his public debut in the guise of a critic" (*Vida e obra de Fernando Pessoa*, 147).

2. An avant-garde literary magazine whose most important contributors were Pessoa, Mário de Sá-Carneiro and Almada Negreiros. Two issues were published in Lisbon in 1915.

3. This assertion is true for much of the Portuguese criticism of this century. Unlike in other critical traditions, a good deal of the best criticism written in Portugal is in fact dispersed among small newspaper articles. Two newspapers currently stand out for the quality of their relatively young critics: *Público*, with Abel Barros Baptista for fiction and Fernando Pinto do Amaral for poetry, and the weekly paper *Expresso*, with António Guerreiro.

4. The literary criticism that João Gaspar Simões claimed to be the founder of had the proven power of correcting authors such as Aquilino Ribeiro. "The dialogues of *Mónica*, whether the novel's protagonist was repeating articles by heart or discoursing about Greek literature out of her own head, were not in keeping with the mentality of this typical, Portuguese bourgeois family. Aquilino was unsurpassable in his rural dialogues . . . and no one could outdo the harangues of his provincial nobles . . . . The same cannot be said about his urban dialogues carried on by people who are very much a product of our times and who were little or not at all familiar with classical authors. And if it is true that Aquilino Ribeiro initially overreacted with a harsh response to punish my insolent irreverence, causing a falling-out in our personal and literary relations, that did not stop me from continuing to express in public the admiration I felt for his work. And for that reason Aquilino Ribeiro, acting nobly, rectified his response to my criticism of *Mónica* in the last edition of his *Abóboras no Telhado*, even confessing that 'after the controversy with J. G. S. [João Gaspar Simões], I took greater care in my dialogues'" (*Crítica IV*, 311-12).

5. Frank F. Sousa, in his recently published *O Segredo de Eça. Ideologia e Ambiguidade em A Cidade e as Serras* (Lisbon: Edições Cosmos, 1996), criticizes the biographical approach of João Gaspar Simões, particularly with respect to Eça's supposedly decadent period. Gaspar Simões goes so far as to censure the novelist for never dreaming of exchanging Paris for Tormes, the two main settings of *A Cidade e as Serras*.

6. A movement that propounded a national art and literature founded on *saudade* "nostalgia, wistful longing," understood as a positive, quintessential trait of the Portuguese character.

7. Pessoa's critical fortune owes a great deal to critics such as João Gaspar Simões and Jorge de Sena, but his status as a great percursor is due largely to poets from the decades following his death. As Pessoa's unpublished work saw print, it proved to be an influence that in many cases was overwhelming. Fernando J. B. Martinho wrote a short book, *Pessoa e a moderna poesia portuguesa (Do Orfeu a 1960)* (Lisbon: Instituto de Cultura e Literatura Portuguesa, 1983), that traces the poet's influence in a number of key writers from the succeeding poetic generations.

8. Aguiar e Silva particularly appreciated the central thesis (and its later development) of Sena's 1948 conference entitled "A Poesia de Camões— ensaio de revelação da dialéctica camoniana":

> Another seminal idea of the 1948 conference, inextricably linked to the stylistic and generational characterization of Camões as a Mannerist, is the thesis that Camões's poetry is eminently dialectical in nature. Partially in accord with Sérgio and Régio's interpretation concerning the speculative and metaphysical aspects of Camões's poetry and adamantly opposed to all those interpretations (by J. M. Rodrigues, Lopes Vieira, Aquilino Ribeiro, Joaquim de Carvalho et al.) that would minimize its philosophical tension and density, this thesis was thoroughly and brilliantly developed in *Uma Canção de Camões* (Lisbon: 1966) as well as (on certain points) in *A Estrutura de Os Lusíadas e Outros Estudos Camonianos e de Poesia Peninsular do Século XVI* (Lisbon: 1970). In light of its important implications and consequences, we may say that this thesis—which presupposes philosophical, historical and literary correlations with Neo-Platonism, with Petrarchan poetics, with certain schools of thought that may be grouped under "Anti-Romanticism," with the Counter-Reformation, etc.—helped in a decisive way to revise, in recent decades, our reading and interpretation of Camões's lyric and epic poetry. (47)

9. It must be noted that feminist criticism—along with gay criticism, and so on—is not sufficiently defined or developed in Portugal to be considered a movement or subgenre in the way of, say, the criticism of *Presença*. In fact feminist criticism is not even a well-established term in Portugal. There is, on the other hand, some excellent criticism produced by women, sometimes about women writers. Paula Morão (*Irene Lisboa. Vida e Escrita*, Lisbon: Presença, 1989) is a good case in point.

10. Nuno Júdice, another poet and critic who began to publish in the 1970s, uses the expression "poesia de 70" (165). Júdice, like Magalhães, notes the limitations of the "Poesia 61" group, due to its "purportedly antirhetorical prejudice . . . . The next generation, emerging in the early 1970s, clearly opposes that prejudice and restores dignity to the rhetorical

and discursive modes. This restoration does not denote a full-fledged return to Romanticism, however" (154). The presence of narrative, everyday, historical and mythological elements in the "poesia dos anos Setenta" ties it to the poetry of modernists such as Pound or Eliot, according to Júdice, and to other kinds of poetry, represented by the likes of Cavafy or Gottfried Benn. For Júdice, as for Magalhães, the relationship with Pessoa is complex and marked by an irresistible attempt to get beyond the poet of many masks. Apropos another poet of the Seventies, António Franco Alexandre, Júdice wrote: "The voice we hear in the poem is receptive to a staging of the poetic being that can result in a physical figure *going beyond the heteronymic dimension* that was mentioned with respect to Pessoa and the poet's guise(s). It corresponds, in a certain way, to the conception of the poet as a character of the language rather than its mere inhabitant" (164, my italics).

11. See, in this respect, the special poetry issue of the magazine *A Phala*, titled *Um Século de Poesia (1888-1988)*, eds. Fernando Pinto do Amaral, Gil de Carvalho, José Bento and Manuel Hermínio Monteiro (Lisbon: Assírio & Alvim, 1988).

12. In spite of this conspicuous aspect of his criticism, Magalhães never explicitly refers to João Gaspar Simões in his two main critical works.

13. This paragraph owes much to a seminar, "Poetic Evolution as Transnational Dialogue," led by Professor Magalhães at the Faculty of Letters, University of Lisbon, in the 1993-94 school year.

14. Magalhães elects Jorge de Sena "as the emblematic figure of the State's ignorance in relation to poets" (*Dois Crepúsculos* 53).

15. For a discussion of narrative in Portuguese poetry from the 1970s on, see João Barrento, "Palimpsestos do tempo. O paradigma da narratividade na poesia dos anos oitenta," in *A Palavra Transversal. Literatura e Ideias no Séc. XX* (Lisbon: Cotovia, 1996), 69-78.

Works Cited

Júdice, Nuno. *O Processo Poético. Estudos de Teoria e Crítica Literárias.* Lisbon: Imprensa Nacional-Casa da Moeda, 1992.

Magalhães, Joqium Manuel. *Os Dois Crepúsculos. Sobre Poesia Portuguesa Actual e Outras Crónicas.* Lisbon: A Regra do Jogo, 1981.

_____. *Um Pouco da Morte.* Lisbon: Presença, 1989.

Pessoa, Fernando. *Obras em Prosa.* Ed. Cleonice Berardinelli. Rio de Janeiro: Editora Nova Aguilar, 1990.

_____. *Páginas de Estética e de Teoria e Crítica Literárias.* 2nd ed. Eds. Georg Rudolf Lind and Jacinto do Prado Coelho. Lisbon: Ática, 1973.

_____. *Páginas Íntimas e de Auto-interpretação.* Ed. Georg Rudolf Lind and Jacinto do Prado Coelho. Lisbon: Ática, 1966.

_____. *Poemas Completos de Alberto Caeiro.* Ed. Teresa Sobral Cunha. Lisbon: Presença, 1994.

Rebelo, Luís de Sousa. "O ensaio e a crítica de Jorge de Sena." *Anthropos* 150, Barcelona: Editorial Anthropos, 1993. 50-53.

Sena, Jorge de. *Dialécticas Teóricas da Literatura.* 2nd ed. Lisbon: Edições 70, 1977.

_____. *Estudos de Literatura Portuguesa—III.* Ed. Mécia de Sena. Lisbon: Edições 70, 1988.

_____. *Poesia—I.* 3rd ed. Lisbon: Edições 70, 1988.

_____. *Uma Canção de Camões.* 2nd ed. Lisbon: Edições 70, 1984.

Silva, Vitor Manuel de Aguiar e. "Jorge de Sena camonista." *Colóquio-Letras* 67, 45-52. Lisbon: Fundação Gulbenkian, 1982.

Simões, João Gaspar. *Crítica IV. Cronistas, Novelistas e outros Prosadores Contemporâneos. 1942-1979.* Lisbon: Imprensa Nacional-Casa da Moeda, 1981.

_____. *Eça de Queiróz.* Lisbon: Arcádia, undated.

_____. *Perspectiva Histórica da Ficção Portuguesa (das origens ao Século XX).* 2nd ed. Lisbon: Publicações Dom Quixote, 1987.

_____. *Vida e Obra de Eça de Queiróz.* 3rd ed. Lisbon: Bertrand, 1980.

_____. *Vida e Obra de Fernando Pessoa. História de uma Geração.* 3rd ed. Lisbon: Bertrand, 1973.

◆ **Afterword**

Literary History:
Are We Still Talking?

Helena C. Buescu

Thirty years after Jauss pronounced it to be one, literary history is still a challenge to literary theory—and I suspect that it will remain so. This "simply" means that we are constantly reshaping not only the *notion* of literary history but its very *possibility*, that is, its *mode of existence* within the fields of discourse. In these several pages I will call this challenge into question, while keeping in mind that if answers do "answer" anything, they also raise renewed questions: that is precisely why challenges never die away—they are simply recast.

I shall argue that literary history may be understood as a *process* or as a *product* and that seeing it one way or the other has definite consequences with respect to its scope and possibility. If seen as a product, according to the largely traditional view, then literary history basically corresponds to paradigm fixation, with effects on the incorporation and exclusion of "objects," obviously in different degrees and levels. Literary history, in this perspective, would be the product resulting in a stable and ideal complete discourse. However, if we consider literary history to be also a process of questioning itself, that is, if we mainly understand it as an *epistemological* activity, do we end with the same paradigm of completion? Do we have to relinquish the label of literary history for those objects which do not propose and see themselves as stable and homogeneous? My answer to both questions is no, and I shall try to show why.

I will point out, by the way, that the same question applies, conversely, to *canon* formation, developments and transformations—the same canon with which literary history (but also criticism or literary theory) actively works and maintains close relations. The ongoing debates about the canon and literary history make apparent, in short, that the understanding of these entities as final and stabilized products comes from a temptation (always there) to view knowledge as quantitative data accumulation, rather than from actual verification of stability and finality in those products.

Traditionally, literary history was, or at least tended to be, the extended report and consistent narration of a literary canon viewed as stable, in which the eventual alterations and revisions were to be felt more as ways of refining the report (in an implicit and progressive movement toward *The Great Report*) than as critical and theoretical variables, as nowadays seems to be the case, involving the notion of the philosophical crisis that extends to the report (any report) itself.

Does this mean that literary history becomes, for this very reason, impossible? To this question my answer would be both yes and no. Yes, I believe, because critical consciousness of literary history effectively prevents it from investing in the production (even if only ideal) of *The Great Report of Literature*. Yes, as well, because the report was conceived of as possible in a particular vision of literary studies, within which literary history was regarded as a privileged field for the organization of critical instruments—and that definitely *is not* the case now. No, however, in the sense that it is possible not to subsume literary history completely under the stabilizing and totalizing paradigm, namely by incorporating the consciousness of the "floating phenomena" that really constitute it: such as the literary and cultural resurgences of residual elements in different historical contexts (Guillén), or the consistent movement between the core and the periphery of the literary system and between various literary systems, both synchronically and diachronically (Evén-Zohar), or even the constant reshaping of canonical objects and of the canon itself (Guillory). This approach in fact is apparent in all the essays in this special issue. They all insist on considering their topics from the conscious viewpoint of heterogeneity and, sometimes, of synchronic contradiction. The literary history practiced nowadays seems to favor tensions, anachronisms, and what Jauss termed the "noncontemporaneity of the contemporaneous"—and it doesn't try, even in the essays of wider scope, to build a panorama of stabilized and homogeneous characteristics.

If this critical movement means that literary history is no longer possible, perhaps we should also wonder if literary theory is possible. This has been done, of course, and some have argued that it is not. I would argue, on the contrary, that only a totalizing paradigm of both disciplines can sustain the argument for their complete disappearance.

Moreover, and due to the fact that literary history is, in fact, a fusion between literary and historical theoretical discourses and fields, we should remember that the epistemological questions asked about it are no different from those of historical discourse itself. Recognizing the narrative mechanisms at work in historical discourse, as Hayden White and Paul Ricoeur have done, does not necessarily entail a step towards *aporia*, by denying the very possibility of that discourse—and the same applies to literary history.

The fundamental question seems to be: What do we *get* from positing the possibility of a critical discourse in the area of literary history? And, conversely, what do we *get* from positing its impossibility? From a functionalist point of view, it seems that the gains obtained from it's being possible are indeed greater than the losses (I would prefer to call them not exactly losses, but "gaps"). For, if we understand that literary historical discourse is feasible only from that stabilized and totalizing paradigm, then we may ultimately have to recognize that *all* discourse is doomed to be abandoned, leaving silence as the only alternative.

Every bit of discourse (and critical discourse is no different in this respect) is made of gaps and fragments, of axiological positions that support choices and exclusions, of coherent procedures entailed by textuality itself. The current crisis of literary history is perhaps the acknowledgement that all discourse is always, not only *in* crisis, but *crisis* itself. As it is, we are still talking—and hope to keep doing so.

212 ◆ HELENA C. BUESCU

Works Cited

Éven-Zohar, Itamar. "Polysystem Theory," "The Literary System," and "The Position of Translated Literature in the Literary Polysystem," in *Poetics Today* 11 (1990): 13-51.

Guillén, Claudio. "Cambio literario y multiple duración," in *Homenaje a Julio Caro Baroja*, 533-49. Madrid: Carreira, 1978.

Guillory, John. *Cultural Capital: The Problem of Literary Canon Formation.* Chicago: U of Chicago P, 1993.

Jauss, Hans-Robert. "Literary History as a Challenge to Literary Theory," in *Toward an Aesthetic of Reception.* Minneapolis: U of Minnesota P, 1982.

Ricoeur, Paul. *Temps et récit.* Paris: Seuil, 1983.

White, Hayden. "The Historical Text as Literary Artifact," *Tropics of Discourse. Essays in Cultural Criticism.* Baltimore: Johns Hopkins UP, 1985.

◆ Contributors

Teresa Amado teaches Portuguese Medieval Literature at the Romance Literatures Department, Universidade de Lisboa. She has edited numerous texts, among which texts by Fernão Lopes and Bernardim Ribeiro, is the author of *Fernão Lopes contador de história* (1991) and the editor of *A guerra até 1450* (1994).

Helena C. Buescu teaches Comparative Literature, French Literature and Portuguese Literature at the Program in Comparative Literature and at the Romance Literatures Department, Universidade de Lisboa. She is the author of *Incidências do olhar: percepção e representação* (1990) and *A lua, a literatura e o mundo* (1995), *Em busca do autor perdido* (1998).

João Dionísio is a doctoral candidate as well as a Teaching Assistant in Portuguese Medieval Literature at the Romance Literatures Department, Universidade de Lisboa. He is the critical editor of Fernando Pessoa's *English Poems* (1993) as well as the author of several articles on medieval literature.

António M. Feijó teaches American Literature and Literary Theory at the English Department and at the Program in Literary Theory, Universidade de Lisboa. He is the author of *O ensino da teoria da literatura e a universidade* (1994) and of *Near Miss. A Study of Wyndham Lewis* (1998), the American editor of a collection of Fernando Pessoa's prose (forthcoming), a translator of John Ashberry, and was one of the editors of the influential literary journal *As escadas não têm degraus*.

Maria de Lourdes A. Ferraz teaches Literary Theory at the Romance Literatures Department and at the Program in Literary Theory, Universidade de Lisboa. She is the author of *A ironia romântica* (1987), one of the editors of *Biblos: Enciclopédia das literaturas de língua portuguesa*, and the editor of the forthcoming *Dicionário de personagens de Camilo*, as well as of many articles on poetics and literary history.

Manuel Gusmão teaches French Literature and Literary Theory at the Romance Literatures Department and at the Programs in Literary Theory and Comparative Literature, Universidade de Lisboa. Among many other works, he is the author of *A poesia de Carlos de Oliveira* (1981) and *A poesia de Alberto Caeiro* (1986), as well as of two books of poetry, and has written extensively on Francis Ponge, of whom he is also a translator.

M. S. Lourenço teaches at the Philosophy Department and at the Program in Literary Theory, Universidade de Lisboa. He has held appointments at several European and American universities. He is the author of *A espontaneidade da razão* (1986) and *Teoria clássica da dedução* (1991), as well as the editor of *A cultura da subtileza* (1995), and the Portuguese translator of Wittgenstein's *Tractatus Logico-Philosophicus* and *Philosophical Investigations* (1987). His work as a creative writer comprises eight books, from *O desiquilibrista* (1960) to *Os degraus do Parnaso* (1991).

The late **Margarida Vieira Mendes** taught Portuguese Renaissance and Baroque Literature at the Romance Literatures Department, Universidade de Lisboa. She is the author of the best contemporary comprehensive study on Padre António Vieira, *A oratória barroca de Vieira* (1989), among many other works.

Victor Mendes, teaches at the University of Massachusetts-North Dartmouth. He is the author of several articles on literary matters as well as of a book on Viagens na Minha Terra (forthcoming).

Paula Morão teaches Modern and Contemporary Portuguese Literature at the Romance Literatures Department, Universidade de Lisboa. She has written on and edited texts of Irene Lisboa (e.g., *Irene Lisboa, vida e escrita*, 1989), as well a book on António Nobre (*O Só de António Nobre: uma leitura do nome,* 1991), and a book of literary essays (*Viagens na terra das palavras,* 1993).

J. C. Seabra Pereira teaches Portuguese Literature at the Universidade de Coimbra. He is the author of, among other works, *Decadentismo e Simbolismo na Poesia Portuguesa* (1975), *Do fim-de-século ao tempo de Orpheu* (1979), and *Do Fim-de-Século ao Modernismo* (1995).

Vítor Aguiar e Silva, currently teaches Portuguese Literature and Literary Theory and serves as vice-rector at the Universidade do Minho, Braga. He has for many years taught at Universidade de Coimbra and held appointments at several North and South American universities. He is the author of *Maneirismo e barroco na poesia lírica portuguesa* (1971), *Competência literária e competência linguística* (1977) and *Camões: labirintos e fascínios* (1994) and of the highly influential *Teoria da literatura* (1st ed. 1967, revised 1984).

Miguel Tamen teaches Literary Theory at the Program in Literary Theory (which he currently chairs) and at the Romance Literatures Department, Universidade de Lisboa. He is the author of *Hermenêutica e mal-estar* (1987), *Manners of Interpretation* (1993) and *The Matter of the Facts* (forthcoming).

◆ Index

Compiled by Juliet Lynd

Confessionalism 111, 198
Consciousness 128, 131, 139; self-
consciousness 134, 135, 204
Cordeiro, Jacinto 70; *Elogio de
poetas lusitanos* 70
Correia, Garção 197
Correia, Manuel 67 (note 16)
Correira, Natália 164
Cortes Rodrigues, Armando 143, 158
Costa Domingos, Paulo 172
Costa Gomes, Luísa 185; *Olhos
verdes* 185
Counter-Reformation 206 (note 8)
Court: private vs. loyal 15; as setting
for baroque literature 61; as site of
Galician-Portuguese troubador
activity 3, 15; and theater 64
Coutinho, Afrânio 59
Crashaw, Richard 140
Crisis: in Cesário 128, 138; as
cyclical in 19th century
Portuguese literature 81; and
Decadence 106, 108, 118; of
epistemology 186; of feeling 157;
and limits of power 182; of literary
history 211; and literary identity
crisis 81; and social crisis in 19th
century 93-94
Criticism: absence of in Portugal
190; and poetry 125-126, 140; and
Decadence 107, 111; feminist 206
(note 9); impresionistic 199; and
judgement 195; and satire and
parody 67, 98; *see also Literary
Criticism*
Cruz, Gastão 153, 165, 167, 168
Cruz, Padre Francisco da 73
Cultural Propaganda Editions 146
Cultural studies 60
Culture: contact with Brazilian,
South-American, Anglo-
American, European literatures
177; contact with Anglo-American
204; cultural citations 167;
degenerate culture and Decadence
107-108; and fin-de-siècle 109,
110, 111, 112; intercultural

relationships 177; and national
identity xix; of poet 167;
Portuguese culture 181, 184;
Portuguese management of 202;
and repression 164; ruins of
Western 140; and self-reflection
186

Dacosta, Luisa 183; *Na água do
tempo-Diário* 183
Dandy 111; dandyish image 113
Dantas, Júlio 113, 115, 116; *Nada*
115
Dante (Alghieri) xv, 154, 192;
Dantesque Hell 144; *The Divine
Comedy* 53 (note 16); and
melancholy 32
Decadence 102, 105-121, 138, 157,
196; Euro-American 116; and
existential trouble 106, 107, 108;
and *femme fatale vs. femme fragile*
116; in Germany and England
108; nihilism and existential guilt
118; as period style 106, 108, 112-
113, 120-121 (note 2), 205 (note
5); and perversion 116; and
pessimistic vision 108, 113; in
Portugal 105-106, 108-119, 149;
social decadence 107
Deconstruction 82, 161, 186
Defaux, Gerard 53 (note 15)
Descartes, René 133, 134
Desire: in Camões 48; and
decadence 106, 116; and
heteronomy 159; and history 29;
and melancholy 47, 51; nostalgic
34; physical 164; to surrender 131,
1132; true love and object of
desire 83
Deus, João de 101
di Medici, Lorenzo 52 (note 8)
Dinis, Júlio 96, 99, 101; *A
Morgandinha dos Canaviais* 99;
*As Pupilas do Senhor Reitor,*99;
Os Fidalgos da Casa Mourisca
99; *Uma Família Inglesa* 99
Diogo, A. Lindeza 158